Praise for

"A primer for anyone consi̲...... fascinating reading for mus........ ...., no matter the experience or ability."

—Tom Druckenmiller, contributing writer *Sing Out! Magazine,* radio host "In the Tradition" WDIY-FM

"*Are You Famous?* is a book about making music and poems, about America, but finally, it is a book about hope. . . . I really loved the book."

—Al Maginnes, music critic and poet, author of *Ghost Alphabet, Film History,* and *The Light in Our Houses*

"A suggested must-read for our staff, Ken reminds us of the passion and tenacity that must stay alive among and between artists and presenters if we are to survive and thrive in these challenging times."

—Scott D. Stoner, Chief Program Officer, Association of Performing Arts Presenters, Washington D.C.

"A fabulous read, chatty, friendly prose, that makes you feel like Ken is sitting right beside you. . . . I love the book!"

—Deborah Smith, Director, Newberry Opera House, Newberry, South Carolina

"If you have ever seriously considered pursuing a career in the music business or any other like profession where you must travel and self-promote, this is a must read."

—Kevin Grastorf, Store Manager, *Employee Reviews,* The Reader's Cove, Fort Collins, Colorado

"A travel guide for aspiring free spirits."

—Maria Browning, *Nashville Scene*

"*Are You Famous?* is the story of a man who is anything but famous (in the traditional sense), but whose generous artistic spirit makes him a compelling and memorable figure."

—Cody Daigle, *Times of Acadiana,* Lafayette, Louisiana

"Waldman makes real life as engaging as fiction."
    —Art Menius, Director, Appalshop, Whitesburg, Kentucky

"Highly recommended for personal, academic, and community library collections, *Are You Famous?* is an honest and candid perspective on the music industry from the inside."
    —Mary Cowper, *Midwest Book Review*

"Are You Famous? is the ultimate DIY guide and inspirational text."
    —Jarret Keene, *Tucson Weekly*

"[Waldman's] need to openly dispel myths of the road, and romantic notions of suffering, may serve as that rare, much-needed reality check for other aspiring artists."
    —Kyle James Shrader, *The Florida Review*

....and praise for Ken Waldman in performance....

"[Waldman] might tempt you to plan a road trip with a journal tucked under one arm and a fiddle under another."
    —*Boston Globe*

"A one-man *Prairie Home Companion*."
    —*Shepherd Express Weekly*, Milwaukee

"Feels like a Ken Burns movie....Always recommended."
    —*Austin Chronicle*

"Picture William Carlos Williams behind a dogsled, Walt Whitman jamming with the Carter Family."
    —*The State*, Columbia, South Carolina

"Waldman is proficient at turning his observations of Alaska life into thoughtful, optimistic work that evokes faith in humanity and the grandeur of nature."
    —*Philadelphia City Paper*

Are You Famous?

Touring America with Alaska's Fiddling Poet

by Ken Waldman

CATALYST BOOK PRESS

San Bruno, California

Acknowledgements

A section of the chapter "Logistics, Technology, Whatnot" was first published in Metro, the Magazine of Oklahoma City Libraries. *"Inner Nome" was earlier published in* International Poetry Review *and in* Nome Poems *(West End Press, Albuquerque).* "Nome Celebrity" *was earlier published in* Nome Poems *(West End Press, Albuquerque).* "Bird School" *was earlier published in* Yankee *and in* The Secret Visitor's Guide *(Wings Press, San Antonio).* "September 11, 2001" *was earlier published in* To Live on this Earth *(West End Press, Albuquerque) and in* The Secret Visitor's Guide *(Wings Press, San Antonio).* "April 11, 2002" *was earlier published in* The Secret Visitor's Guide *(Wings Press, San Antonio).* "Adrift" *was earlier published in* And Shadow Remained *(Pavement Saw Press, Columbus, OH).* "After Hearing John Haines Read" *was earlier published in* Ice-Floe *and in* To Live on this Earth *(West End Press, Albuquerque).* "Buster Keaton, Romancer" *was earlier published in* Natural Bridge *and as part of the longer poem, "Comedy Hour" in* Conditions and Cures *(Steel Toe Books, Bowling Green, KY).* "Railroad Days" *was earlier published in* Crucible *and in* And Shadow Remained *(Pavement Saw Press, Columbus, OH).* "George W. Bush: On Health Care" *was earlier published in* As the World Burns *(Ridgeway Press, Roseville, MI).* "At the Survival General Store" *was earlier published in* Quarterly West *and in* To Live on this Earth *(West End Press, Albuquerque).*

Catalyst Book Press ISBN 978-0-9802081-2-2

**To order additional copies of the book, contact Catalyst Book Press
www.catalystbookpress.com, info@catalystbookpress.com**

Jessica Powers of Catalyst Book Press would like to thank Kathy McInnis for her excellent book cover, Dennis Powers and Sara Juday for design help, Chris Gibson for emotional support, Casey and Denise of New Pages *and the Byrds of Cinco Puntos Press for failing to talk me out of this and for getting excited instead.*

"Are you famous?"

Asked by a fourth grader in Sullivan County,
New York; by a fifth grader in Winnemucca, Nevada;
by a fifth grader in Lancaster, California; by an adult
in Winslow, Washington

Ken Waldman's Answer

"Well yes, maybe. In this room right now, anyway,
for this instant, and maybe a little while longer."

Also by Ken Waldman

Books
As the World Burns
Conditions and Cures
And Shadow Remained
The Secret Visitor's Guide
To Live on this Earth
Nome Poems

CDs
55 Tunes, 5 poems
As the World Burns
Fiddling Poets on Parade
All Originals, All Traditionals
Music Party
Burnt Down House
A Week in Eek

Table of Contents

Introduction

Ken Waldman, Alaska's Fiddling Poet (and America's most versatile, steadfast, and far-ranging "troubadour" since Carl Sandburg), has written a unique and even astonishing book of vital importance to American readers for numerous distinct, if interrelated, reasons.

First, *Are You Famous?* provides both poets and folk musicians, green and seasoned, with the most extensive and detailed cultural map and guide book currently (or perhaps ever) available. From Nome, Alaska to Austin, Texas; New York to Seattle; DC to San Francisco; Atlanta to Minneapolis; New Orleans to Chicago, and countless stops beyond and in-between, Waldman ranges back and forth across the continental USA, observing people, cities, trends, and making lists upon lists of everything that might prove useful someday (from a survivor's perspective) or already serves as a source of dismay or delight.

As with any indispensable guidebook, however, it is the discerning commentary interlaced throughout *Are You Famous?*—observations both witty and wise, savvy and philosophical, meticulous and meditative—that makes a lasting impression and a very great difference. In this respect, *Are You Famous?* is more a scout's field manual than a TripTik from AAA. Want to learn the parking intricacies of Manhattan or where to find the finest zydeco in New Orleans or Lafayette? Want to know the computer access hours in scores of US public libraries or where to photocopy for 3¢? Want to discover the best poetry bookstores in Portland or Seattle; the cheapest, most nutritious restaurants, buffets, coffeehouses, diners in Flagstaff, Albuquerque, Austin, Asheville, Buffalo, LA; and all the lowdown taverns? Or how (and where) to sleep off-road in Oklahoma City or Atlanta; stage a show for kids in Eek, Alaska; bike Chicago; survive a plane crash; compose music; record CDs; score a gig at DC's Kennedy Center; read with Creeley, Rich, Cisneros; and publish a very considerable stack of books? Well then, consult *Are*

You Famous? Ken Waldman tells all and in the telling weaves a moving personal story about the loneliness of transient life, the yearning for hearth and home, the ceaseless, sometimes heartbreaking, desire for love.

Moreover, this is a book about the dynamic, mysterious art of healing and the healing power of art. During the past two decades, Waldman has possessed neither the time nor the financial means to access traditional health services (much less dental care), and has, for an extended period, fallen desperately ill. Yet today he is thriving—in itself an inspiring (if cautionary) story and a profound amazement, especially given the stressful, cutthroat, privatized, petty, bureaucratic, and toxic environment to which he daily submits his body, his talent, his vision, his hope. Indeed, though Waldman's story is finally a cause for celebration—here is an American who persists, damn fool, in believing he is both talented and free—it is not without travail and the unnerving gnashing of teeth.

Because, finally, this is a book about the American dream tipping toward nightmare: the corrupting effects of the "star system," the crippling impact of "celebrity," the debasing temptation of our quest for "fame," and one brave, modest, generous man—an artist of persistence and integrity—who helps us make it through the night.

Robin Metz
Director, The Program in Creative Writing, Knox College
Producer and Contributing Artist, Vitalist Theatre Company, Chicago

1
Between Old Life and New:
Into and Through Disease

Inner Nome

This spirit road of ghost
shrub tundra, an air current
spiraling uphill beyond fog,
wind, the memory of trees,
toward a small clearing
of blackened rock, burnt grass,
all that remains of the cabin
fire that took a life—

and continues past that spot,
past unmarked grave, gravel,
past ice, hail, drizzle, the gray
cloud countries of ancient grit,
past salmon creeks, blueberries,
reindeer, past a world shiny
and rich, the sun in love,
past everything but source.

Mid April 1992, Juneau, a Sunday night festival jam session with friends, I was fiddling in an upstairs room at the Alaskan Hotel when I felt something give in my right elbow, as if I'd been bitten deep inside. The sharp pain almost made me drop my bow. *Oh shit,* I shrieked as I stopped playing, then quickly stuck fiddle and bow in the case. Moments later, right arm dangling by my side, six words, an insight from out of nowhere: *This is going to kill me.*

Then I hurried downstairs to the bar in search of ice.

The next two days I remained in Juneau, tending to my throbbing elbow with ice and aspirin, and in the evenings led writing classes over the phone. As an assistant professor at the Nome campus of the University of Alaska Fairbanks,

I mostly taught via audio conference: at a specified time the students would dial in, and I'd facilitate what essentially was a conference call. Theoretically, I could have done this from anywhere—and, in fact, since September one colleague from Bethel had been teaching his classes from Denton, Texas, where he was on a fellowship—but for the past two years, since beginning the job, I hadn't strayed farther than Anchorage or Fairbanks during the academic year. Juneau was still in state, sure—after all, it was our capital city—but it was fifteen hundred miles and a $450 plane ride away, a completely different Alaska. And three days after the festival, I'd be attending a conference in Minneapolis.

Planning the week, I'd wondered about the logistics. Occasionally I'd traveled to villages to meet my students. It was one thing to lead classes on the phone from one of my students' sites, another from distant hotel rooms in Southeast Alaska and Minnesota. During the Monday evening class, mind on my physical discomfort, sitting in my room in the Alaskan, I felt like I was off the continent. Tuesday felt worse, like I was off the planet.

This trip was supposed to be a celebration, a paid vacation of sorts. Getting to Juneau had been my responsibility, but from there my college would pay for travel to Minneapolis, a hotel room there, my conference fees. With only a few weeks left in this second year of my tenure-track job on the Bering Sea coast, I'd survived the hard part; and there had been hard, dark times since arriving in Nome. But I'd learned from them, and this year had been easier. Now that it was mid April, the light had returned, and though it was still cold and windy, at least there was the promise of May. It seemed simple to cruise into summer, which I looked forward to spending in Seattle.

Outside the Pacific Northwest, Seattle is often viewed as way out in a corner, cool and gray, always drizzly. According to the *New Yorker* cartoon map of the world, it's just this side of Japan. For many Alaskans, Seattle is the big city oasis, the middle of everything, south and east, warm and lit, full of color, fine weather, lots to do. Awful traffic maybe, but music, culture, commerce, and airplane connections come with a price.

But before my summer in Seattle, I still had another month. An easy month, I reminded myself, since I wasn't even going to spend all of it in rural Alaska.

Between Old Life and New: Into and Through Disease

First, the festival in Juneau, where I'd not only see friends from throughout the state, but show what I'd been doing musically the past winter. Single since moving to Alaska in 1985, I'd been fortunate to land in rentals where I could play music late at night. In lieu of a steady girlfriend, I had a fiddle, I joked, though really it wasn't much of a joke. For a much better one, here was how Alaska women described the abundance of eligible men up north: The odds are good, they'd say. But the goods are odd.

So I was one of those odd goods: a single guy in his mid-thirties passionate about writing, teaching, and fiddling. My three years in the graduate Creative Writing program in Fairbanks, I'd lived several miles from town in a rental cabin that had no plumbing, where I played music each night before going to bed, making that long slow transition from awful to mediocre. The first two years I didn't even have a phone. In Juneau—living for a year in another cabin in the woods, another year without plumbing, and juggling three part-time jobs— my playing rose to passable. In Sitka, where I was a visiting assistant professor for a year, I had my spacious sublet right on a cove, a beautiful spot a block from downtown with, yes, running water, and there I could hear it myself—my fiddling now had its moments. And in Nome, though I never found much of a social life, I loved fiddling more than ever as I'd lose myself for hours in the living room of my little house on the corner of Third and Division. For years I'd wondered how it felt to put personality in the music; somehow I'd learned and was having so much fun that I'd even bought a mandolin, then a banjo, and begun picking and frailing.

I'd been especially looking forward to Juneau since a few years earlier I'd made my festival debut performing on the big main stage, and just last year had enjoyed my all-time favorite public session, playing with friends for one of the evening dances. I'd moved there after leaving Fairbanks, and would have remained if I hadn't received the offer to teach full-time for a year in Sitka. Juneau, a cool cloudy place, where downtown averages a hundred inches of rain a year, always felt glorious for one week in April, overrun by hundreds of musicians escaping the end of winter ice-snow-mud mix further north. It was the best party in the state, with music all day, everyday, throughout downtown.

And I was even more excited about Minneapolis, where I'd be attending a conference of more than a thousand writers, virtually all affiliated with colleges and universities. AWP was the name of the event, and the acronym stood for the Associated Writing Programs. Since finishing graduate school, I'd completed a story collection, begun a novel, and written a few hundred poems. Dozens of these poems, as well as a handful of stories, had been published, or had been accepted to be published, in national journals. In Alaska seven years now—the past two in Nome, population 3500, a small community accessible only by air—I was eager to travel to a big place other than Seattle, and meet other writers and teachers, maybe even an editor or two.

But flying to Minneapolis, I could only focus on my achy elbow, and arrived distracted. Monday, Tuesday, and now Wednesday had been the first days in over ten years I hadn't played music, at least for a few minutes, and the forced withdrawal was disorienting me even more. Once I settled in the hotel room, to feel better I picked up the instrument, put it under my chin, and grabbed the bow. But a quick stab of pain halted me. I wanted to feel better, not worse.

In a strange place, feeling unwell, I didn't know what a doctor could offer, so I struggled privately, continually applying ice. The only times I felt like myself were Wednesday and Thursday evenings, in my hotel room, phoning in to teach my classes, talking with my students. As I wandered the conference sessions, I couldn't wait to return to Nome on Sunday, where I hoped my elbow would improve.

But back in Nome my elbow didn't improve, and the first morning it ached so badly I could barely use my right hand to scrawl comments on papers, could barely use it to type. I counted days: two weeks left to teach, a week of exams, and then one more week on my contract before I could leave for Seattle. I'd just gut it out, I thought, and at worst spend June, July, half of August repeating the previous summer's successful regimen.

The preceding year I'd struggled the whole second semester, as difficult a time emotionally as I'd ever had. Day-by-day—sometimes it felt more like hour-by-hour—I fought to leave behind whatever mystery had caused me to almost instantaneously crack up in Seattle over New Year's week, a period of mania that led to my late-night admission into the university hospital's mental wing. Though I checked myself out the next morning, I wasn't feeling better, and for months felt I

14

was barely surviving the world. But I survived to spend the summer in Seattle playing music, visiting friends, biking everywhere, seeing a therapist. Seattle had been healing, and I remembered returning to Nome in late August feeling as if I was within a month of being whole again. This past year I'd fiercely protected that near-wholeness, though, no matter how conscious I'd been, it was as if week-by-week I'd been slowly leaking energy.

So why live in Nome if I was facing such difficulties, you might ask; after all, there were easier places.

First, I loved my job. Not only did I have a knack for teaching, but I had a knack for the challenges found in this setting. A single developmental college writing class might have gifted-and-talented village high-schoolers along with a Native elder or two, along with students from prison, along with a cross-section of Natives and whites from Nome, all with stories to tell. A composition class might have a similar make-up. A lower-division literature class might have a wide range of accomplished non-traditional students from rural communities all over the state, larger-than-life folks it was a huge pleasure to come in contact with. When I taught short-term Creative Writing classes on site in Nome, several students had lives that were startling and they were looking to capture them on paper.

I enjoyed improvising ways to turn the hardships of teaching in rural Alaska into advantages. For the audio conference classes, I asked students to mail me photos, which in turn I'd mail out, and we had a contest to see who could match the most names with the faces. I assigned pen-pals, which not only provided writing practice, but in some cases worked as an extra support mechanism to allow a struggling student to continue with the class. Sometimes it even led to genuine friendship. We had class parties over the phone, a kind of talent show, where students would play music or sing, and where one Nome student had the genius to mail cookies to classmates ahead of time with the instruction to bring them to class on a specified day. For her party turn, she invited us all to bite in simultaneously. Also, there was money in the budget for me to fly to villages to meet with students who, it seemed, needed a doctoral level of commitment just to survive remedial classes. When I traveled like this, not only was it rewarding to meet my students, but, since I was already there, I'd also offer to visit the village school to play fiddle and lead writing exercises. I found I had a talent for entertaining youngsters and teaching them writing. At the same time, I also began volunteering in the Nome City Schools.

Granted, the physical setting wasn't for everyone. Did I say the nearest trees were fifty miles away? And I'd heard Nome described more than once as the perfect minimum security prison. And it was true—you really could do almost anything you wanted, except leave, that is unless you had $350 to fly to Anchorage. And then there you were, *Los Anchorage*, the Los Angeles of Alaska, where you needed to rent a car to get virtually anywhere in a preposterously strip-malled landscape, which meant ultimately you were spending double or even triple the plane fare for other expenses on even the briefest getaway.

But I wasn't everyone. I didn't mind the tundra or the weather, and the job suited me: fulfilling work, adventure, more than reasonable pay, summers off. I wasn't contracted to remain forever, but did have security for the next few years, and probably much longer if I wanted. I wasn't looking that far ahead. Mostly I taught, played music, wrote, felt productive. The previous fall I'd mailed up a bike, and had become one of the intrepid handful who rode everywhere all winter long. Sundays I'd bake bread and cook a big pot of soup, another of rice. All week I ate the leftovers. I may not have loved everything about my life there, may not have felt fully whole, but I'd felt fully alive, at least until the elbow had seized up there in Juneau.

Seattle would be easy, and already I was looking forward to fall, and my third year in Nome. Since I'd already developed effective lesson plans for distance delivery, I wouldn't have to spend so much time in the office. Rather, I saw myself continuing with the fiddle, playing more of the other instruments, and, best, returning to my half-finished novel that I'd put aside my first Nome winter. Plus there were always more poems to write, more journals to send to. I wanted as many publications as I could get. And with virtually no expenses besides rent, food, and an occasional flight out to play music, I'd be saving two to three thousand dollars every month.

My second night back in Nome, protecting my right elbow, I gingerly reached into the refrigerator, took out a loaf of homemade bread I'd made a week and a half earlier, unwrapped it, and placed it on a cutting board. Gripping a serrated bread knife with my left hand, I leaned in to slice the hard cold bread, and again felt something give, this time in the left elbow. *Shit,* I hollered, and dropped the knife to the counter. *I can't take this shit.*

The next morning I walked to the hospital, where a doctor examined me, diagnosed a pair of mild strains, prescribed anti-inflammatory medications, and handed me a sling. Both elbows aching, unable to play music, uncomfortable now on my bike, I spent the next three weeks walking everywhere, my head down, and felt transported to the previous year's difficulties. How I hated it when time just didn't progress, those long cold spring days that were mysteriously torturous. Now I lived for those short periods the pain relented and I felt I could write; taking advantage, I finished grading papers in bursts. Otherwise, I took care of what little Nome business I had, and just hoped this sad episode would pass. I'd never concerned myself with my elbows before, and now they were the crux of my life. Having already planned to spend a few days in Anchorage before flying to Seattle, I made an appointment with a sports medicine doctor there to get a second opinion.

Like the doctor in Nome, the one in Anchorage diagnosed mild strains, nothing major, possible depression, and told me to throw away the sling, to stretch and gently strengthen the irritated tendons. He handed me a few illustrated sheets which demonstrated how. Within a few weeks, if I took it slow, he said, I should then be fine to resume a full range of activity, able to fiddle or do anything else. Happy for that kind of news from a specialist, I envisioned healing quickly, then a mix of strenuous exercise and relaxed bliss from mid June on. Last year's challenge had been emotional. This year, I figured, I'd be facing the physical. I vowed to make myself strong.

Arriving in Seattle, I arranged a few days in one friend's guest room, a few days in another's, until I learned of house-sitting jobs that might last anywhere from a week to a month. With luck, I wouldn't need to pay any rent the whole time in the city. I bought an inexpensive mountain bike, something to knock around on for a few months. Most important was to find people who could help me with this elbow pain, and its accompanying issues. Though I had health insurance from my job, and was happy to use it, what was essential was to get well any way I could, and

17

I was committed to spending what I needed to in a way that felt right for me. Already, I was viewing the pain as an invitation to go deep within. Quickly, I made appointments for the following week with a pair of counselors, a body worker, and an acupuncturist. Evan, a friend who worked at the university hospital, told me about an orthopedist there who specialized in musician's injuries. Though she was booked for months, because of a cancellation I was able to schedule one more meeting for that next week.

Almost immediately, I learned this was going to be nothing like the preceding summer. Despite continuing with the anti-inflammatory medicine and beginning to practice easy physical therapy exercises, my elbows ached continually, sometimes excruciatingly, except for the day I went to see the orthopedist, a gorgeous June morning, where I biked to her office feeling the best I had since Juneau. Examining me, she found little wrong other than perhaps a minor strain, some weakness in the joint. I left her office optimistic but perplexed. Fifteen minutes later, pedaling back to where I was staying, I suddenly felt the sharp pain deep in my right knee, seemingly inside bone. There was no apparent reason for it. None at all. I wasn't biking that hard; I hadn't even been going uphill. Dismounting, I had to walk the bike home. So, in addition to the pain in my elbows, which varied, there was now the pain in my knee. Acupuncture helped only minimally, so I stopped treatment after three sessions. I stopped taking the pills. I saw one body worker, another, then settled on a third. Unable to decide between the two counselors, I saw both for a few weeks until one went on a vacation, so I began seeing the other twice, then three times a week.

No matter what I did, the pain worsened. Unable to bike, increasingly having difficulty walking, my left knee now troubling me too, I spent days riding buses, journeying from one appointment to another. Guessing it might be something internal, I saw a doctor who ran blood tests, pronounced me normal, but, since I was obviously severely depressed, prescribed anti-depressants and an appointment with a psychiatrist. This prescription I didn't fill, feeling that though I was now certainly depressed, and getting worse, something bigger was surfacing. I wanted to get to the bottom of it, didn't want to mask the symptoms, and didn't feel like adding a psychiatrist to the mix. Wasn't seeing a psychologist three times a week enough?

Between Old Life and New: Into and Through Disease

Three months earlier I could exult biking around Nome in minus twenty-five wind-chill. Now I couldn't comfortably climb steps in balmy Seattle. Who wouldn't be depressed, I thought, since there was no obvious cause? I knew it wasn't merely depression that was causing all this joint pain. Still, despite the therapy, despite all the appointments, I had no idea what was happening, only that I needed to continue receiving as much help as I could. One week, house-sitting, the pain in my knees was so bad I had to crawl up and slide down stairs in the house, could no longer comfortably walk two blocks to the bus stop. That was the week I began renting a car. I no longer missed the fiddle; I couldn't even fathom playing.

In addition to seeing health practitioners, I began relying more and more on a few good friends who had time to occasionally sit with me and listen. Like going one step forward, two steps back, I'd tell them. Or like a slow-motion fall from a mountain, I'd say, then narrate my latest round of bad news. I was going down, and no matter how fiercely I was digging to find a hold, it wasn't helping. Somewhere I'd read of bee venom therapy as a safe, effective, non-invasive approach to relieve chronic pain. By early July, more than ten weeks into it, I certainly thought of the pain as chronic, so made an appointment with the M.D. who'd pioneered this. First dose, I had a reaction that several hours later felt like I'd been dropped off a building. I remember a weekend house-sitting in North Seattle, unable to sleep, unable to sit, stand, move or be still, the pain in my elbows and knees somehow transformed to dark wavy body-wide cords of impossibly knotted tension as I clung desperately to televised images from the British Open golf tournament, needing anything to take me out of myself. Sometime in those worst weeks I received my mail from Nome. Included was a letter from a friend of a friend, Toni, a voice teacher from New York I'd never met but who I'd corresponded with that past winter. She had experienced chronic pain herself, I recalled, remembering previous letters. Taking this new letter as a sign, I called her. She was happy to hear from me and invited me to call anytime. Since New York was three hours ahead of Seattle, I began phoning her during my worst nights, at 4:30 or 5:00 a.m., when I was unsure how I'd hold on until dawn.

Early August I changed therapists, hoping to at least slow what had begun to feel like a runaway descent. It was around that time I remember what my body worker, Richard, told me. A sweet man, he played Irish music on mandolin, and taught at one of the local massage schools. There, he was held in such esteem that he regularly drove to Eugene to work on world-class track and field athletes. Previously, he'd helped a number of Alaska fishermen whose bodies, he said, were the most gnarled and wretched he'd ever seen. And you, he said, I think of you as the anti-Alaskan. Really, there's not much wrong with your body, but you're obviously suffering and you're no con man. I think you're in a disease process.

One session, he gave me Darla's name, and mentioned she was a naturopath who specialized in cases like mine. The healer's healer, he called her. But when I phoned Darla's office that afternoon, I was told the next opening was in nine months. Nine months? That sounded no better than sometime the next century.

Also in August I called the director of my campus, told her what had been going on. I didn't think I could return for the fall semester, I said, but expected to be back in January. Receiving permission to take a leave of absence, I continued shuttling from one house-sitting position to another, one health practitioner to another, one empathetic friend to another. August crept by. On good days I'd drive to Green Lake, stroll its two-mile loop, no problem. Buoyed, I'd work harder at the latest physical therapy I'd been prescribed. But the bad days, no matter what I did, I'd invariably encounter a setback, the sense of tendon giving way under even the mildest of pressures. It felt like what little reserve left was being used up, despite all the help. Attending an arts fair, desperate for a sign, I treated myself to a pair of card readings. One psychic predicted dark times ahead; the other, that I'd be unlucky in love, and would die prematurely. Just what I needed to hear, I thought. The next afternoon, filling the rental car with gas, I couldn't even remove the cap to the gas tank without a yank that aggravated my right elbow, the exact spot I first hurt. That was in the midst of a very bad day, and it felt like if I didn't watch out, if I couldn't take care of myself any better, I'd soon have to be institutionalized. One pre-dawn September morning, in the midst of yet one more phone call to Toni in New York, I received an invitation: if I ever needed a place to stay, she had space in her apartment, and I'd be welcome for as long as I needed.

After one more bad day, I discussed New York with my newest counselor, with my body worker, with the friends who'd been witness all summer. The consensus:

whatever I'd tried hadn't been working, so why not fly to New York City to stay with this woman I'd never met? As one of my friends put it, upon learning of her East 53rd Street address: Midtown Manhattan, you'll be going exactly where the outer environment will match what's going on within.

I shrugged my shoulders. Leaving the virtually unused bike and a few small bags with friends, I rode to the airport carrying a daypack and my fiddle, a one-way ticket to New York City. Never had I traveled so lightly or in such bizarre circumstances.

Toni and I became lovers almost immediately—not unexpected in retrospect, since we were both in physical pain, were both needy, and there wasn't much space in her one-bedroom apartment. Meeting Toni was to fall through a spiritual trapdoor and face a lost shadow family. I didn't particularly like Toni but there I was, sharing her bed and meeting her friends—like Andrew, a laid-back Australian acupuncturist, who came over every few days to give me treatments; and Sherry, a waitress, who used to take voice lessons from Toni and now offered both of us herbal remedies. Mainly, though, we sat on the sofa, talked, watched TV, played cards, comforted one another. The big love of Toni's life had recently passed away, and she was disconsolate, just wanted company. Me, when the pain would hit, I'd chatter nonstop, doubting if I'd ever turn this around. My responsibilities each day were simple: get out of bed, sit, go walk around the block with Toni and her little Chihuahua, Elsie. Eat breakfast. Read the newspaper. Watch TV awhile. Hang out with Toni. Eat lunch. Talk. Listen. Lie down and read. Maybe nap. Walk downstairs and out a few blocks one way or another for take-out to bring back for dinner. Watch more TV. Walk Elsie. Go to bed.

Gradually, the days grew more expansive. I'd walk further. I'd take the subway. I'd make a few phone calls and set up appointments. Near Soho, I started seeing a body worker who had once suffered similar elbow pain, and who each visit managed to find deeper and deeper spots, making the discomfort disappear for longer and longer. I called old friends in New York, who I met for meals. Twice a week, Toni played in a poker game that I was invited to join. One weekend I took a poetry workshop led by Galway Kinnell. For my birthday in October, I tuned my fiddle, tightened my bow, and scratched out a weak happy birthday to me. The next day, I walked to Central Park, where I watched the joggers. Later that week, I somehow found myself able to jog a half mile with no ill effects. One night, when Toni revealed she was a clairvoyant and knew I'd be coming to stay awhile, I just nodded. Nothing made sense, and yet this here was my life, unfolding. Through November it was more of the same: one day I'd still be in pain, but the next would feel normal, or at least well enough to begin making plans, always beginning with returning to Nome in time to teach the second semester.

The better I felt, the less I wanted to spend time with Toni. This she was reconciled to, though with her powers maybe she knew this was our fate from the start. Thanksgiving weekend, I took a train upstate to visit a music friend, a visit that was cut short when we tried playing music. I felt my elbow seize and couldn't stop crying. Returning to Toni's place in New York—the middle of the big, dirty, busy city—I was reminded of what that Seattle pal had told me: Midtown Manhattan, where the environment matched what was going on inside me.

If that was so, at least I was getting used to it.

A few days later I was feeling better again and had even received an invitation in the mail to housesit for a friend in Arizona over Christmas. Since meeting a year and a half previously at a music camp, we'd been corresponding occasionally, Evie and I. She was an artist, who made a living as a school counselor. She owned a small house in a high-country town more than an hour north of Phoenix, *a healing place*, she'd said, underlining the phrase, mindful I'd replied to her latest letter by explaining that I'd been having difficult times. But how difficult, I hadn't said, and she had no idea.

With the invitation, though, a plan took hold. What had remained unchanged: I wanted to return to Nome and the life I'd created there. Though New York had somehow worked out far better than I had any right to expect, I didn't trust the big city, and didn't want to stay longer with Toni. It seemed too complicated to find another place in the city, and besides, I belonged in Alaska. This, then, was the plan: I'd fly to Arizona and stay at Evie's between Christmas and New Year's as a kind of test. At least I'd be back west. If I could rest there peacefully, as I thought I could, I was confident I could return to Nome, go back to my job, reclaim my life.

Between Old Life and New: Into and Through Disease

Saying good-bye to Toni, I was grateful that at least I was returning to a world where once again I had a multitude of choices. Or so I assumed.

Here's what I knew about Evie: she played fiddle; she threw pots; she knew Meg, one of my former professors in Fairbanks. And though I guessed she was single, I hadn't felt attracted to her.

Arriving at her place after a long flight and an hour and a half shuttle from Phoenix, I reflected she was right about one thing: her house *did* feel like a healing place. Every piece of furniture, every space, seemed to have been properly thought out, and in proportion. Evie, too, was prettier than I remembered, though I felt no spark there, nothing. We had a day and a half together before she was to go East to visit her parents.

After Toni, who I felt I had little in common with but neediness and disease, yet who I had also become involved with, it was a pleasure being with Evie, whose tastes and interests felt familiar. We stayed up late talking that first night, and it was easy to let the conversation wander, especially without a sexual current. When I detailed what I'd experienced the past eight months—eight months, I couldn't believe it—she offered to call a body worker friend of hers the next morning.

So I received a full-body treatment from Evie's friend. Later, as I jogged the hills near her house, inhaled the dry cool December air, took in the brown hills and white pines, marveled at the clear blue sky so big and deep that it seemed the perfect midpoint between water and space, I reflected that, yes, this was a miracle: I was really getting well.

That night unfolded like the first, but started earlier, and Evie cooked lasagna, opened red wine. We had one glass, a second, and I don't know when or if she touched me, or I touched her, but there was a hug, a kiss, and then we were kissing and kissing. When she invited me to bed, I didn't know what to do, but just let it all wash over me, all of it, happy at least I was pain-free and able.

The next morning I drove Evie to the Phoenix airport, then spent a week alone at her house, then three more days together with her, seventy-two inseparable hours. My body didn't hurt, at least not like it had in the depths of summer or even fall, but it certainly didn't feel right either. No, it certainly didn't feel right.

23

I liked Evie, I knew, but didn't love her, and questioned whether I could, even though we had become lovers. About relationships, everybody has theories, and I had mine, which was chemistry was an ineffable thing, but whatever that thing was, at least at some level it was apparent from the start. And though our first night together had been passionate, it had also felt like an aberration, a one-time thing. Evie certainly seemed capable of loving me. Was I scared to love? I asked myself. Why had I let this get started? Could I learn to love Evie? Maybe we just needed more time.

In New York, I hadn't especially liked Toni, certainly hadn't loved her, and yet had allowed a season-long relationship with her that had run a course, had felt neither good nor bad, but just was. I was grateful for the help, but now I was elsewhere, wondering what I was going to do next. I loved my life in Alaska, was supposed to return in the next days, yet feared I wouldn't be able to make that return. Maybe this relationship was a variation of the same thing I'd had with Toni—a tenderer, more compressed version.

Or maybe I was still sick. After all, I was someone whose job was to plan lessons weeks in advance in order to teach successfully over telephone and now I couldn't get it together to buy an advance plane ticket. Was I really going to be okay? When I finally called the airline, I found I could get to Seattle no problem, but to get to Nome on time for the first day of classes, I'd have to pay more than $1100, double the usual. I decided to fly to Seattle, pick up the bags I stashed there, and see how I felt before buying a ticket to Nome. Evie offered to drive me to Phoenix. Kissing me good-bye at the airport, she said I should do whatever I needed, but if I wanted to return to Arizona, she'd be happy to make space for me to stay as long as I needed. Crying, I walked into the terminal.

A few hours later, back in Seattle, I felt stretched three ways: one part up to Alaska, another part down to Arizona, a third part held right there in Seattle. Maybe that was why, I reflected, my body felt like it was falling apart again: one more round of drama. And I was sick of drama. I tried calling the director of the campus, my boss in Nome, to ask how things were in town. It was hard tracking her down, but I finally found her in one of the Anchorage hospitals. Her son had been badly hurt earlier that day in a snow-machine accident, and had been airlifted to the city in serious condition. She'd flown in early in the evening, had just arrived at his bedside. I could hear her weary sigh.

You know what it's like here, she finally said. If you have any doubts at all, don't come back now. It's dark and cold. We can get by without you. What's important is that you get well.

I thanked her, told her I'd let her know as soon as I could one way or the other, and that I'd pray for her boy.

Thanking me back, she hung up.

A day later, suffering increasingly sharp pains through my knees and elbows, I called Evie to tell her I'd be flying back to Arizona and to expect me the following evening. Then I left a message with my boss in Nome requesting a second leave of absence.

Looking back, it was no wonder Evie had difficulties making sense of my condition. Two weeks earlier I'd arrived from New York City, shaky from the long months of illness, but temporarily pain-free, able to jog, capable of responding to a flirtation. When I returned, it was with many of the same symptoms I'd battled for months. Where Toni was able to accept that I was sick, Evie wanted to take a more active hand in the healing. Why didn't I sit in the sun, she wondered, as she saw me spend the afternoon on the couch reading and napping. Why not go for a walk, or a ride with me up to Jerome or Sedona, or at least if you do have to lie around doing nothing, at least be more positive. I shrugged my shoulders, went back to one more of the health and healing books I'd been consuming throughout the process. Though I felt much better than I had the preceding summer, my arms and legs were still hurting. It would have been fun playing music with Evie, but I couldn't. I wished my knees didn't hurt, but they did, and for now I couldn't go further than a couple of blocks, down the street and back. The next week I began seeing a therapist, a body worker, an acupuncturist, a naturopath, a macrobiotic counselor. I joined a wellness group, this my latest round of healing.

By early February, we were well into a routine. After Evie went off to school I'd amble down the street to the convenience store, pick up a newspaper, slowly amble back up to the house, and linger with the paper over breakfast. Days I had appointments, Evie would catch a ride to work with a fellow staffer, and I'd use her car. My counselor in Arizona, George, I considered the best I'd ever had. He was a friend of Evie's, a hypnotherapist who often led wilderness retreats in which he trained other therapists. I only saw him a half-dozen times, this after meeting with one of his associates for four weeks. Each session, we'd talk a bit, and then he'd put me in a trance. His final diagnosis: He'd never met anyone with as much determination to get well, and all he could say with certainty was that my condition was not the result of somehow being depressed, but that I was in the midst of a particularly tenacious disease, and that I'd been doing, and would likely continue to do, everything I could to heal, but, unfortunately, he could make no promises in this case. I might end up perfectly fine in a week, or just as likely continue to suffer the effects for years. There are some mighty powerful bugs out there, he concluded soberly.

Still, the diagnosis, which truly resonated, heartened me—the closest I had to proof that I hadn't somehow just imagined the misery or subconsciously concocted an elaborate ruse. The other Arizona practitioners were also helpful, though it was all too late to save my job. One bright February afternoon, I received a letter stating that since there had never been a conclusive diagnosis of my condition, and since there had been no consistent insurance claims, no duly authorized doctor overseeing the case, my request for a continuation of the leave of absence had been denied.

The news that I was now out of work—my connection to Nome officially severed—made me cry: one more loss in an inexorably long season of them. But once I'd flown back to Arizona, that life in Nome seemed worlds away. This wasn't the worst that had happened. What mattered now was surviving each day, lessening the discomfort, incrementally regaining sustainable health. Though I was hemorrhaging money, I still had enough saved so that wasn't yet a main concern.

The late afternoons, once Evie returned, we'd run errands together, cook dinner, eat, spend the rest of the evening talking, reading, or watching a video, then go to bed. If her band had a rehearsal, she expected me to attend. She loved that we were a couple, even if our relationship had immediately stopped being sexy. Evie had her hopes. I was only grateful I was now well enough to write. One Saturday, disturbed by yet another downturn with my health, frustrated I'd never get well, I picked up a pen and wrote a draft of what was clearly a poem—the first poem in months, not the occasional tortured journal entry I managed when the pain in my elbow relented. By the end of the afternoon, I'd crafted it to what felt like completion. I shared it with Evie, who was clearly happy for me. Sunday, I wrote another. And this, too, became part of the routine—most days writing poems, similar to ones I'd written before, but different too, focused as they were on health-related issues.

Evie didn't have a computer, but did have an old electric typewriter, which I lugged to the small table in the side room, and plugged in. The first time I used it for any length of time, at first I reveled how my fingers remembered the keys, until I felt the pain now shoot through new places, my right palm, and then my left, spots I didn't know could have such pain. Amazing, I thought, that I could still be surprised at how my body might react. I stopped typing for a few days, continued with the handwriting. Later, when I returned to the typewriter, I figured a way to type which didn't hurt, using only my thumbs. Through April I wrote more than forty poems.

The saddest time was May. Not yet feeling well, but consistently better, I'd been fighting with Evie for weeks; we hadn't made love in months. I was not in love with Evie, hadn't been in love with her, and couldn't imagine how I was ever going to be in love with her. One night in bed, crying, she told me this was the best relationship she'd ever had, being with me the past months. Tears in my eyes, I shook my head. Evie had been married twice. I felt so sorry for her, and for myself. At forty, she'd been so worried about spending the rest of her life alone that being with me, even like this, had been an improvement. I'd treated her respectfully, listened to her, confided back.

But to me, just three years younger, also afraid I'd never meet someone to share my life, this had not been the kind of relationship I'd ever imagined or wanted. I'd been sick from the beginning. That was part of it. Now, as I was improving, I realized not only that I didn't love her, and didn't want to live with her any longer, but that I had to go, the sooner the better. To get well would mean to find health and passion in every aspect of my life. Listening to her cry, feeling my own tears, I reached tentatively for her hand and she reached back. Then we hugged once, twice, hugged harder and harder.

After that night, we continued fighting, but fought more gently. We never made love again. And for the first time in my life, I understood how people could become so impossibly trapped in unhappy relationships that they remained in them for years, despite desperately wanting out. It was hard leaving Evie. But a few weeks later I did and returned to Seattle. What needed doing there felt unfinished. This summer would have to be an improvement.

I may not have been healthy yet, but I was healthier. I may not have known what exactly I suffered from, but the past year I'd become an expert on that suffering. This time, arriving in Seattle, I had a better idea how to proceed.

It helped that one of my friends, Jamie, invited me to stay in the basement of the house he rented in Wallingford. Jamie, no stranger to the occasional dark time, had been the one who originally told me about the old Chinese curse: *May you live in interesting times.* He was a banjo player I'd occasionally played music with, had been a stalwart pal the preceding summer, and was happy I was clearly doing so much better and that he could offer me a convenient place. Immediately after moving in, I called Richard, the body worker who'd been so good to me the year before. I only saw him a few more times that summer, long enough to be encouraged that, yes, even if I doubted it now, I'd be playing music again. In fact, he insisted I buy his old Flatiron mandolin, since he was having a new one custom-made by a luthier. No hurry, he said; he'd save it for me. I tried again making an appointment with Darla, the healer's healer, the naturopath he'd referred me to the preceding summer, the one I'd have needed to wait nine months to see. When I called now, I learned she was no longer taking new patients. But since she shared office space with a second doctor, I decided to try that other one, guessing the magic in the building would still find me.

I didn't feel well, but didn't feel badly either, and luxuriated in the normalcy of being virtually pain-free. When I walked too much, I could feel heaviness in my knees, even my toes. There was a cloudiness, too, in my arms, wrists, and hands. But as long as I was conscious, it was something I could handle. Fibromyalgia? Maybe. An exotic auto-immune disease? Perhaps. Chronic fatigue syndrome? Possibly. I'd been through all those avenues, and more. This was my disease even if I still didn't know what it was. One naturopath for now was enough. I'd buy an occasional bodywork session if I felt like it. I had no desire to play music or go dancing. I didn't want to date. I was just glad to be doing this well.

July, I attended a wedding near Mount Rainier. Later that month, I moved into the upstairs of a house twenty-five blocks from Jamie's, the southern end of Wallingford, close to the Fremont neighborhood, owned by a musician, Anita, who earned money writing for high-tech companies. August, I flew to Nome, where I gathered what of my belongings I could find, selling a few, giving away more, mailing the rest down to Seattle. Busy place, Nome. Forever timeless. As always, I loved it and hated it—that hadn't changed. Returning to Anita's, I set my old computer on a card table there in the upstairs room, and pulled up a chair. That was my office. Mornings, I'd lie in bed and write, usually completing a new poem, sometimes two. That fall I was writing more about disease and disability—my own process and others—but also poems about family, and plenty about Nome, as well as whatever else might strike me. For further inspiration, I'd dip into the heap of poetry collections stacked by the side of the bed. Regardless, I'd type until I walked the mile to downtown Fremont, where I'd find a cafe for a bowl of soup, a salad, a look at the newspaper. Then back to the house, where sometimes there might be another session on the computer. More often I'd nap, and then walk uphill to the center of Wallingford, or further to the University District for a cup of tea, a dessert, maybe a movie.

Anita and I would occasionally sit at the kitchen table and talk. She was long estranged from her family in California; I'd been long estranged from mine. In my case, my parents had split up bitterly once I'd left for college. Almost immediately, my mother had moved to Florida, not far from where her own widowed mother, my grandmother, lived. My father had remained in our hometown of Philadelphia, remarried, and several years later also moved to South Florida, within a few hours of my mother. My own move out west in the mid-80's, and then up north, had put an appropriate distance between us, I thought. Those two years in Nome, I could not have been further on the continent, which was not a bad thing. Ever since I'd begun writing poems, I occasionally wrote about them, but the new poems put family relationships into another perspective. So much about my family was toxic. The poems were not gentle.

Late October, when I complained during an appointment that the heaviness in my legs was still present, that it still hurt when I walked too far, the naturopath furrowed her brow. A minute later, she said I really should be seeing improvement, and that she didn't think she was the one to help me, and would refer me to another practitioner.

Well, refer me to Darla, I said, naming her office partner.

Nobody sees Darla, she said.

She's next door, I said. If you feel like you can't help me, you can at least ask.

Okay, she said wearily. I'll ask Darla for you, but she's not seeing anybody new. I'll call around and let you know who you might see.

Later that week, the naturopath phoned. When I answered, she said, I can't believe it, but Darla said if your schedule is flexible, she'll see you when she has a cancellation. It still might mean you won't see her for months. Or that you'll have to come in on extremely short notice.

Fine, I said. I can do that.

Then she named several other naturopaths I might want to consult.

The next day, I received a call from Darla and saw her that same afternoon.

More than fourteen years later now, I still don't know what it is Darla does—her mix of homeopathy, bodywork, crystals, talk therapy, astrological charts, and God knows what else—only that once I started seeing her, I started healing more quickly. My witch doctor, I took to calling her. Remembering that convalescent time, it was as if I was slowly sloughing off the disease poem by poem, and what remedies Darla gave me catalyzed the process. In fact, that fall, when I showed her some of the poems I was writing, she was quick to say they helped point to what she needed to prescribe next. They weren't necessarily the strongest poems or the ones quickest to be accepted in journals, I found, but they did feel honest in their lyric treatment of body symptoms—the one about the divorcée vomiting up years of marriage, another about the insomniac remembering years of abuse.

You were a mighty sick man, she said to me towards the end of one session, shaking her head. In fact, I think we're pretty fortunate you're still here.

So what did I have? I asked. Other than George, the hypnotherapist I saw in Arizona, no health practitioner ever acknowledged the severity of what I'd been through. I wanted to know more.

There's no name for what you've had. If people ask, you can say chronic fatigue syndrome, but that's not it either.

It's not? I said.

She shook her head.

That was the end of it, but for an insight I had several months later. I could at least recall the little house I rented in Nome. Maybe it had a faulty heater, maybe low levels of carbon monoxide leaked into the house—not enough to kill anybody but enough to gradually make someone very, very sick. I'll never know, but it might explain that tumult I experienced the first year in Nome, when I arrived as healthy as I'd ever been, then months later experienced such frightening lows, especially the New Year's week in Seattle, days of non-stop dementia that led to a strange night in the university hospital psychiatric ward, an even stranger release, the flight back to Nome, and the struggle to continue through the spring semester. It might explain how I'd felt so much better after being out of that Nome house for three months, and then returned to it, only to slowly fall into sickness again, so by the end of the year, it was in me so deep that there was no way to quickly heal.

I'll never know, but it was what I accepted in order to go on.

During that year in Anita's Seattle house, as I regained my health, I fought to reclaim other aspects of my old life. In addition to writing all those poems, I was again submitting poems and stories for publication, and was quickly receiving more acceptances than I'd ever had. I led a few writing workshops around Seattle, and while only a handful attended, they showed me I still wanted to teach, and enjoyed doing it. In February, realizing I'd written so many poems about Nome, I made a list of even more poems I should compose about specific people and places there, wrote them in a rush, and there I had it, a 120-page full-length collection. March, I flew to the Aleutians to lead a writing workshop at the branch campus there, where I also visited classes in the school, and since I was back in state, flew to Fairbanks to visit friends. One night at a party, I met Michael Nye, the husband of a writer from Texas, Naomi Shihab Nye, who was in state for a month to lead writing workshops throughout Alaska, including Nome. Since I'd just finished the manuscript, and I thought it would be of interest, I passed it along to him. The next day, Naomi called. She'd already read it and wanted to meet me. Keep sending this book out, she said at the end of our conference. These poems deserve readers.

Into June, then July, I felt confident that I was truly getting well. I might not have felt like playing fiddle just yet, but thought I'd certainly be getting back to it. One afternoon I called Richard. True to his word, he'd been saving his old mandolin for me, had recently been thinking of me, in fact. I stopped by his house, intending just to look at it, but Richard's price was so reasonable, I left with the mandolin and case. That same summer, my friend Stephanie was low on money. I was running low too, but still had some, enough at least to buy the banjo she was selling. One evening, I tried jogging a few hundred yards, and it felt fine. The next evening, I tried again, felt an ache in my toe, and said, no, not yet for that. Days, I went back to the novel, and finally finished the story within the story at the end of the long second section, the part I'd abandoned my first winter in Nome.

August, I flew back to Juneau for the first time since the folk festival. Ostensibly there to see friends, I was visiting to scout about moving back. Just as I'd felt I'd left Seattle the previous summer with my work there unfinished, my time up north felt similarly incomplete. After all, I was still an Alaska resident. But first I needed to check if I really wanted to return full-time, and, more importantly, whether it was in the interests of my health to return. Hedging my bets a few months earlier, I'd applied to join Alaska's artists-in-the-school roster. While I wasn't certain when I'd be back playing fiddle, I could always go into schools and teach writing, and I had more work connections in Alaska than anywhere.

Spending a week in Juneau, exploring opportunities, confident I could find work, I was convinced to return. Southeast Alaska was close enough to Seattle so it would be reasonable to continue with my naturopath, yet I'd still be in Alaska, where I felt most at home and where I could more likely find work that mattered. And I needed to work. After twenty-seven months without income, one health expense after another, I was finally going broke.

2
How'd I Get Into This Racket, Anyway?

Nome Celebrity

Two years writing, teaching,
fiddling, sharing all I could,
I was known in Nome, maybe,
as one of the crazies
who rode a bike winter-long.

Then I walked from a plane crash.
Old-timers I didn't think knew me
now greeted me by name. I saw
how others watched, and whispered.
I let drunks touch me for luck.

I flew to Juneau late October, arriving on a cold, crisp fall day. The state capital, Juneau, wedged tight by mountain and water, accessible only by plane and boat, is notorious for its lack of housing. But I had friends, and until I found a permanent and affordable place somewhere downtown so I wouldn't need a car, I planned a mix of spare rooms, housesits, occasional sublets, the odd short-term rental. Through New Year's, I'd already arranged for a two-month sublet, and had leads for others. I had no job and almost no money, but I did have credit cards, and I was getting more and more poems published. No money there, but at least my vita was growing. Now that I'd returned to the novel, which I'd started in Juneau the year after graduate school, and which I'd always felt had merit, I was going to finish it. I didn't yet feel 100% healthy, but I was getting closer, which was the most important thing. Though I wasn't playing fiddle, the big house I was living in, which I was sharing with four others, had a history of musicians. Thanksgiving, when I did take out the fiddle and played a few tunes, my right elbow felt fine, just minor discomfort in my left hand, forearm, wrist, and fingers. Playing almost felt natural again. The only thing really hurting was my pride: I sounded so rusty.

Mostly, my return to Juneau meant a return to full-time income-producing work, or, in my case, full-time job hunting which, in theory, would lead to income. My first week back, I led a session at the state literacy council conference in Juneau, meeting two teachers that led to a pair of invitations late February in the interior of the state. I researched grants and applied to every one that fit my skills. Getting word I'd been turned down for the artist-in-the-school roster surprised me, but the next week I received news that I'd been invited to give a reading and lead a workshop at the state's bilingual-multicultural conference early February in Anchorage. And the week following, I received an invitation to teach a month at the summer fine arts camp in Fairbanks. Weekend mornings, I led writing workshops in a used bookstore. Attendance was usually slim, but I met people, and it always felt useful, even if only one or two others came. Back in Fairbanks when I was in graduate school, I used to teach in the prison. One week we had a visitor, Joe Bruchac, from upstate New York. Taking part in his workshop, listening to us share what we'd written, listening to him read his own piece at the end, I thought that was the trick: to not only get paid for inspiring others to write, but to get paid for your own writing practice.

For my conference in Anchorage, my friend Penelope, who'd once taken classes from me, offered to help gather a few dozen of my poems set in Nome and design a chapbook—that is, a stapled pamphlet. My computer, an ancient double-floppy-disk contraption suitable only for basic word-processing, was useless for this task. Penelope lived on a boat and had a new laptop. I'd visit to type the poems on her computer. Three short sessions and we were nearly done. The last day, she chose fonts, offered several options for a cover, and, once I approved one, proofed the manuscript. Then she copied the file onto a disk, which we carried to a print shop. The next day I carried home a boxful of chapbooks, one hundred copies, which cost a hundred and fifty dollars. It was that easy. If I needed a sign, a few days later a check arrived in the mail for $100 from another former writing class attendee, Barbara, in Seattle, who felt she wanted to support whatever I was up to now, and hoped the money would be useful. It felt wonderful handing one of the chapbooks, signed, to Penelope, and shipping off another to Barbara.

How'd I Get into This Racket, Anyway?

At the conference in Anchorage, I read aloud from the chapbook, played a few fiddle tunes, and, by the end of the three-day event, had sold twenty-two books at $5 each. The conference had paid for my flight up and back. I'd rented a car and had stayed for free on a couch at a friend's upholstery shop in South Anchorage. Factoring the incidental expenses in participating, I calculated that with the $210 I'd brought in—adding Barbara's check to my book sales—I'd not only already paid for that first run of chapbooks, but still had seventy copies left. Self-publishing had its stigma, I knew. But Walt Whitman had done it. And I'd recently read how James Joyce, T.S. Eliot, and Virginia Woolf had self-published at various times of their lives. Obviously, I was no Whitman, Joyce, Eliot, or Woolf. But still, it meant others had taken this path. I liked having the book to show off and sell. Yes, I thought, I'll take to this small-press book business.

Later the same month, I flew back to Anchorage, and rented a car to drive to Fairbanks and then the schools in Delta Junction and Tok that had hired me to visit. Having free time after arriving in Anchorage, I had the notion to stop by the office of the woman who administered the artists-in-the school roster. The past months, querying for jobs, occasionally having to admit, no, I wasn't on the list of artists approved by the state arts council, I'd returned to that rejection. Having recognized many of the names that had been chosen, for the most part writers that didn't have half of my credentials, I wondered what my application lacked. Had it been my illness? My time out of state? I hadn't talked about that on the application, and it wasn't common knowledge, but still, I thought, that was the explanation that made the most sense. After parking the car, I quickly found the office. The door was half-open, the administrator in. I knocked as I approached her desk, and explained who I was and what I wanted to know.

I'd caught her by surprise. How else to judge the candid response that followed?

Oh, I remember your application. It was red-flagged. No one knew who you were, so the committee didn't believe you did the work you claimed.

I don't remember if I shook her hand. I left her office stunned, and remained stunned driving up the Glenn Highway, taking the left turn onto the Parks, the ride through Wasilla, and up past the Talkeetna turnoff. A beautiful day, I can recall, sun out, clear and cold, in the winter light each mountain an impossible treat. It was a ride I ordinarily loved, though this trip I just kept shaking my head. I'd arrived in Alaska nearly ten years earlier. Granted, I'd been ill and out of state for much of the past three years. But I'd lived in Fairbanks three years, Juneau a year, Sitka a year, Nome two years, and now I was back in Juneau. I'd taught full-time for three years in the university system. I'd received an MFA from Fairbanks. I now had over a hundred published poems and stories, a good number in top-flight national journals. This was Alaska, for God's sakes, where everybody knew every-body, and I'd been a legal resident nearly ten years, and if no one knew who I was, I had a problem, a real problem. Worse, whoever was on the committee not only didn't know me, but didn't even care enough to bother calling my references. *They didn't believe I did the work I claimed.* By God, 38 years old, I hadn't done all that much. After all, I wasn't Joyce Carol Oates. Past Trapper Creek, I vowed to do a better job of making myself known. How else was I ever to find work?

A month later I returned to the AWP Conference, the one I'd first attended in Minneapolis. This year it was held in Pittsburgh. Here the arts council did offer support, a third of my plane ticket, $150. Otherwise I paid my own expenses, shaving costs by staying several blocks from the conference site in a sad rundown hotel above a strip club. Walking back and forth, making a trail from my cheap little room to the conference panels and readings, I felt like I was psychically hiking each morning from Nome and returning there to sleep each night.

Prior to the folk festival in April, Penelope was busy, so I had another friend help design what would be my second chapbook, to include all my poems about old-time music and dance. Positive it would sell, I ordered 500. And when I did my solo set which combined fiddling and poetry, I was able to read from it, and mention from the stage I had books for sale.

This new one didn't immediately sell as well as the first, but I liked how it looked and read, and one thing was sure: I now had plenty to peddle. At the fine arts camp in Fairbanks, I loved the lit June and July nights, the long hot days. After what I'd been through, it astounded me to be actually enjoying a Fairbanks summer. It was my favorite place in Alaska, my favorite time of year. Riding my bike every-where, hardly leaving time to sleep, I felt healthy. Free moments, I found myself pulling the fiddle out like I used to; during the camp sessions, I wrote poems along with the campers, strong poems it felt like. All my expenses were taken care of and I even received a reasonable paycheck at the end of the month. I only wished the camp had lasted longer. As it was, I stayed in Fairbanks an extra two weeks in order to use the computers on campus. Learning as I went along, I designed four more of my own books—two more of Alaska poems, two about relationships. As an afterthought, I even designed a dozen poetry postcards similar to cards I'd seen elsewhere.

Returning to Juneau for August, I found myself back at the other work, querying for jobs by letter, phone, or else in person. When I discovered disks from the Fairbanks university computers didn't work at the print shop I used in Juneau, I decided on a more old-fashioned approach, pasting the poems in proper order side-by-side, and asked the print shop to photocopy the pages, card stock for the cover. The results were more than adequate. One sunny afternoon, I hiked the trail up Mount Roberts, and easily summitted, though I hadn't intended to, had only meant to climb a short way. The descent was joyous. Mid month, performing in Haines at the Southeast Alaska State Fair, asked to provide a description of what I did, I thought to call myself Alaska's Fiddling Poet. Why not? The three words accurately described the act and might even be catchy.

A few weeks later, I traveled to Seattle for Labor Day weekend, and the big arts festival, Bumbershoot. I bought table space there at the book fair, had even printed my first catalog for the occasion, and sold enough of my six chapbooks to pay for the table and my naturopathic appointment. Now I had seventy names on a Seattle mailing list, which might also be of use someday. One night several months earlier, in the bar at the Alaskan Hotel, concerned about money, I'd been talking with a friend about grants when another friend, Bob, sitting a table away, overheard and interrupted, Grants are all well and good if you can get them. But the trouble is you can't ever depend on them. And that's where credit cards come in.

Dumbfounded, I looked at him. I'd never trusted credit cards, never had thought about them like that, always used them with extreme caution when I used them at all. But the remark stuck, and as the year went on, realizing my bank account had emptied and that I needed to continue growing this business, I saw he was right. This was a unique time and I needed to do everything I could to promote myself. I hadn't thought twice, then, about using the cards to fly to Pittsburgh, or to publish the second chapbook, or the next four, or to buy stamps, buy office supplies, even pay for rent and food. Every time I saw Bob after that night, I updated him on my financial status.

After awhile, he just shook his head and winced. You're not supposed to go from three to five to seven under. You're supposed to pay them back.

I will, I said. I will. Besides, one of these days I'll get a grant and get caught up all at once. Anyway, I just found a place to rent. Only $300 a month for a studio apartment without a kitchen. The yellow Coast Guard house near Cope Park. I'll get by. I know it.

Smiling, my friend shook his head one more time.

Settling into that room in the old Coast Guard house, I worked more hours, it seemed, than I ever had when I taught. There was always so much to do, between querying for gigs, to keeping unpublished poems out in the mail, to writing new ones, to keeping current with my new-found interest in local, state, and national politics. The capital city Juneau was all about policy, and it was almost impossible to avoid thinking about the repercussions.

Each summer, as more and more cruise ships docked in Juneau, the downtown felt more and more overrun. That was one thing, but as rents rose, the more unique shops couldn't afford to stay as bigger businesses filled the spaces. A local corporation was well on its way to building a tramline from the pier to the top of Mount Roberts, this in seemingly direct violation of city ordinances. Some state legislators were also proposing building a road to Juneau as a way to ease access. I wondered what they really meant. This particular project would entail building seventy miles of very expensive road along an avalanche-prone coastline to a spot where motorists would still need to catch a ferry. Residents from Anchorage and Fairbanks, the two big population centers nearly a thousand miles away, would continue to fly in for business. Summer tourists in cars and RV's might be happy about the shorter ferry ride, but Juneau streets were already clogged during those months. People who wanted to come already had their access. Juneau was always going to be a far place, and the majority of people liked it just the way it was. The ferry system worked fine.

How'd I Get into This Racket, Anyway?

October, I flew to Fairbanks to lead teacher workshops at that year's state literacy conference, and then visited an elementary school there. Later in the month, I flew to Oregon to attend Arts Northwest, a conference for presenters in the region —big and small arts councils, performing arts centers, and theaters mostly— who had budgets to book artists, often those they met on site. November and December, I remained in Juneau, putting together two more poetry chapbooks—one of comedy sonnets, one of newly written political poems. Meanwhile, my bills continued increasing. Though I never stopped thinking of the novel, it was a challenge making time. I must not have been ready. There was only so much I could do.

Mid February, I flew to Nome for a week in the schools as a visiting artist, my first time back since moving my possessions out two and a half years before. It was to be the start of a five-week tour in the region, and would include nine villages in the Bering Straits School District. I'd spent months arranging the details, and while it wasn't going to be huge money, the $7000 I'd be earning would cut my spiraling credit card debt in half. I looked forward to reconnecting with old friends in rural Alaska, meeting former students, enjoying March Iditarod festivities.

As long as I didn't live in Nome, it was a fine place to visit. I used to think of the bar scene as a perpetually frozen Mardi Gras with no hint of Lent, which in short doses was hugely entertaining. People seized on any occasion to drink, invariably to excess. Friday nights were always good, as were Thursdays, Wednesdays, Tuesdays, and Mondays—hell, a former Nomeite returning for a visit was good for several nights out in a row—so I'd had one fun week in Nome, and then spent a week on St. Lawrence Island, working in Savoonga and Gambell. They were the only two settlements on the island, though Gambell was especially notable. Just forty miles from Siberia, it was a collection of approximately a hundred and fifty houses, many no better than shacks, on a desolate strip of gravel. Most slept seven or eight in two or three rooms. There were two stores, an administrative building, a school. Siberian Yup'ik was the first language, English a distant second. Visiting Gambell when I used to teach in the region, I'd once taken my fiddle to the school, and a teacher told me most of the kids had never before seen a violin. And while to my eyes, the community always appeared impoverished, I learned on earlier trips that beneath the surface was a close-knit, complicated place where virtually everybody was related. They were intensely proud of their culture and homeland, and saw *me* as impoverished because I lacked a similar family structure.

Returning to Nome, I spent a weekend hanging out in the bars with friends, then flew to Teller, where I worked two days in the school, did a public performance, and visited my friends teaching there. I left Teller Wednesday morning on a snow machine, and rode the seven miles across sea ice to the village of Brevig Mission. I repeated my Teller schedule and worked two days in the school, then performed Thursday night in the gym, a show notable because the large crowd paid little attention at first. They were there for the chance to win the raffle that was to follow my set. Early on, my hour looked to be a disaster as the adults talked loudly in the bleachers, their children running unsupervised throughout. But then I had an idea. First, I asked the younger kids whether they wanted to play some games. A few were agreeable, so I requested they all form a big circle. Quickly, they arranged themselves into a ring. I'd always thought I might call dances someday, and here was my chance. As I continued playing the fiddle, I called a simple circle dance, which led into an impromptu Simon Says kind of game, where I asked the kids to pretend to lie down and go to sleep, then to dream they were puppy dogs, then kitty cats, then birds, and then bears, all with the appropriate sound effects. The dance went on for twenty minutes as I stretched the game as long as I possibly could. Succeeding in front of that audience, I remembered feeling like I could go anywhere, do anything.

The next day, Friday, I was weathered in at Brevig. Early Saturday afternoon, trying to return to Nome on the scheduled Grant Aviation flight, the only passenger on a six-seater plane, flying through more bad weather, we hit a hill twenty miles from Nome, near the mouth of the Sinuk River.

Really, it was no big deal: we didn't go down. Visibility had been poor and the pilot thought we were over the frozen ocean; instead we'd drifted inland. We'd been lucky to clip a hill, which meant we'd hit, skipped, then hit again for good, but a bit slower. Any lower, we'd have hit straight on and been killed. Any higher, we'd have missed the one hilltop, hit something else, and, once again, likely died. The plane was totalled, the pilot uninjured but in shock, and I'd somehow hit my head on the co-pilot wheel, gotten briefly knocked out, and had come to, profusely bleeding from head wounds. Fortunately, we were found three hours later, with enough daylight so we could be hauled to town on a snow machine just before nightfall. I needed more than a hundred stitches and spent a few days hospitalized. Doctors were unsure whether I'd fractured vertebrae, so I had to be flown to Anchorage for tests. It was only when I was released, no internal damage found, that I tried walking out of the hospital and felt all wobbly. The effects of the concussion lasted well into the fall.

When I told this story, most people thought it strange that the pilot panicked as he did. Knowing he'd made a critical error, he'd wanted to run to town for help, even though he was in tennis shoes, and didn't know where he was. And they thought it stranger that I remained calm throughout, so calm that a few hours into it, when the pilot panicked yet again, fearing we wouldn't be found, and asked me if I had anything to talk about, anything to read, I responded by going into my backpack and reading him poems from my chapbooks, literally giving him his own personal poetry reading.

What I thought strangest, though, was afterwards, the realization that not only had I grounds for a lawsuit, but it was Grant Aviation I'd flown with. *Grant Aviation.* Somehow or other I was going to get my grant. The crash may have cost me up-front the forty-five hundred dollars I'd have earned the following three weeks, but I was going to receive more than that in the end. Even before leaving Nome two weeks later, I'd made an appointment with an attorney there, who had agreed to take on the case.

Ultimately, it was as my friend, Dan, from Haines said. *Ken's plane crash: Good career move.* That said it. Not only was I in position to make money from the pilot's error, but it was a story I could benefit from in the telling and the writing.

Still, in my case, the truth was something different. As difficult as the concussion was, as much as I'd never want to experience another one, that plane wreck experience was easier than the illness time. About the plane wreck: there was nothing for me to do but keep my wits about me until rescue. It might sound romantic to survive a crash, and for some people, maybe it is. But mine was not romantic. It was just something that happened to me.

A month and a half after the crash, I boarded a plane from Juneau and flew to Atlanta to attend the upcoming AWP conference. My plans had been made prior to the accident, and though I wasn't fully well, I saw no reason to cancel the trip. The fresh scars on my forehead certainly made for a story if anyone asked, though nobody did since I spent most of conference alone in my room, within myself. I did meet John Crawford, publisher of West End Press in Albuquerque, who had a table in the book fair. He specialized in multicultural, Native American, and political poetry. After introducing myself the first day, I asked if he'd like a copy of my first chapbook, the one set in and around Nome. He nodded yes. When I checked back with him later in the conference, he invited me to send a complete manuscript.

May, I saw a neurologist in Seattle, as well as my naturopath. Head injuries, I learned, were difficult to track. At least the scars were slowly fading. Still, as much as I wished to return to full speed, I was content to go at what pace I needed. Returning to Fairbanks for the Fine Arts Camp, I didn't even tempt myself by bringing a bike. Instead I led workshops as best I could, spent the evenings in, typing. Since I didn't feel well enough to go out, or even to write much, I'd type poems into the computer. Over the four weeks, I put together eight new poetry chapbooks and designed dozens of new poetry postcards. Now I had a chapbook of sports poems, a book with poems about disease and healing, a book with poems about writing, and five more. In August, I spent an evening with a Juneau friend who had recording equipment, so I stood in front of a microphone, read the few dozen poems I'd written about my plane wreck, played fiddle tunes, and made a cassette. Labor Day, when I went down to Seattle for the Bumbershoot book fair, I now had a catalog with 16 chapbooks, had the cassette in production, and was even selling a deck of 52 poetry postcards. That year I'd been invited to read at the festival, a ten-minute opening slot one evening in a big theater. Taking out the fiddle, I played a tune, then read a few of the plane wreck poems. It seemed like the large crowd enjoyed the combination of music and poetry.

Unable to follow up on jobs the preceding spring, I only had a single two-week residency in Hoonah that fall as well as a few days of work in Anchorage, so I spent time scheduling school dates for February, March, and April. Fortunately, I was able to return to the Bering Straits region for repeat visits to several villages as well as to finally get to the schools I'd missed the previous year. Also, thanks to a storyteller I met who lived in Bethel, and was a teacher there, I received an invitation to visit several schools in the Lower Kuskokwim School District, based in Bethel. And the end of the year, I was invited up to the North Slope for the first time—one day at the Middle School in Barrow, a week in Nuiqsut.

From Thanksgiving to New Year's, I finally had the time and energy to return to the novel, and I worked on it for five weeks, completing the third section before flying to Seattle to see my naturopath and perform in the city. From there, I performed in cafes and bookstores in Olympia, Portland, Eugene, Corvallis— a successful tour, I thought, fun dates with reasonable turnouts, even newspaper and radio coverage. Returning, I had to prepare for nine weeks of touring, first to Anchorage, then to the Nome region, then on to Bethel and beyond.

More than ten months after the plane wreck, I felt near fully recovered. Now I was mainly concerned with my debt. Though I'd been a Management Sciences major as an undergraduate at Duke University, I'd never gotten in the habit of keeping strict financial records. This had been no problem in my twenties when I waited tables, nor had it been a problem in graduate school, nor when I'd been a professor. It wasn't even a problem now, I reflected, since the credit card statements that arrived every month were a better record than anything I could invent, as long as I was careful to save them in a place I could find them. One February evening on this tour, my second week out, I calculated my debt to the dollar, estimating my expected take for the next few months. That moment I was within two thousand dollars of my final credit limit, closer than even I was comfortable with. Though I'd be netting several thousand dollars through the end of the school year, and had another good month in Fairbanks lined up for this summer, I had no jobs yet for the fall. The money wasn't going to last. The biggest trouble, I realized, was the longer at this business, the more I learned of opportunities that would enable me to continue, but to take advantage of these opportunities invariably meant spending money up front. The past three and a half years, even cutting corners as I could, using every last frequent flyer coupon I'd had saved, I'd averaged just over an eight thousand dollar deficit a year. At that pace, I'd be bankrupt by Christmas.

In Nome, I made an appointment with my attorney, who felt good about my prospects. He didn't think it would have to come to trial, he said, but it might, and if it did, it would likely be this coming summer in Nome; he advised me to be ready.

Working continuously took my mind off my debt, and it felt triumphant those weeks in rural Alaska, boarding small planes for the first time since the crash, visiting those villages rescheduled from the previous year, then moving on to the Yup'ik villages outside of Bethel, communities which felt both familiar to the Inupiat villages near Nome, but wholly different, places with names like Eek, Kwigillingok, Kongiganek, Tuntutuliak, Kipnuk. The end of March, I flew back to Juneau, attended the festival there, jetted to the AWP conference, and returned to Juneau via Northern California, where I worked three days in schools near Grass Valley, performed one night in San Francisco. After spending two weeks back in Juneau, I flew to Barrow.

There, even this deep into the year, despite nearly twenty-four hours of daylight, wind-chills were below zero. Having finished a successful day at the middle school, I decided to stop at the elementary, where I sought out the principal, who strode out of his office, waited impatiently on the other side of a counter for me to begin. I quickly explained what I was doing in Barrow, and what I'd be doing the following week in Nuiqsut, and how I was a writer and musician, a former college professor in Nome, who played fiddle, got kids excited about writing and reading. I mentioned the day at the middle school had gone well, so was here inquiring about returning in the future to share my talents in his building.

No, there will never be interest or money here for the kind of thing you do, he said abruptly, waving me off. Then he turned back toward his office.

I left the building embarrassed and confused. No, I hadn't set up an appointment, I thought, but wasn't it self-evident that I was offering something of benefit? And not only that, this was Barrow, the northernmost settlement on the continent. Here, of all places, since I was already working in town and taken the time to offer my services personally and politely, shouldn't I at least have been treated a little more courteously, even if it somehow was the wrong time to stop by? And what did the principal mean by that anyway: there would never be interest or money in the kind of thing I do? Did he mean he was somehow anti-reading and anti-writing? Was he anti-music? Not only that, this was the North Slope, home of the Prudhoe Bay oil fields, which made this, per capita, the wealthiest borough in the state. If anywhere could afford what I offered, it was here, and at the time I wasn't even charging that much for my work in schools: $350/day plus expenses.

I took a deep breath, another, wondered if I'd ever learn to take rejection more graciously, wondered why I bothered with this or any of it. Then the wind kicked up. I slid, lost my balance, barely caught myself. Continuing to walk toward my hotel room, I chuckled. By God, I was in Barrow. To the north, it was white. To the west, white. East and south, white. Except for the buildings, and the sky, everywhere was white. Dirty white, bluish white, ice white. So many whites, everything the same and different. Somewhere out on the sea ice, whaling crews were camped, waiting. Tonight I'd eat at Pepe's North of the Border, the furthest north Mexican restaurant in the world. Tomorrow morning I'd fly to Nuiqsut, where I'd spend a week at the school. A week from today, I'd fly back to Barrow and would perform here Friday evening. An old college pal was joining me, a doctor in Louisville, who loved winter and snow, and for more than a decade had been joking about meeting me in Barrow. When the job came through, I wrote him, and he was taking a week off work and from family. We'd spend the weekend here before flying to Fairbanks for a few days. So what that the elementary school principal had summarily dismissed me? So what that I was nearly bankrupt? Today I'd inspired some Barrow middle-schoolers. Tonight I'd sleep well.

Two weeks later, my attorney called. He'd just received a call from the lawyer for Grant Aviation. The airline company, he said, was willing to settle for $75,000.

What do you think? I asked my attorney. With my two-thirds share, I'd come away with $50,000.

What do you think? he said, answering my question with his own.

I'll need more time to think, but I just don't know. It's a lot of money, sure, and it would help me out, but it doesn't sound just right. I don't know. It just seems like it should be $100,000. When do I have to let them know?

Monday. They said it was on the table through the weekend. Anyway, that's the offer today. It could change Monday. My own sense is there's another offer out there because they don't want to risk a trial in Nome. They'd probably split the difference, and call it $85,000. But I can't guarantee that, or anything else other than they've offered $75,000 today.

Listening, I imagined the lawyer's work, the thousands of these kinds of conversations he'd had in his career. $85,000. The additional ten thousand would mean an extra sixty-six hundred dollars, almost four solid weeks of school visits.

I told him to tell Grant Aviation that if they could come up with $100,000, I was ready to settle.

Done, he grunted.

Within a week, I'd settled for $95,000, and was congratulated by my lawyer, who said I'd shown guts at the end, that in this instance he himself wouldn't have pushed past the $85,000 that had been the next, and, supposedly, last offer.

There was nothing about the plane crash that took guts, I thought, even this settlement; it had been the illness time that had been so hard, that I was never going to forget.

Still, it felt so good to be in Seattle a few weeks later, performing at the big Memorial Day weekend Folklife Festival, reading at bookstores in Bellingham and on Bainbridge Island, seeing my naturopath, Darla, who thought I was making strides. It felt especially luxurious to write the big checks to MBNA, Bank of America, Citibank, and Chase. One friend gave me the name of a financial planner, who I called to ask how to most sensibly invest what I now had in my bank account. I hoped I'd never experience a similar financial crisis.

There was no time to change my life, even if I wanted to, which I didn't. Besides, it wasn't that much money. So, I'd gone from $25,000 in debt to $40,000 in the bank. What was I going to do differently? That summer I returned to Fairbanks where, in addition to the writing classes, for the first time I taught fiddling at the camp. Returning to Juneau, I recorded a second cassette, this one combining fiddling with all my music poems, and in a burst managed to finish the novel that I'd begun eight years before. Immediately, I started querying agents. I even finally received a response from John Crawford, the West End Press publisher, who'd asked to see my poetry manuscript sixteen months earlier. While he didn't want to publish it as it was, he suggested I cut it nearly in half, add a section, and send it back. He wouldn't promise to publish it even then, but guessed if I managed to make those changes, even if he didn't want to, someone would. I made the revisions within a week, adding a section with several poems about my plane wreck, and mailed it back.

How'd I Get into This Racket, Anyway?

The end of August I flew to Anchorage to lead in-service programs for high-school and middle-school writing teachers, and from there traveled to Seattle to again take part at the Bumbershoot Festival Book Fair. After seeing my naturopath at the conclusion of the fair, I remained south to perform twice in Oregon, where I also attended the Pacific Northwest Booksellers conference.

Finally, I was learning what must have been obvious: to even have a chance at making this work in the long-run, I had to meet as many professionals as I could who were involved in the field, although in my case there were several overlapping fields. Afterwards, there was the follow-up, which meant phone calls and letters, sometimes occasionally dropping by an office if I was in the area. There were endless variations to getting jobs, and often one job would lead to another. For instance, I was not only paid well to lead that particular in-service—a vast improvement over the amount I was paid for the workshops I led for the state literacy conferences—but the full day of sessions introduced me to school district teachers who might later in the year hire me to visit their classes. Savvy teachers had budgets for this.

The hard part here was getting hired for the in-service. How did I make this happen? On one of my many trips through Anchorage, I managed to corral an appointment with the school district's director of language arts, who I'd been trying to meet with for several months; it was her I impressed, there in her office, which led to the invitation to lead the workshops for teachers. Past all the challenges of marketing and self-promotion, which sometimes could seem like a silly, stupid game, there was the fun part: the travel (which was sometimes paid), then the actual teaching or performing (which I loved and which was the reason I did all the rest of this), and finally the paycheck (without which, I couldn't continue).

Early October I was flown back to Nome and Shishmaref to visit schools. Stopping in Anchorage on the way back, I worked a day at Steller Secondary, where I now had a standing invitation from the principal to work. Later in the month, I again attended the Arts Northwest conference, this time in Idaho, and made it part of a tour that included performances in Boise, Moscow, Pocatello, Salmon, and a drive to Denver to take part in the Rocky Mountain Book Festival. Completing this tour of new places was like starting from the beginning again, and I could only have booked these dates after receiving the settlement money. Though

I lost money, I met plenty of new people.

Home in Juneau through December, I turned my attention back to the novel. Having gotten no reaction from the first agents, I queried several more. I didn't ignore the poetry, so also continued sending poems in the mail, a practice which had been harder to find time for, but which I'd never abandoned. The Sunday between Christmas and New Year's, mindful in Juneau I'd never celebrated the settlement, or the completion of the novel, or was in position to throw a party of any kind, I decided to rent out the whole Silverbow Inn, and invited old-time musician Fiddling Wolf to be the guest act. I flew him up from Southern California, where he was tending to family business, and made a mini-festival of it, even having the whole affair catered. The Permanent Fund Party, I called it, my budget being the $1500 each Alaskan received that year through oil revenues. It was better than the Nome celebration I'd held ten weeks earlier, when I invited everyone I knew to show up at the Anchor Tavern at midnight, Friday, where I'd ring the bell and buy drinks for the house. It had been a slow evening, and I escaped spending less than a hundred dollars. In Juneau, we had several acts play onstage amidst plentiful food and drink.

January, I flew back to Seattle, where I performed at a coffeehouse concert series that was well attended and which received a feature, with my photo, in the *Seattle Weekly*, my first big-city notice. Later in the month, I flew back to Anchorage, where I performed at schools and a festival, then returned to Lower Kuskokwim schools for two weeks.

March, I came closest to what passed for vacation. First, I flew to Atlanta, where I visited an old friend, then rented a car and drove to the North Carolina Piedmont, where I'd once lived. There I read and played music at a bookstore, and visited friends I hadn't seen in over a decade. Returning the car to Atlanta, I took a train to New Orleans, where I read at a college that a friend from Fairbanks now taught at. Renting a car, I explored New Orleans clubs, and then drove to Lafayette, where I'd heard there was a terrific music scene, which was certainly true. I flew back to Juneau for a few days, then was back in Oregon and California for the annual AWP conference, as well as for more performances and school visits.

After returning home to Juneau and playing at the folk festival, I flew to Anchorage not only to work at several schools, but also to explore moving there.

How'd I Get into This Racket, Anyway?

Los Anchorage. By now I could look beyond the aesthetics to understand its place as the commercial center of the state. The move made sense for a number of reasons. Not only had I begun working there more and more, but I was occasionally dating someone who lived there. In Juneau, my social life often felt miserable—most everybody was coupled up. Also, my work had evolved. Every job involved getting on an airplane, so I was flying more and more and was in town less and less. Though I'd met with local administrators, the schools weren't interested in having me, and there didn't seem much else for me in the community. A Seattle director had at the time been interested in making a play out of some of my rural Alaska poems, but she was having trouble finding funding. I'd passed those same poems to the director of the local theater, who wasn't interested, but suggested I show them elsewhere. The lead went nowhere. I did receive one small grant from the local arts council, but then had been turned down for a pair of others, as well as for grants for specific writing projects. For income, I was flying to Anchorage and north, or else Seattle and south. I remembered the first show I did in Olympia, when afterwards someone asked if I'd ever played back east. I shook my head, unable to fathom the concept. East? I'm in Olympia, I said. I already am east.

And we all chuckled at my little joke.

But now I was going to conferences where I was meeting people who were making it possible for me to go east, or at least further east to Boise and Denver. And the past season I'd gone to North Carolina. It was a big country. I was living in a place where just to make money, or to have much of a social life outside of the one week of the folk festival, I'd have to get on a plane. No wonder I'd almost gone broke. Even now, working as I had following the settlement, paying the same low rent, owning no car, but accounting for the expense of plane ticket after plane ticket, rental car after rental car, I imagined myself slowly sinking if I remained in Juneau. What was the point? I remembered a poem I'd written, "Migration," several years earlier. It was about moving on, and there was a line: *content people don't move.* That happened sometimes with writing poems: you say something that's smarter than you. While I wasn't unhappy in Juneau, I wasn't content there either.

So I spent a few days in Anchorage figuring the logistics of what appeared to be a midsummer move. The details weren't clear yet, but that was okay. I'd already turned down an invitation to return to the camp in Fairbanks. Instead, I'd spend time in Seattle, attend a fiddle camp there, maybe a publishing conference, and buy a used four-wheel drive car or truck, which I'd drive to Juneau. There, I'd pack up, drive to Anchorage, and find a place.

The plan made sense—most of it, anyway. For a while now, things had been going my way. From Anchorage, I'd be flying back to Barrow, where I'd been hired for a week: two days at the middle school and three days at the elementary, where last year's elementary school principal had been replaced. I was now billing $500/day. With a new administration in that school, there was now interest and money for me in the community, even though my rates had gone up. For my part, I was happy to return to where it could be so light and so cold in late April and early May, where I could eat in the world's furthest north Mexican restaurant, and where I could view families gathering in front of houses to watch the man of the house saw whale meat. This next trip I'd even learn there was a cable TV channel dedicated to showing where the three buses that made up Barrow's bus system were at any time. Late April was one thing. Mid winter, when wind chills might hit minus sixty, minus seventy, or colder, the buses would still run, so the TV was a way for people to know when the bus was approaching, more accurate than a timetable. When I wanted to relax after a day of teaching and performing, I'd turn to the bus channel for a few minutes, glad to see that at least in one small place there was perfect knowledge, and everything could be predicted, no surprises.

The end of May, I returned to Seattle and shopped for four-wheel drive vehicles. The first day of looking, I found a truck well within my price range, under two thousand, which I bought directly from a mechanic, not without misgivings. It was the first vehicle I'd owned since living in Sitka eight years before. Though it ran rough, at least it ran. What sold me, finally, was the camper shell. I imagined packing the bed with the boxes I still had stored in Seattle, then driving to Juneau, there loading it utterly full to save on mailing, and two or three days later arriving in Anchorage ready to move into a new life.

There was one other thing. Before leaving Anchorage the previous month, I'd had an almost certain invitation to move to a house near the top of the Hillside, a spacious home with a living room where you could look out and not only catch a gorgeous view of the city below to the north, but, on clear days, even glimpse Denali hundreds of miles further. The woman who owned it lived alone, was near my age, was familiar with what I did, and thought it would work for her to have a part-time housemate. Living there in winter, though, I'd need four-wheel drive for the steep neighborhood streets. So I bought the truck thinking it could first be my moving van, then my Anchorage town car.

But the truck had over 200,000 miles. The mechanic offered to help with any initial repairs, which was the final selling point. After flying back to Juneau to pack, I returned a week later to spend more than a month in and around Seattle, taking care of business in a leisurely enough fashion to enjoy the summer.

Quickly, I learned this particular truck would need tending. When it overheated, I had the mechanic replace the radiator. One morning it didn't start: new battery. Next, the water pump. Since I was still having to use a bike to get around, it seemed like nothing had changed, except I was spending money on repairs and insurance for a vehicle that was mostly parked in a shop. July, driving back to Seattle from a fiddle camp in Port Townsend on the Olympic peninsula, the truck started shaking, then making a new noise. I made it back to Seattle, barely, and early the next day returned to the mechanic, who sighed, and explained I'd need to replace the universal joints. The past month I'd been keeping the guy in business. Still, after each repair, the truck did run. As long as it got me to Anchorage, I thought, it would pay for itself. And in Port Townsend, I found I not only slept comfortably in the back, but stayed dry from the rain.

The next week, I stayed at a friend's place in a neighborhood near downtown. Riding my bike one afternoon, I spotted a For Sale sign in a car window, a clean little Nissan Sentra, the price under a thousand. I stopped and jotted the number. When I called later, the owner was in, so I hopped back on my bike to check it out. I'd had the idea to keep a second car in Seattle, which I'd use on the West Coast instead of paying for rentals.

The vehicle, which had 118,000 miles, ran perfectly, and was only being sold because the owner had finished graduate school, gotten married, and was moving across the continent with her new husband. I had the car checked by a mechanic, not

51

the one who'd sold me the truck. Told there wasn't a thing wrong with it, I was happy to buy it. Two months of use, and this car would pay for itself. Sean and Suzanne, married friends who were struggling with having to share their one car, were happy to keep this one in their driveway, and now had their own back-up vehicle.

After attending a conference near Seattle, where I once more tried, unsuccessfully, to interest agents and editors in my novel, I loaded my truck and took off north. The vehicle could barely hit 60, but it continued running, and I kept fingers crossed as I drove two days to Prince George, then turned west toward the coast. Past Smithers, I slept in it off the side of the highway, awoke early, and was off again. That third morning I arrived in Prince Rupert, where I had a reservation on the ferry. Despite mountains and weather, flying into and out of Juneau was relatively easy. By car from the south, Juneau was difficult and expensive. Taking the ferry from Bellingham would have been too expensive. Driving to Prince Rupert had saved me several hundred dollars.

After packing in Juneau, I boarded the Kennicott, the one ferry that crossed the Gulf of Alaska. I bought a ticket to Seward, just 120 miles from Anchorage. While I thought the truck would have made it from Haines—a 900 mile drive after a much shorter ferry ride—the savings weren't as dramatic, and now that I'd made it to Juneau, it seemed more prudent to get the truck to Anchorage with the least worry. I was glad I made the choice. Driving uphill out of Seward, I heard noise, and pulled off the road. This time, the tailpipe. I had to apply duct tape so the metal wouldn't drag. Nursing the truck up more hills, this last leg took more than three hours. The next morning, first thing, I was at a muffler shop.

Truck fixed again, I continually shook my head the first days there, driving on Seward and Minnesota, the two freeway stretches that ran north and south, and then the cluttered east and west roads like Northern Lights, Benson, Dimond. Picking up a used desk here, used bookshelves there, hauling them across town. I was happy the truck was not only running but of real use. After leaving the furniture temporarily at my friend's upholstery shop, where I'd so often stayed when visiting town, I'd go pick up another load, shaking my head yet again. I'd actually done it. *Los Anchorage.*

The move made sense professionally, but I still needed to convince myself personally. I remembered arriving in Alaska thirteen years earlier, almost to the day, and living the next three years in Fairbanks. There, nights in my cabin without running water, I used to wonder why anyone chose Anchorage, where even the residents joked that it was a half hour from Alaska. Now I knew. So Anchorage was a half hour from Alaska. Still, that was three hours closer than Seattle, which was closer than anywhere else down south. Anchorage was a compromise. Some adapted by living thirty miles south of the city in Girdwood, where there was a ski resort, or above the city on the Hillside, or north of the city in Eagle River, or Chugiak. Others embraced what the city offered: the network of excellent bike and cross-country ski trails around town; the multitude of restaurants and stores.

A year later, after I'd lived in the city awhile, I heard Anchorage described as an oil town without a college, which struck me as just about right. There was no university district and the big college, University of Alaska Anchorage, was primarily a commuter school, a place unto itself. The biggest businesses in the city—indeed, in the state—were the oil companies, which all had stakes on the north slope reserves. The city had grown quickly since statehood in 1959, and the tragedy was that with the whole history of urban planning to draw from, the city ended up a cluttered sprawl of strip malls and junky facades. Compared to Houston, Anchorage might be charming, but it could have been much more. I gave myself two or three years in the city but was willing to be surprised. Maybe my business would succeed in ways that would change where I'd need to live. Or maybe it would fail in ways that would similarly catalyze change. Then, too, there was the woman I was casually dating, who lived here. The relationship probably wasn't going anywhere, but in that too I was willing to be surprised.

The more I thought about moving to the Upper Hillside, the more I doubted the location. I liked the woman who owned the house. I loved the layout and view. But what would happen in six months if we didn't get along and I needed to move? What would I do for an address? What would I do for a phone? And how would I get around this winter if my truck remained unreliable, which was likely?

At first, I decided on another compromise, which was to rent office space, which meant even if the Hillside didn't work, I'd have my own permanent address, my own phone, my own place to sleep if I was stuck in town. But there turned out to be a last-minute problem with the space just as I was about to sign a lease. Later that afternoon, in the midst of picking up more bookshelves, just south of the downtown park strip, I saw a For Rent sign in a yard and a man in shorts watering the lawn. I stopped, introduced myself, and was given a quick tour of the downstairs two-bedroom apartment he was eager to rent. He'd lived in the space for several years, had recently bought the house and moved upstairs.

The next two days I was torn between renting the two-bedroom apartment, which I could use for my home office, and which was a convenient location where I could walk or bike to virtually anywhere I'd need go, or, for the same price, rent both a room in a big house with a view and a small office somewhere, either in the building where there were still issues with the lease or elsewhere. But just as the man was eager to have a renter, I was eager to be settled, and it just seemed simpler to have a more central convenient location, one where I had plenty of room, which felt all mine, where I could cook. Most of all, though, I wanted to unpack and get to work. The next week, I found a used computer shop, where I bought a McIntosh desktop model and a laser printer for the office, a Mac laptop for travel. I compared it to my double-floppy PC that I still used for my poems, and had used for my novel. Now that I owned equipment from the same decade, I felt positively modern.

That very week, the publisher in Albuquerque accepted my collection of rural Alaska poems. It would still be more than a year before the book could be released, he cautioned, not until late 1999 or early 2000. But if I could wait, he'd do it.

Finally, I thought. Finally.

By the end of the month, I was as settled as I'd been in Juneau, which also meant resuming the touring schedule. I flew back to Seattle for my fourth Bumbershoot book fair, remained a second week, and was pleased how the changes I'd made were working. Though from Anchorage the flight south was now double the distance as from Juneau, the fare was less, and now I had a car waiting. Following Bumbershoot, I performed twice in Seattle, once in Portland, and appeared live on radio. Sunday evening, I was back in Anchorage.

The next few months, I was able to pick up small jobs in Seward and Palmer, shows I ordinarily would have only done, if they could even be arranged, when I was already in the region. Now based in Anchorage, I had more flexibility. I worked a few days in Anchorage schools, then a day in Moose Pass, less than two hours away. When I was invited back to the Lower Kuskokwim School District that fall, the flight to Bethel was so much easier from Anchorage; being one flight closer made a major difference. Also that fall, returning to the Colorado Book Festival, I played a coffeehouse in Boulder, where I was joined by my friend Woody, a local banjo player I'd first met when he was visiting Haines, Alaska. It was my first time doing a full show with an accompanist. On the same trip I performed in schools first in Cheyenne and then Casper, where I also did a solo show in that community's performing arts series.

Every day was always so different and challenging, and though I loved what I was doing, and felt good about it, I still wasn't making money. Just like I made to-do lists for calls, I tried figuring my budget. My Anchorage rent was more than double, I rationalized. And now I had to pay car insurance. I'd bought the computers and the printer. And moving had been expensive. Still, though I felt I was certainly moving forward, the woman I was dating, who I went out with no more often than when I lived in Juneau, didn't see it that way.

I can't be your girlfriend, she answered one time, when I asked if I could see her again in the next few days, not have to wait for a week, or two, or even three. I don't want to see you any more than I'm seeing you now.

You're delusional, you know that, she said, another time. It's kind of sweet, really, she said, putting a hand on my shoulder. But, still, I really think you're delusional. I could never really be with someone who didn't have a steady income. Have you ever thought about getting a real job?

Indeed, I had, but not the kind of jobs she meant, which, when I pressed her on it, included managing a bookstore or administrating in an arts organization. Though I liked teaching in schools, my particular knack was to be able to go in once and inspire, whether it was a classroom of twenty or an assembly of four hundred or more. I'd come to prefer the day-long residencies, though was always happy to consider visiting longer if there was a budget. But I didn't have an education degree, and, now in my early forties, didn't want to go back to school to write papers and read about teaching theory. I'd already done graduate school once, and besides, when I was getting invited to lead teacher workshops, I was getting positive reviews.

Since I was accomplished enough already to be invited to teach certified teachers, it just didn't make sense to go back to school to get the basic certification to be a classroom teacher.

If the right position came along to teach at a university, I'd consider it, but it had to be the right one. Though I liked returning to rural Alaska, I didn't want to live there again. And even though I regularly continued to have poems published, and now had my first book accepted, the kind of jobs I was most interested in—semester-long or year-long sabbatical replacement positions—were out of my range until I had the one book or likely two or three. As is, I'd applied for such a position in Anchorage and another in Eugene. For the Anchorage position, I thought I'd at least have a chance at an interview, living five miles from campus, a book due out. But I wasn't going to count on it. How could I?

Juggling so many projects, planning to begin another novel, I didn't feel so much delusional as busy. I didn't have much time for a girlfriend anyway.

In early 1999, invited by the local arts council, I drove to Homer for a weekend-long residency that included a writing workshop and a show. On the way back home to Anchorage, I stopped in Seward to work at the middle school and high school. Then I flew down to Seattle, picked up my car and performed in Washington, Oregon, and California. Once I was out of Alaska, I joked, everything was close and convenient. So from northern California, I decided to fly to Albuquerque, where I met with my publisher and attended Folk Alliance, yet one more conference, one that had been especially recommended. There I met an entirely new community of peers, more than a thousand people, from performers to presenters to agents to disc jockeys. I learned how professionals arranged tours, built press kits, grew careers, and realized I already knew a good bit. Flying back to the Bay Area, I picked up my car, headed back to Seattle, performed once more, and then flew back to Anchorage.

Early April, I flew east to attend AWP in Albany, combining it with small shows in Ithaca, New York City, and a school show in Boston set up by my sister, where I visited her and her family. Afterwards, I drove into Vermont and Maine, visiting new friends who were involved in some way with the music business, and old friends from twenty years earlier, when I used to teach tennis outside Boston and lived with a girlfriend, Frannie.

The end of the month I was back in Barrow for another week, then returned to Washington state to perform at a pair of festivals over Memorial Day weekend. Most of the next three months I spent within biking distance of my basement apartment. Midwinter, the truck's alternator had needed replacing on the Homer trip. Now, when I did drive, it seemed there was almost always a problem. One week, a fuel pump; another, simply a flat. Most mornings I sat in my office, stared into the monitor, typed poems to the computer. Afternoons and evenings, I'd climb on my bike or else make calls for future tours. By the end of the summer, I'd completed ten more chapbooks, which included *Leftovers and Gravy*, all about food; *Dream Week*, about dreams; *Dear Mother, Dear Dad*, which I subtitled *not-so-nice parent poems*; and my favorite of all, *All Originals*, which included notations for twenty original fiddle tunes (barely able to read music, unable to write it, I'd played the tunes into a tape recorder which I'd shipped to a fiddler in California who freelanced as a transcriptionist) paired with twenty original poems and a brief story how each particular piece had come to be. That was the last one, the twenty-sixth, and once I finished designing all ten new ones, I took them to the shop to be photocopied and stapled. A few days later, hauling the boxes full of chapbooks to the truck, which was running that day, I realized I was done with the project, having gone from A-Z.

The only time I'd been out of state that summer had been for a week and half in late June and early July to play a couple of small shows, and to attend the fiddle camp in Port Townsend, which I'd attended the previous summer and had been occasionally attending since moving west in 1984. I owed much of my development as a fiddler to the annual gathering. That summer I met a banjo player from Vancouver B.C., Andrea Cooper. Everyone liked Andrea. In her early thirties, she was smart, personable, and a terrific Celtic flute player as well as an excellent banjo player. Towards the end of the week, we played tunes one afternoon for a half-hour. Not only did our styles mesh, but when I tried one of my original tunes, she picked up enough of the melody almost immediately so we sounded rehearsed. When I tried another of mine, she picked that one up as well, and an idea came to me. Before leaving, I asked if she might want to tour with me sometime, maybe in Alaska. Try me, was all she said.

Through the rest of July, back in Anchorage, working on the last chapbooks, thinking of touring with Andrea, I had an idea. Living in this particular apartment, I didn't need the truck, and now that it had become increasingly expensive to maintain, I wanted to sell it. But I still needed a vehicle. So I came up with a plan. If Andrea was interested, after the Labor Day book fair in Seattle, as I'd drive the Sentra up to Anchorage, she could come along for the ride, performances en route.

When I called, she was surprised, and glad, to hear from me, but thought driving to Alaska was overambitious. Something closer, no longer than a week to ten days, maybe that she'd be able to do.

Encouraged, I scheduled dates from Vancouver to Eugene, mostly coffee-houses and house concerts, though we also performed at an outdoor market, at a school, and over the radio, ten dates in all. We didn't make much money, but we made some. More importantly, we had fun traveling and performed well enough together that when I invited Andrea to fly to Fairbanks in November to join me for a pair of school residencies in the Alaska Interior, she accepted. Spending time like this, we got to know each other better. Spare moments, Andrea was quick to find a phone, search out computers at libraries and internet cafes, or else write old-fashioned letters. Earlier in the summer, she'd met someone on the East Coast. Now she was showing me a long-distance romance could work if both partners were committed to regular communication.

After our tour, I drove the car onto the ferry in Bellingham, sailed to Haines, and from there hurried straight to Anchorage in a single long stretch, winter weather approaching up north. Having the car in Seattle had been useful, and I wished I could have kept it. But it wasn't essential, not now when I needed a reliable vehicle in Anchorage. Several days alone on the boat and on the road, I'd done more of the thinking I was always doing when I had the time. Though I was always busy, and did have money coming in, I was still spending more money than I was taking in, just like when I lived in Juneau. I needed to get smarter somehow. Or more efficient. Something was still missing. Maybe Andrea would help with that.

Andrea's trip to Fairbanks, Nenana, and Anderson was a success, and especially notable for a last-minute problem with the car, which necessitated taking the truck. I doubted every time I stuck the key in the ignition, but it ran fine for the entire nine-hundred-mile tour, even north of Talkeetna, where the temperature never rose above minus twenty. *Just driven to Fairbanks and back,* I could proclaim in want ads, which helped sell it two months later, once I had the heater fixed, the last of its problems I'd ever deal with.

In December, Andrea flew back to join me for jobs in Bethel and Eek, where I'd become a regular, my fourth trip to the Yup'ik Eskimo village. "A Week in Eek" was one of the fiddle tunes I'd composed, making it up after first writing a poem with that title. It was one I played with Andrea, and it was especially fun experiencing the school and kids this time partially through Andrea's eyes and ears. *kenwaldman,* she called me, mimicking the elementary-schoolers, who pronounced my name quickly, making it one word, three rapid-fire syllables, all lower-case. Andrea, they'd squeal. Play the banjo more! Play the flute! You're real good, you know.

February, I returned to Folk Alliance, this time in Cleveland, and booked dates elsewhere in Ohio, and in Michigan, since I was already in the region. This year at the conference, I attended more of the sessions. In this community, I was certainly one of the last holdouts. I'd never gone on the internet, didn't use e-mail, and insisted on conducting all my business in person, through letters, or over the phone. Maybe this idiosyncrasy was a shortcoming, as most everybody suggested. Or maybe this method was a strength, because I was still getting jobs, and I'd hear the odd comment that I was smart not to get hooked on e-mail. All I knew was that I was already so busy, I couldn't imagine finding time to add to my tasks. During that tour, a free night in Michigan, I called Andrea, explained what I'd learned about making CDs, and asked specifically whether she might consider doing one with me. Sidestepping, she didn't say yes, didn't say no.

Flying back to Anchorage, I reflected this trip had been like so many others. I'd made money, but not enough to cover the travel, the conference fees, the hotels, the rental car. Though I still had a healthy reserve from the settlement and was now down to just the one car, I couldn't keep from dropping $10,000 a year. But at least attending this conference, I'd come away not only with new contacts, but with ideas that would help sustain my little business. It seemed obvious I had to keep doing more, not less, if I wanted to have a chance.

Mid March, I taught a week at a fine arts retreat for high-schoolers in Port Townsend, the same organization that administered the fiddling workshops I'd so often attended. Then I had two weeks before flying to Kansas City, the host city of this year's AWP Conference, and where my publisher at West End Press had promised the book would be available. For months, I'd called all over the Northwest and Midwest, but couldn't fill the dates. Then I had another idea. Back in Anchorage at the end of February, home briefly between tours, I called Andrea, and said I'd have free time in a few weeks when I'd be just a couple of hours away from her. If we found a studio, would she have two days to record a CD? She said that since our previous discussions, she'd been talking to a band mate, who had a home recording studio. If we all could coordinate schedules, and agree on details, she said she didn't see why we shouldn't make a recording.

And that's how Monday morning after my workshops in Port Townsend, I came to be sitting with Andrea in a living room in a little house in Point Roberts, Washington, one of the more absurd places in the United States. A community of several hundred residents, located in Whatcom County, it's more Canadian than American, connected to Washington State only by water. To drive the road in or out is to drive through British Columbia, which means every trip anywhere to or from Point Roberts, no matter what, you have to cross the U.S. and Canada border, with all the accompanying hassles.

From Andrea, I began learning what some of these hassles might be. I heard how U.S. customs agents had sometimes opened her instrument cases, even asked her to put together her wooden flute and play for them. She had to play her banjo. She had to say she was coming to the States for leisure, not work, which sometimes meant stretching the truth, which sometimes felt dangerous. A current band mate of hers had once been found crossing the border with a single marijuana joint in the pocket of an old jacket. The band mate hadn't even known it was there; it had been months since he'd even worn it and recalled a friend borrowing it. The result? Though he owned land in the States that he still paid taxes on, he was banned from entering the country. Now that Andrea's boyfriend, Mark, had moved to Seattle, and she was crossing the border more regularly, it had gotten more complicated not only for her but also for him. I'd never been too concerned about the border, nor was I this time. I was back to renting cars, and except for my fiddles and a couple of bags, I wasn't hauling much. Just in case, though, I left chapbooks and anything else that might raise questions at a friend's in Seattle. Though you could drive into what passed as the center of town in Point Roberts and mail a letter with U.S. stamps, and use U.S. currency everywhere, it felt like another place altogether.

Wearing headphones, we looked like a pair of musical pilots set to face off. I held my fiddle. Andrea, her banjo. Cords from the headphones dangled awkwardly, making it difficult to get settled. Late morning now, the session hadn't just started poorly a few hours earlier, it had been worse. I could imagine the clock ticking *bad idea, bad idea, bad idea*. Aside from my cassettes of solo fiddling with poetry, this was my first recording, and despite having attended a few conferences and reading articles about what to expect, I'd been thrown off. The first tune we tried, "Old Joe Clark," one we usually played to warm up, had sounded so weak when we listened back to it, we wondered if we'd made a mistake coming and shelved it for later. The next, "A Week in Eek," which was going to be the title cut, was not much better, though here we decided to try a second take, then a third. Listening back, thinking we could improve, we played it again, and then listened back once more. Not perfect, but good enough, useable. As we were getting set to play the next tune, "Texas," the engineer cut in from the other room: he might have punched a button by mistake or else something just went haywire on the computer. Either way, trying to save the cut we'd just recorded, he feared he'd erased it somehow. We sat for several minutes as we waited for him to figure if he could find the other cut and manage to save it. Finally apologizing that he couldn't, he advised us to record that same tune again. This time it wasn't right, but the engineer insisted he could fix this one in the mixing process, and that we should go on, not get hung up on this particular cut. Now we sat, poised to go back to that tune, "Texas." When we heard the engineer give his go-ahead through the headphones, we started to play. First time through, this one actually came off as it should. Still, at this rate, it was hard to imagine the project succeeding, at least in the time frame we had. After more than two hours, we had completed a single tune.

Early afternoon, Andrea's boyfriend, Mark, arrived. He'd not only been deeply involved in the music business for more than twenty years, but had played in bands that performed at major international festivals. He had also played on, or produced, dozens of CDs in virtually every imaginable circumstance. Though he'd been invited to come, he hadn't promised and we weren't expecting him.

Still, there he was, and after we ate lunch and talked about how the day had gone and what we hoped to accomplish, he was happy to help. By early evening, we'd successfully recorded eight more cuts, including the ones I'd been most worried about. Having Mark there changed everything. Two cuts where Andrea played flute, he played banjo. Elsewhere, he joined us on guitar or else sat out listening, thinking. Even the engineer was quick to defer to Mark's judgment, whether that might mean replaying the whole track or punching in a note or a phrase to salvage a track that needed only that quick fix. Returning Tuesday, just me and Andrea, we found most of the CD was already completed, so there was no time pressure. Wednesday and Thursday, the engineer and I mixed the CD while Andrea went to her part-time job. The following week, before leaving for Kansas City, I completed the rest of the process, which meant approving the final mix, getting the disc mastered, getting photos and text to the graphic designer, and contracting with a Seattle CD manufacturer.

At AWP, I bought a table at the book fair and was happy to have the *Nome Poems* collection with color cover and flat spine—a real full-length volume to go along with the chapbooks, postcards, and cassettes. From Kansas City, I flew to Denver, rented a car for two weeks, performed throughout the Southwest on behalf of the new book. While setting up for an event at an art gallery in Albuquerque, I met an artist who was there to re-hang one of his paintings. He asked what I was doing and nodded his head vigorously when I explained.

Every time he was ready to quit, he said, a gallery from Los Angeles or New York would call, or one of his galleries in Santa Fe or Taos would tell him he had just sold something big, or else he'd win some award, not as much as needed—*never as much as he needed*, he emphasized—but enough to convince him someone out there was noticing, and that he should continue. How'd we get into this racket anyway? he asked, and smiled crookedly.

I didn't know, but told him about the man who came up to my table the previous September at the book fair at Bumbershoot in Seattle. He kept looking at my display of 26 chapbooks, and then all he said is that sometimes you'll have lots of money, sometimes you won't have anything, but even when you have nothing you'll have just enough to keep doing what you do and it'll be worth it, because you're supposed to keep going, because you're an artist. *Who are you?* I asked him. *Sign my mailing list.* He waved me off. I'm nobody. My wife's an artist. I just appreciate. You're supposed to be making things. *Buy a chapbook then. Or a cassette.* I pointed to the display. And you know what he said? Not right now, he told me.

That's typical, said the New Mexican artist.

Then we both laughed.

Back in Alaska, I did an Anchorage show in a brewery to celebrate the book release, then flew up to Barrow the end of April for another week-long residency at the elementary school. Returning home for a few days, first I drove north to Healy and Fairbanks for a mix of school visits and book release concerts, then south to Kasilof and Homer for more of the same. Memorial Day weekend, I flew back south for events in Bellingham, Seattle, and Portland, and to pick up my CDs.

That weekend in Seattle, at the Folklife Festival I ran into a fiddler I knew. Doug was a bit older, a furniture maker with a ponytail. He'd always seemed interested in what I'd been doing with the fiddling, the poetry, the touring. I had my fans, but others in the Seattle traditional music scene seemed annoyed by what I was doing. Doug was a fan. Whenever I saw him, he'd stop to ask about my touring, how I was feeling, whether I was enjoying it. He'd invariably be smiling during these exchanges, even if he did seem a bit wistful.

I saw you played last night, and I wanted to tell you, Doug said. It's all about momentum. No matter what, it's all about momentum.

I looked at him quizzically.

I wanted to make that one. It was at a bookstore, right? But I was playing myself last night.

You were? At the time Doug was a decent fiddler, but not great. I wondered what kind of show it was.

Yeah, I was in a band a long time ago. It was semi-famous in some circles.

Some people liked us. Some didn't. Last night at the Crocodile, some people who liked us got a few of us together.

The Crocodile? I'd never been to a show there, but knew the venue, though knew nothing about the bands that played except they were usually hip rock bands with a buzz. Sounds like fun. Was it?

That same wistful smile. Some of it.

So, what was your band? I asked him. I was getting curious.

Maybe you've heard of it. The Velvet Underground.

You were in the Velvet Underground?

Doug smiled, punched me lightly on the shoulder. Remember, I'm watching you. It's all about momentum.

In Anchorage for the summer, I did a few small shows around the state, spent several days with other artists at the downtown art museum where we personally sold our work to tourists, and for the first time waded into the computer terminals at the library. From Folk Alliance, I'd heard of folk-dj, a listserv for almost everything relating to folk music on the radio. Now that I had a CD, I wanted to do what I could to publicize the CD on my limited budget. Earlier in the year, after finding a listing of addresses, I'd written to every library in Alaska, which had resulted in book orders and a few paid gigs. Now I was researching disc jockeys who posted play lists. Not only did I find names and addresses, but by viewing what they played, I could make a calculated guess what they'd do when a CD of old-time fiddle and banjo combined with poetry arrived unsolicited in the mail.

The time was well-spent. Though virtually no one had known of me beforehand, by getting the CD in the right people's hands, almost immediately I was getting airplay on folk shows on public and community stations nationwide. Getting played on one particular show in Madison, which was broadcast on a dozen other stations, meant people in Wisconsin heard me statewide. I received airplay in college towns like Eugene, Bozeman, Bloomington, and Columbia, and big cities like Miami, Chicago, and San Francisco, as well as numerous smaller communities. One folk disc jockey in eastern Iowa played the first half of the CD on one broadcast, the second half on another. More confident now how it sounded,

How'd I Get into This Racket, Anyway?

I worked harder marketing both the book and CD to stores throughout Alaska

It should have been easy, I thought, selling what I did in my home state. The book's title, *Nome Poems*, readily identified place, and the color photo on the cover, taken near Fairbanks, might easily have been set in rural Alaska. The book was not only distributed nationally by the University of New Mexico Press, but the blurb on the back was written by a respected writer, Naomi Shihab Nye, who had praised many of the book's poems six years earlier when we'd met. Still, because it was poetry, most stores shied away. Even the main distributor in the state was reluctant to carry the title, until the manager of the airport bookstore, one of the few stores in the state that had given the book a chance, ordered it and reordered it, because when I'd given her a sample copy in the spring, she'd read it and liked it. By displaying the book all summer on a table that featured new Alaska titles, she sold dozens.

Because poetry still had a stigma, at least I could understand some of the challenges to overcome in selling the book. It was harder to understand the difficulty with the CD. After all, everybody liked music, and while fiddle music wasn't necessarily commercial, people liked it, and could associate it with wilderness places, like Alaska. Though the CD included poems, they were accessible ones: poems about playing fiddle, playing banjo, or visiting the village of Eek. There was nothing the least bit controversial or dark like some of the poems in the book, unless it was controversial to mention kids smoking, or adults drinking. Still, despite a fair price, an attractive package, and excellent early reviews, the CD was not an easy sell to the shops.

As I continued making plans for the next year, what was hardest, I thought, was understanding the difficulties I'd faced in scheduling appearances in state, especially in schools. The past year, I'd expected the rejection from the local university for the one-year fill-in position, though I'd have appreciated a short personal note acknowledging I'd at least been considered and owned all of the requisite qualifications. More frustrating was that while I understood more than ever all it took building an audience for shows, or to insure a successful visit to a school, I had few opportunities to put what I'd learned into practice. I was disappointed that now having the book and the CD meant virtually nothing to in-state media, or to various Alaskan arts councils, or to other local and state agencies I assumed would be interested. While I was no worse off than before, I was also little better.

It seemed odd. Though there were countless fiddlers and countless poets, and some dozens I'd run across who both played traditional music and wrote good contemporary poems, there was no one else combining the two. No one else was writing poems about playing fiddle, who could then read the poems, then play a fiddle tune to demonstrate, maybe even a good original one that sounded a couple hundred years old. And no one, certainly, could entertain and educate high-schoolers or middle-schoolers with fiddle tunes and age-appropriate poems, and then go entertain and educate elementary-schoolers with a different set of fiddle tunes and age-appropriate poems. For the younger ones, I could do a variation of the show I did back in Brevig Mission in 1996, and turn a fiddle tune into a Simon Says kind of a game, complete with dance calls, which could then turn into an effective writing exercise. For all ages, whether for a class of thirty or an assembly of more than three hundred, I found that by making noises on the fiddle and asking students to guess the sounds, I was offering a fun exercise that invariably led to pieces that often had the characteristics of successful poems.

As I grew more experienced, I thought it would have been easier finding jobs in schools in Anchorage, or up in the Matanuska Valley, or down on the Kenai Peninsula. I felt sure there would be more demand. But it was no easier; there was no more demand. When the language arts director for the Anchorage School District left the state to take another job, her replacement never returned calls and would never meet with me to discuss a possible workshop even though I lived in town and the previous in-service had been a success. When the principal at Stellar Secondary retired, I no longer had an open invitation to visit that school and I never worked there again. The preceding year I'd met the director of library services for the school district, who invited me to make a brief presentation for the middle-school and high-school librarians, another for the elementary-school ones. In retrospect, I should have played fiddle. Instead, for school district personnel I thought it would be sufficient to explain that while I lived locally, I was working more and more out-of-state. Passing around a sheet explaining what I did, emphasizing I'd had success getting kids excited about writing, I mentioned I wanted more work closer to home and was looking for reasons to remain in Alaska.

One middle-school librarian hired me for a day. A few others expressed interest at the time, but afterwards never returned phone calls. In this business, I was used to people not returning calls. But this was home. I'd always felt comfortable charging less here. But now, if I was not going to have calls returned even as a courtesy to say no, sorry, we're not interested, and if people didn't see I was offering a service of real value, I had little choice but to continue putting more and more of my effort outside of Alaska, where there were so many more opportunities and I was developing a reputation. The business was hard enough. I didn't think it was too much to ask for recognition and appreciation in my home state.

I thought then of my experiences in Seward. One of the middle-school language arts teachers, a former Alaska teacher-of-the-year, learned I was performing in town and invited me to a class once. He had become a supporter. Referring to me, he said I was not just an artist, but that I was a teacher. So he invited me a second time, for a full day, which again went well, and when we had a free minute between classes mentioned he thought what I did was great and that he might want to try something similar when he retired. Sure, I said, but tried to explain that this was the easy part of the job, visiting classes, playing fiddle, and getting kids excited about reading and writing. I wasn't sure if he heard me. He only looked at me a second, then said to let him know if I ever had time to come back, and he'd set up two or three days for me in town. When I returned for that third time to work one day in the high school, another in the middle school, he shook his head. I hereby stop being your booking agent, he said. I tried for months and I still couldn't get you in the elementary school, and I live here, work here, and know they have the money. I don't know how you do it.

Shaking my head, I said what I'd said before: the teaching and performing, that's the easy part.

This time, I was positive he heard me.

As I readied myself for another season of touring, first another trip to Seattle, where I was to perform at the Bumbershoot Festival—though this time my publisher from New Mexico had a table at the book fair, not me—then to Texas for a few shows, then back to Oregon for a few more and the regional booksellers' meeting, I thought more deeply about what I needed to do next. Though I considered myself frugal—everything was going into either writing, the music, or performing, and I cut corners where I could without sacrificing quality—starting this business had been intrinsically expensive. I'd made a thousand copies of the first CD for just over $5000, which was incredibly cheap, yet it was professionally designed and mastered, so it looked and sounded like anything a major label might produce. At $15 each, $9 for wholesale, I'd sold enough this summer to not only almost break even, but to think about reordering, where there would be real profit, since much of that first outlay was for one-time only expenses. And now that the first CD had done so well, I needed to follow up with a second as soon as I could. I certainly had the material to make one. Friends had a studio in Fairbanks, and already I'd reserved time in December, when Andrea had said she could come up. But another CD would cost money. Everything cost money, and I'd been spending heavily. What could I eliminate? What could I change? Where did I need to go and who did I need to meet?

Ever since I'd left Nome, this path had felt like an accident. Adventurous and exciting, yes, but an accident. But it also felt right, so I continued. Ultimately, what I wanted most was to stay in and write, find a girlfriend I felt passion for, who I could love and who could love me back, someone to marry. But if there was one thing about this lifestyle, the constant travel was not conducive to sustained writing or slowly growing a relationship. And then there was the matter of income.

The Fiddling Poet, I understood, was a persona, an-almost-but-not-quite-me, a way of being so as to become known, to develop a readership, to segue into the life I most wanted. And though I wasn't making a profit yet, at least as The Fiddling Poet there was the possibility of money, real money. I knew there were jobs that paid $3,000-$5,000 and more, and though I wasn't getting them yet, I thought it possible. When I started, I'd be embarrassed if I asked for more than $500 a day. No longer. I wrote well enough. I played fiddle. I could talk onstage. I enjoyed teaching and was good at it. All I needed was to have the right book get published or else win the right award or else somehow meet the right person somewhere.

Once you were established, I was learning, you were always established. But getting established, that was the hard part. Even though my work was set here in

How'd I Get into This Racket, Anyway?

Alaska, and I was, in a sense, established here, I was never truly established, not in the way it took to make a living. I remembered what I'd heard the previous year in Wyoming. With only 400,000 people, many of the same people shoulder much of the work. With only 650,000 people in all of Alaska, not enough of them would ever care about what I did, and there was never going to be money here. To succeed, I'd have to continue touring. Sometimes all it took was meeting one right person at one right time.

That summer in Anchorage I started playing occasionally with a local music teacher, David McCormick, a multi-instrumentalist who also used to write and edit at the *Anchorage Daily News*. He understood more about what I was doing than virtually anyone else in the state. He urged me to get out of Alaska as much as I could. There's nothing up here for someone like you, he said.

October, Andrea met me in Nevada and we toured there and California. Later in the month, I returned to Washington and Idaho, where I showcased at the Arts Northwest conference. November, I returned to Anchorage for a month. Thanksgiving weekend, I rented a table for the first time for the holiday book fair at the museum. The next week, Andrea flew up. First we worked in schools and performed in Kotzebue, then in Fairbanks, where we recorded our second CD, *Burnt Down House*. Like the first one, we recorded quickly and successfully. Unlike the first, we were experienced in the process, at least a little, so we knew what to expect. And thanks, too, to the graciousness of Pat and Robin, who ran the studio, the week felt like a party.

I spent the rest of December home in Anchorage, readying the CD for the graphic designer in Seattle, and struggling to begin a new novel, which I worked on fitfully. Conferring occasionally with David McCormick and calculating my budget, I began formulating a new plan. My trips outside were becoming longer and longer. What was stopping me, I wondered, from giving up my apartment, and its $9,000/year rent, and going on an extended tour? By driving out in the Nissan Sentra, I'd have a car down south and the flexibility to get from place to place to place. Now, every time I performed at lesser-paying venues, I had to factor in the cost of the flight down, the rental cars. It wasn't efficient. Yet to make a career in this work, there were often reasons to work lesser-paying jobs. By driving out of state, I'd be giving up full-time residency. But I'd be increasing the odds of establishing myself. Sometime in the spring I'd have the second CD to mail out, and to sell. And I'd already signed a contract with West End Press for the second collection, tentatively due out in early 2002. When I mentioned all this to David, he said, Hell yeah.

If I needed a further sign, I got it Christmas morning when a pipe began leaking in my apartment. I spent that Christmas Day packing boxes of books and old record albums, and then hauling everything out of the living room and into the laundry room so we could lift the carpeting and assess the damage. Those boxes never did make it back into the living room.

Early January, I flew to Nome to work in the schools, lead writing and music workshops, and to celebrate the book, which had been set there. I saw a few of my old pals who still lived there. Others had moved on and others were too busy with one project or other to come out to visit. Though my time around the Bering Straits had long seemed done, it also felt oddly unfinished.

The next months were more of the same: Seattle, Vancouver, Cleveland, New York City, Buffalo, and several Midwestern dates from Michigan to Minnesota. The good jobs were better; the bad ones weird in new ways. The end of April, Andrea joined me for my fifth consecutive year in Barrow. That had been a good one. We'd been featured on the public radio station, and our evening show had a good turnout. The elementary school principal mentioned afterward he'd just returned from a conference in New Orleans, had attended Jazzfest, and thought my performance with Andrea in Barrow compared favorably.

I spent most evenings that May and June slowly moving out of my apartment, getting rid of the furniture I'd bought nearly three years earlier, parceling out books and kitchenware. Most of what I owned I was storing in friends' closets and garages for the next year. I'd be traveling in a sedan, hauling plenty of books and CDs. There wasn't going to be room for much else.

Days, I'd mail the new CD to disc jockeys, or bike to the midtown library where I'd get on the computer. I was back to studying the folk-dj listserv, or else researching venues. Several days I'd been invited back to the museum, where I sat at one of the artist tables and sold books and CDs. Already I was planning to record another CD this winter up in Fairbanks, sometime between Thanksgiving through Christmas, maybe even the same first weekend in December we'd recorded this latest. One morning at the museum, mulling over this new third CD, I took out the mandolin, somehow started picking a sweet little waltz, something new. This was how I most often made up tunes, unconsciously, only recognizing the melody was worth saving after I'd been playing it awhile. I played this new one over and over, switched to fiddle, made up a notation so if I couldn't remember how it went, I might look at the jottings and be able to resurrect it. If I could conjure up this particular one again, I thought, I had the waltz to complete the third CD. The first two both had original waltzes. The third was ready to be recorded anytime, but for the lack of such a waltz.

I'll be here two to three years, I'd guessed when I first arrived in Anchorage, and I was approaching two years and eleven months. That's what I might have liked best about living there full-time: it was neither more nor less than I'd expected. I could leave for a week, a month, or longer, and return ready to turn around and leave on another tour. I never really minded living there, but never missed it when I was gone.

My last night in town was a Friday, a few days after summer solstice. I'd at last moved everything out of the apartment. Everything was clean. I only had the car left to pack tight in the morning, and even that chore was half done. I wanted to thank David McCormick for some of his help the past months, so treated him to dinner at a downtown seafood restaurant he favored. We lingered over another beer, and then I walked home to my apartment, arriving just past midnight in the midst of one of those long slow delicious northern summer sunsets. An hour later, about to go to sleep, there was a banging on my door. It was David.

You may not be lucky in your love life, but you're lucky with your work.

What do you mean? It's 1 o'clock. What are you talking about?

Follow me. It's a beautiful night, he said, and sighed. I have something to show you. Then you're free to come back and fly this coop in the morning.

I nodded, with no idea what he was talking about. I followed him down L Street and onto Minnesota. Every light went our way. In five minutes we were on

Spenard, crossing 36th, and seconds later we were turning onto his street, pulling into the driveway of the house he was sharing. He led me into his room, pointed to the computer.

I just checked Ken Waldman dot com and it's available. I suggest you reserve the domain name right now. You don't know how lucky you are. David McCormick dot com is *long* gone.

But I don't even do e-mail yet. Why do I want to reserve it?

Just do it. It's $50 to reserve it for a year. Just do it. You'll thank me.

But I don't even do e-mail.

Look, this isn't e-mail. And you're going to want to have a website.

You sure I want this? I asked. I was tired and wanted to go to bed.

Believe me. You want this. $50. Type in the credit card number. Then you can drive back. And I can go get to sleep myself.

The next day, almost noon, my car impossibly loaded down, I struggled with an awful headache as I drove the Glenn Highway to Tok. There, I performed that evening at Bud and Heather Johnson's. Though we'd all lived in Alaska for years, we'd never met until Folk Alliance in Cleveland. Bud's radio show was syndicated around the state, and occasionally he presented concerts.

One more day, and instead of a headache, I battled car trouble. The six-hour ride to Whitehorse took over thirteen. I limped into town past 2 a.m., grateful that at least I'd made it. After two days in the Yukon awaiting the repair, the car was fixed, and I sped south, the first night napping as I sat slumped in the front seat, the next sleeping in a Prince George motel after a sixteen-hour stint on the road. What I'd earned at the well-attended show in Tok was supposed to get me to Seattle with money to spare.

Now I had to think again.

Out of Alaska, my grand tour had begun.

3
Bedrooms I Have Known

Bird School

When we cracked the window,
a small crow glided to our bed,
roosted a minute, preened
and squawked, delivered
its raucous lecture.

So we removed all glass,
let in the birds—all sizes,
colors, songs—and studied.
For graduation, we took off
outside, opened wings, flew.

The second week of July 2001, I slipped into Portland for a few days. Portland was always a safe haven. My friend Ned lived there with his wife, Tia, and their boys, Amos and Louie. I'd known Ned almost half my life. We'd met nearly twenty-one years earlier, back when Ned was courting Tia in Portland, a time he was also renting a small house in Carrboro, just outside Chapel Hill, North Carolina. In July that summer, one of his housemates moved out, and another, James, moved in. In August, the second housemate moved out, and James posted an ad for the living space, which I answered. When Ned returned to North Carolina in October, he found two strange men perfectly at home in his house on North Greensboro Street.

Ned was a banjo player, a dance caller, a storyteller, a gardener, a botanist, a carpenter. James was a clogger, a harmonica player, a woodworker, a baker, a cook, an activist. I was the boring housemate, the one who worked in a bookstore, hung around the house reading, didn't play music, was slowly mending after my first love, Frannie, had joined the Peace Corps. Though our monthly rent was only $165, and we were only paying $55 each, none of us, it seemed, ever had money, which didn't stop us from throwing terrific parties or living creatively. James and Ned were always making scones or else baking bread, but Ned wouldn't stick bread in the oven without giving the loaves real shape, making what he called James Brown bread or Elvis Presley bread. We hung chairs on the walls. We heated exclusively with wood, which we'd scavenge, chainsaw, haul, pile, chop. For Christmas, Ned made me several long postcard racks so I could hang the more peculiar ones of my collection in our kitchen. He built his cats, Leon and Hazel Bunny, a solar cathouse.

One night that winter a friend of Ned's, a furniture maker from Raleigh, left a fiddle, bow, and case at the house, and told me if I wanted to try playing, that was fine with him. He'd never taken to the instrument and, low on money, was hoping to sell it. Low on money myself, I'd eye the instrument greedily every time I walked into and out of the living room. He was only asking a hundred dollars, which was reasonable. But for me, that was a full week of bookstore wages. I couldn't afford to buy much of anything those days. Yet one evening I dug into my wallet, quickly handed Ned five twenties, and told him to take the money and give it to his buddy. Later that night, trying to wrestle the fiddle into tune, I broke a string. Ned and James just laughed. The instrument sat in its case the next six months until I mustered the courage to change the string and try tuning it again.

My two housemates were both excellent musicians. Friends who came by with fiddles and guitars were among the best in a region full of people playing old-time string-band music. I'd listen, mystified how the fiddlers could just sit there with fid-dle, bow, and right arm, and get all that sound. It seemed magic. When no one was in, I'd take out my own fiddle and bow, stiffly scratch every last note of "Soldier's Joy" or "Fisher's Hornpipe," learning from a tune book I'd bought, which I couldn't quite read out of, but thought held the answer to getting the right sound.

Hey, you're scaring the cats. *Quit scaring the cats,* Ned would shout if he caught me trying as he strode through the door, flinging off his cap. I'd quickly put the fiddle down, then pick it up again as soon as he and James were both gone.

We lived together in Carrboro for more than eighteen months, which included my twenty-sixth birthday dinner, when Ned cooked us chicken tagine from the Moroccan cookbook I'd given him. He used the exact recipe, even down to pricking his right forefinger and adding two drops of blood. Spring 1982, the landlord sold the house. Ned left for Portland and Tia. James moved in with his girlfriend, Nettie. I migrated to Hillsborough, fifteen miles north, where I continued fiddling, and commuted to town almost daily. By then I was waiting tables, and had started once again to teach tennis. Our time together in the Carrboro house hadn't been all that long, but for me it had been memorable.

Later, when I moved to Seattle in 1984, I saw Ned in Portland. I'd been seeing him ever since, staying at his house—the first one on Rodney Street, with the huge basement; the next one on NE 20th, off Prescott; and most recently, the one near Mount Tabor. Each retained some of the flavor of the house in Carrboro. Always, he'd been like the smarter, older brother I'd never had, the one who already knew everything I wanted to know, if only I knew where to look. World music and literature, outsider art, environmental politics: impervious to pop culture, his interests sometimes anticipated mainstream trends by a decade. I always wondered what he'd been doing recently, what he planned next. I was always happy for his approval.

In Portland, Ned had started a family and had returned to school to become a teacher. He'd worked in the same elementary school for years, and now rarely played banjo, but had joined a Brazilian marching band that played festivals. One time, after attending one of my Portland shows, he paid me my all-time favorite compliment.

You ought to start painting, he said as we sat nursing beers in the kitchen.

Painting? I can't paint.

Precisely, Ned said, raising his eyes. You forget. If you could learn to fiddle, you could learn to paint.

He'd said it. If Ned said I'd learned to fiddle, I'd learned to fiddle.

This trip, summer 2001, the same kitchen, his wife and boys upstairs, Ned and I were drinking beers again. I told him I was heading east to a music festival in West Virginia, and September I had work in Texas, October I'd be in Arizona, November in California, and then probably be back through here, no gig yet, but I was hopeful. Thanksgiving, I'd be up in Anchorage, but I'd given up my apartment. Early next year, I had another book coming out and was scheduling dates around that. I was not only on tour, I told him, but on perpetual tour. In three or four years, I'd either be established or bankrupt.

On tour? Ned interrupted. You call yourself on tour? Why, you're homeless.

75

I'm on tour.

Homeless, Ned corrected. But no matter. You'll likely find a few patrons of the arts, like me and Tia, or Danny and Nancy, to feed you and keep you sheltered. By the way, did you call Danny?

I shook my head. Through Ned, I'd met Danny when he lived in Seattle in the mid 1980's. Now he'd been in Portland for years, living a few miles from Ned, and ran a used record store out of his house. When I was in Portland and not staying at Ned and Tia's, Danny and Nancy put me up. Ned had his fabulous collection of staplers in the basement, two boys who were growing into interesting and eccentric young men, a wife who shared Ned's humor. On his walls, Danny had old board games: Candyland, Clue, Chutes and Ladders, several models of Chinese Checkers and Parcheesi. Adjoining the house was a shop where he mailed rare vinyl record albums to collectors world-wide. Danny adored the unusual. His wife, Nancy, was an architect, an artist, and a professor. Their black lab was named Easy. And me, I was their occasional house guest. The minor folk celebrity. The writer and observer.

The next morning, as Ned walked me outside, I ticked off an itinerary. Danny's house first. Then shoot out 84; make my way to a reading in Moscow, Idaho; see friends in Boulder and Denver; do a radio show in Bloomington, Indiana; spend a week camped at Clifftop and play old-time music.

Ned shook his head as he glanced at the Sentra.

At least I'll see the country, I said. At least I'm driving.

Good grief, Ned said. That overloaded car has broken down once already this trip. He smiled as we hugged good-bye. Well, at least you're in the tradition.

What tradition is that?

An American man. His Japanese car. The so-called quest.

From the sidewalk, Ned watched me start the engine. As I pulled from the curb, the car groaned from the weight. Out of the rearview, I saw Ned chuckling.

August 2003, I'd been on tour two years and two months. Like any life, this one had its rhythms and I'd been learning to adapt as best I could. Some weeks, in the midst of a particular series of jobs, or a particular landscape, or a particular temporary routine, I felt full of energy, and, no matter what, effortless productive days unfolded before me.

Bedrooms I Have Known

Other weeks, everything was a struggle.

To find a specific photo, or a letter, or a simple piece of tape, I'd have to go into my vehicle and rummage fifteen minutes through a dozen or more boxes. Or maybe it was one of those sad days where I had to unload the whole sorry mess and rearrange. Or else maybe I'd be cruising through rural Georgia or southern Illinois, nowhere near a city, and hit one of those freak two-hour traffic jams. Or else maybe I'd been booked to appear at a venue on a night of record cold weather or rain, or in a community where the state high school football championship had taken my audience, or in a town where the publicity had gotten overlooked and there was simply no interest in a fiddling poet because no one knew a fiddling poet was even there. Or maybe I was restless, or hungry, or tired, so tired I'd forgotten what usually kept me going during the lulls: that in addition to being my main source of income, all of this touring was also research, and I'd eventually write about what I was learning.

Beginning late April, I spent nearly three months house-sitting and dog sitting for my friend Patrice in New Orleans, a small house in a changing Mid City neighborhood by the bayou, and enjoyed being in one spot. Intending to write, I wrote little, and instead got sidetracked on a more pressing side project. Comfortable in my routine, I could have stayed longer. But then Patrice returned. It was tempting to remain in Louisiana through early September—after all, I had to be somewhere—and get to the writing that had gotten delayed. But already mid July, Clifftop beckoned.

I'd been to Clifftop the past two years. Where the festival in Juneau was a huge indoor northern spring music party, the one in West Virginia was even larger, a gigantic outdoor old-time music gathering atop a big hill. Elaborate and not-so-elaborate campsites stretched every direction, from the open fields into the woods. By Thursday the grounds had turned into a dense tent-city. Virtually everyone attending played, most at a very high level. Though I certainly played adequately, I always felt pedestrian. During the days, it was easy to get sidetracked for hours, visiting friends to play a few tunes. Nights, wandering in the dark from site to site, hearing unimaginably satisfying combinations, could feel like fantasy.

So I drove to Clifftop, running errands en route: Alabama (where I stopped in the arts councils in Tuscaloosa and Opelika, querying for future jobs); Georgia (where I stopped at the university in Columbus, and later met a woman friend outside Atlanta); North Carolina (where I spent a few days in Asheville, and confirmed dates for September); Tennessee (where I visited the national storytelling museum in Jonesborough, and met the festival director); and Virginia (where I bought tires and got an oil change in Salem, had dinner and saw a documentary film in Blacksburg). This was how I traveled when not feeling pressured, making strategic stops where I thought there might be benefit. Finally in West Virginia, I spent another terrific week camped at the festival while deciding what next. And deciding what next, I also felt torn. I wanted to get back to my projects.

When friends from near Asheville invited me to house-sit for a week, I accepted, which solved the problem about where to go immediately next. Arriving, I settled in, taking care of their pets and enjoying the proximity to a town I liked. I also did some writing, completing three grants as well as a short essay. Once my friends returned home, I still had four free weeks. I could have gone anywhere, I knew it, and was invited to remain in the same house, downstairs in the guest bedroom. But I didn't want to go anywhere. I just wanted to be in one spot, and I didn't think this was the one. I couldn't say why. It was just a feeling.

If I had the money, it might have been easier. I could have bought a motel room in Asheville. But that didn't seem right either. And while I had other friends in Asheville, this was one of those times where I didn't just need to be in one spot, it had to be the one right spot. I thought of Sarah then, the woman I'd seen in Atlanta on the drive up. She loved Asheville. Though I'd invited her to see me the previous week, it hadn't worked out. She'd grown up in the south, disliked Atlanta, left there after a divorce, and had spent several years in Durango and Sedona, two places she also loved. But she'd gotten sick out west, which exacerbated her financial problems. Her boys' father was still in Atlanta, so she returned. Back a year now, she was still struggling with the decision and her finances. We talked on the phone. If I wanted to stay at her place, she had a spare bedroom, and would be happy to rent it to me for a week or longer.

Atlanta wasn't all that far, I decided, and if I was going to drive, at least I knew of another venue or two to stop at on the way to check about jobs. Mostly, though,

Bedrooms I Have Known

I wanted to see Sarah. I liked her. And she seemed to like me. When I'd driven through a few weeks before, I'd met her boys, and we'd all gotten along fine. Why not? I thought. I'll spend a week at Sarah's. I'd been feeling tired. But having spent the late spring and early summer in one place, I should have been refreshed, not tired. Maybe I was just tired of being alone.

Quickly, it was apparent that Sarah and I were going to be just friends, not lovers. Her life was busy and complicated. So was mine. We liked each other, but not enough to make our complicated lives even more so. Though she disliked the circumstances of her life—from the gated apartment complex she chose because it made her relationship easier with her ex, who also lived there, to the awful suburban traffic north of the perimeter—she managed. And because she was so welcoming, I stayed three weeks even though I disliked the traffic, the apartment complex, and the whole suburban culture just as much. Completing one task after another, I reordered poetry manuscripts, made phone calls, confirmed jobs, mailed packets. But I also read two novels. We shared occasional meals. One evening Sarah insisted on giving me a card reading. We sat beside one another on the living room sofa. Following her directions, I picked a card from one of her special decks, set it down. Then I picked a second card. Then a third.

Studying the pictures, Sarah said the meaning was simple. I'd been a guest at many homes, she said, and would be a guest at many more. Sometimes I felt awkward visiting, as if intruding. She said there was no need to feel awkward. My presence was a blessing in a home. Or, rather than a blessing, I was giving people a gift. These might be people who wanted to travel, but couldn't. Or people who wanted to create, but couldn't. Or people who wanted to give more freely, but couldn't. If anybody truly made me feel uncomfortable, she said, then it was their problem. As for me, she said I was fine, and would continue to be fine as I remained on this path.

A part of me said, Yeah, sure, maybe you're saying that because you want me to stay and pay another week's rent. But a bigger part said, Sure, why not, there must be some reason I'm doing what I'm doing, other than researching a book. There were easier ways to make a living, and to make it through a life.

Mindful of Sarah's card reading, I first was taken back to Nome, a conversation

I had my first winter with Cecilia, who worked with me at the college as an administrator. Watching my struggles that second semester, she took me aside one day, said I'd been brought to Nome for the purpose of learning about the culture in order to write oral histories. That was my true job there, whether I liked it or not: to go out and gather the old Native stories. But I never could fully trust Cecilia. She was the one who months earlier had denied that drunks lurched up and down Front Street, and accused me of exaggerating the problem, even though I witnessed it almost nightly as I walked home from the college.

But Nome had been a long time ago. This month I was in suburban Atlanta, paying rent by the week, enjoying the little bit slower pace, and once more taking stock of my life, so ridiculous sometimes on the surface, but not without its rewards. Sarah was right that I sometimes felt awkward when I visited people's homes. Still, I took comfort that for the most part I was an easy guest to have around for a day or two, or longer; at least, I sure hoped so. But who ever knew, which was where the doubts crept in.

I recalled some of the houses and bedrooms I've known on tour. After leaving Ned's in Portland I'd traveled to Moscow, Idaho. My friend there, Peter, had a radio show, and presented concerts, or at least used to. Once he had arranged a successful coffeehouse appearance for me. He also was a long-time cancer survivor, had recently survived a stroke, was now a damaged man. I hadn't known him long or well, but had always been fond of him, especially his warped sense of humor. In addition to working together, we shared a room at two conferences. Once I gave him a ride to an event off site. He had the map. Straight? I asked, as we came to a possible turn.

Always forward. Never straight, he answered, waving me on.

That was Peter.

This trip through I was reading at a bookstore, appearing on his radio program. He hadn't invited me to stay with him, but mindful of my budget and remembering he still owed me for one of the conference hotel stays, I asked for a place to crash for the night. Though I could tell he was hesitant, he was also too polite to outright refuse me. After the radio show, I bought him dinner. Later, entering Peter's house, I realized why he'd been hesitant. Newspapers and magazines were piled several feet high everywhere, every surface, but for a thin trail from the front door to his bedroom to the bathroom. I didn't say anything, just took it all in. Peter sighed wearily. He did collages, he explained, so needed images, which he culled from what he collected. I did end up sleeping there, but not before moving several armfuls of materials in order to find a flat place to lay a sleeping bag.

And I recalled one late night near Kansas City after a daylong drive, pulling up to my friend's house, a friend I didn't know very well, another acquaintance from a conference who'd offered hospitality if I was in the area. Though he'd invited me to stay, once I actually arrived he ran to meet me outside and rescinded the offer because his house was a mess. But I have an idea, he said. Follow me. We drove along empty suburban roads to some apartments. I'll be sleeping here, too, he said, and I assumed we were at his girlfriend's. The next morning I learned it was his parents' old place, everything as it had been, though they'd passed away several years before.

In Denver, I stayed at Bob and Beth's. Bob was an excellent poet with several books, and far more prolific than me. The guest room was in the basement, as was the library. Every visit I marveled at the bookshelves and bookshelves of poetry journals. Though I knew the field, I'd invariably come across obscure titles I'd heard of for years, but had never seen. Bob had poems in every one, in thousands. We'd joke we were a pair of small-press all-stars. But he was the king, steadily sending out worthy poems for more than two decades, toiling with little appreciation outside of a small circle of devoted editors and readers. I'd had a few good years, and now was sidetracked with the touring.

Near Boulder, I stayed with Woody and Chris, and would play with Woody when I had dates on the Front Range. A fine banjo player and guitarist, he was in several bands, and had played publicly for more than thirty years. Once he joined me on tour to Grand Junction, Durango, Flagstaff. You're living one of my dreams, he said.

An accident, I said. This was never my dream. Anybody could do this if they made a lot of phone calls.

I couldn't do it, Woody said, adding, *Besides, you have something to really offer.*

In Flagstaff, I stayed in a trailer off Route 66 with Mike and Janet, and their sweet little girl, Aria. I'd met Mike when my first book had come out. He was a playwright and actor, and a teacher who taught English at the charter high school where I visited. The kids, at least the ones I met in Mike's classes, were brilliant. Mike not only loved what I did, but invited me to stay anytime in his small home. Sometimes I slept on a couch in the living room, sometimes on the beanbag or on a cushion on the floor in the extra room. Several months after we met, he wrote to let me know Flagstaff schools had been awarded three years of arts grants, and told me who to contact about returning to the community, and getting some of that grant money.

In Phoenix, I stayed with Bill and Michelle, and their three dogs. I'd met Bill in Albuquerque, my first Folk Alliance. He was a guitar player who used to present concerts, and once managed a band. Now he was officially out of the field. But that didn't stop him from putting me up for several nights—once helping me celebrate my birthday—and offering helpful input on my CDs. When the first one had come out, I had no e-mail account, so it was Bill who posted a notice on the folk-dj listserv.

In Las Vegas, I stayed with Jarret and Jennifer. Jarret was a much-published poet and fiction writer, who was the arts and entertainment editor for one of the city's three weekly newspapers. Jennifer was a sociology professor at the university. Jarret had a Ph.D. and a book out with a good independent press, but like me had one foot in academia, one foot out. We'd originally met at AWP. Since he regularly wrote about touring bands, he was especially intrigued with my choices and how I marketed myself. With two good incomes, they'd invariably treat when we went out to dinner, and I was happy to let them. They knew a different Las Vegas from the tourist guides.

In Southern California one night I stayed with Lois and Tim, who hosted concerts in their backyard. Tim was a singer-songwriter, who also worked a factory shift. Lois managed his musical career. One night I stayed with Andy, a guitarist, who was on faculty at Cal Tech. One night I stayed with Barbara, a banjo player who worked in an office at USC. And one night I stayed with a couple, Barb and Walter, who lived near West Hollywood. Walter played several instruments, worked in the movie business. Barb was one of my favorite old-time fiddlers in the country. She'd moved from the Bay Area to be with Walter. Once in San Francisco I stayed at her old apartment near Potrero Hill. That had been one of the tour's first really dark moments, early January 2002, a Sunday just before midnight, when the Sentra broke down climbing uphill a half-mile from where Barb lived.

But Barb had been wonderful. She helped me load everything into her car, making two quick trips to her place to unload. When AAA came to tow the car, it was empty, which made it safe to leave outside the repair shop. The next morning, I rode my bike to see the shop manager about what to do. The good news: only $400 to replace the broken axle, and it would be fixed by the end of the afternoon. Later, when I returned once more to pick it up, the mechanic who'd worked on the car looked me in the eye. The bad news: an older car, more problems awaited. When I mentioned I was a touring musician, and was about to embark on a trip east cross-country, the mechanic was incredulous—*what kind of adventure are you looking for anyway?*

The next night in Berkeley, I led a four-piece band that consisted of Barb, her banjo-playing pal Maggie (in whose apartment I'd stayed my previous trip to the Bay Area), and a guitar-playing friend, Mark. We performed at the Freight & Salvage, one of the premier acoustic music venues in the country, and the show was well-attended for a Tuesday. In forty-eight hours, I'd gone from helpless to temporarily prominent, which wasn't atypical.

Winter 2002. Over the next four weeks I drove from the Bay Area to Flagstaff (where I stayed with Mike and Janet), to Albuquerque (where I celebrated my second book with a performance, and spent a night at Dave's, a friend from Nome), to Las Cruces (where I saw my pal Rus, another fiddler and writer, in his Mesilla adobe) to Marfa and Alpine (where I stayed with the owners of the bakery, where I performed). In Austin, I stayed with my music partner there, Jerry Hagins, and his family. In New Orleans, I visited my friend Patrice in her old uptown house. Near Beaufort, North Carolina, I spent two nights at Barbara and Bryan's, friends from Clifftop. My heroes, I called them. Barbara, a writer who specialized in maritime issues, was a guitarist. Bryan, a boat builder, played accordion and fiddle. Their band alternated between Cajun and zydeco. At Clifftop they pitched a huge circus tent from the top of a monstrous old truck and cooked plenty of food, inviting everybody to party and play. When I visited them on the North Carolina coast, I headlined at the local coffeehouse. Despite the mechanic's warning, the car made it across the continent, no problem.

In Chapel Hill, I spent a night with Jim and Cindy, friends from the restaurant we'd worked in twenty years before, who had a small shrine to the Three Stooges in the guest bedroom. Then I moved to Isabel's. Isabel was a shop owner and craftswoman I'd also known twenty years before, primarily through her boyfriend. Now she owned a house within walking distance of her downtown shop, taught tai chi and meditation, was politically active. To help her own shaky budget, she had housemates. When that became problematic, she decided to divide her house and make one of the side rooms a studio apartment. Several months earlier, my previous trip through, she'd just finished the remodel. Now her house had a second apartment, so her own space had shrunk further. She'd also recently converted the meditation studio in the backyard to a rental. Like my friend David up in Anchorage, she offered keen insight on my particular challenges.

You must have been very very kind to me in a past life, she said one evening, because I really feel I'm supposed to help you along in this one.

February 2002, I stayed for nearly two weeks, time enough to buy a Plymouth Voyager minivan with 116,000 miles and sell the Nissan Sentra, all while working several college jobs in the region. Despite the chaos of travel and work, there did seem to be a purpose to what I was doing, or at least a synchronicity. Those two weeks in North Carolina, I earned just enough to pay for the vehicle without having to take an advance on one of my credit cards.

I recalled the last bustle of errands while at Isabel's. Once I'd signed papers and registered the vehicle, I drove to Goodwill, ripped out the back two rows of seats, tossed them on the donation pile. That evening, repacking, the minivan's roominess felt spectacular. Though I'd need one soon enough, I didn't even have to immediately buy a rack for the bike. There was plenty of space now.

Then I left North Carolina to work a pair of jobs in South Carolina. After the second, in Sumter, I bought a motel room, where I stayed an extra two days to get caught up yet again. The main project was upgrading the minivan. Though I'd always thought I'd build a cabin sometime in Alaska, I'd never gotten to it, one more dream lost to the busyness of days, to circumstance. In truth, I'd never built much of anything. Ned had always ridiculed my ignorance of tools. But now, by God, I was going to build.

Treating the job as I would a poem that needed contemplating, I jotted notes, a few diagrams. Starting at the absolute beginning, I first bought a tape measure, then a hammer, some nails. Later, I drove to the big hardware store where I shopped for boards and 2 x 4's, both of which I had cut to size. Back at the motel, I certainly amused the cleaning crew with my hammering. Asked what I was doing, I told them I was building a platform for the back of the van, something I could sleep on but which I could store boxes underneath; it was the largest thing, I said, I'd ever built. First thing the man's building himself is a bed, one of the maids chortled. The others started laughing, and I couldn't help smiling myself.

Done, I thought an hour later as I pounded in the last leg. Setting down the hammer, I circled around it in the parking lot, studying my handiwork from every side. I sat on the bed. I laid on it. The initial attempt was almost perfect. The platform wobbled slightly, not because it was uneven, but because I could feel it needed more support. After a second trip to the hardware store, I nailed a few more 2 x 4's to make the platform more stable, then lifted it, and wrestled it in straight and snug against the side. Not only did it fit lengthwise, but the height had been just right. I was proud I'd wasted none of the wood.

Then I was back on the road to Folk Alliance in Jacksonville, a school date in Alabama, AWP in New Orleans, then north.

Ten months earlier, April 2001, I stayed with Kent, my first time to the Twin Cities since AWP in spring 1992 when my elbow hurt, when I'd lived in Nome, the beginning of my illness time. Though Kent and I had never met, we'd been corresponding for years. Someone with a sense of humor had sent him one of my photocopied poetry postcards. *Nomadic Press Postcard Poetry Series,* it said in small print, and beneath was the return address for the Nomadic Press, the legal name of my Alaska-based business. Kent was a letterpress printer, and a long-time member of the Twin Cities book arts community. He did extraordinary work. The name of his business: Nomadic Press. I was living in Juneau when I received a letter one day, that the Nomadic Press of Minnesota sends greetings to the Nomadic Press of Alaska.

For years afterwards, we exchanged gifts. I'd send him a chapbook or a cassette. Later I sent him my first book, then my first CD. He sent me broadsides. Once I knew I'd be reading at the Loft Literary Center in Minneapolis, I contacted him, giving several months notice. When we finally met, he asked where I was staying. Several places had fallen through, I admitted, and told him I thought I might be buying a room. Nonsense, he said. Stay with us.

And I did, three nights, though Kent and his wife had to move their little girl into their even younger son's room. You could have been a jerk, Kent said, hugging me as I was set to go. But you're a good guy and we like each other. This has been great.

We parted as great pals, who now shared more than a business name and a correspondence.

My second time through, noticing I now had the van, Kent asked to take a closer look. We walked outside. Peering through the windows, admiring it, Kent asked whether I slept in it. I nodded, opened the side door, pointed to the platform, buried that moment under several boxes. I'm just getting used to it, I said. But what I'm learning is to pick my spots, like getting out of a city late at night, so I can get an early start on the next day. Or nights when I'm driving and it makes no sense to buy a room. Anyway I try never to sleep in it two nights in a row.

He nodded back. It can be a slippery slope, he said.

I knew what he was alluding to. It was easy to justify saving $40 or $50 motel bills every now and then, but the more I saved the money, the more I might be tempted to make that the norm. And that had its awkwardnesses. It was counter-productive to pop in at an arts council or a performing arts center and talk to a presenter about the possibility of setting up an event when the presenter might be wondering whether I'd ever had a shower. That was a problem. Still, I said, every time I've slept in it so far, I've slept really well.

Kent patted the hood. Home sweet home, he said fondly. Your midget RV.

It shouldn't have been so surprising that even from the beginning I slept well in the van. Staying at friends, everyplace was different. Big beds, small beds, hard beds, soft beds—no two alike. Sometimes I slept on sofas—both long-enough and too-short. Sometimes I shared rooms with cats and dogs—and the occasional cat

I could be allergic to. Sometimes there were bathrooms that I'd have to patiently wait for in the morning—and might have to tiptoe through my host's bedroom in the middle of the night to use.

In the van, I could shuck my shoes and socks where I wanted, turn, clamber up between the front seats, and crawl onto the thin air pad atop the wood platform where I'd sprawl face-down. There I'd turn on my back, wriggle out of my pants and into the sleeping bag, find a pillow or two. Maybe I'd flick on my flashlight and read. If not, I'd take off my glasses. Invariably I slept well, through the night, though if I had to crawl back through to the front seat to let myself out to piss, that was no big deal either, even if it sometimes meant a dark scurry to a restroom, bladder dangerously close to bursting, hoping I didn't trip over my untied shoelaces. Still, why shouldn't I have felt comfortable? Even though the back of the van was fairly cramped, and I could barely extend to my full 6'4" length on the platform, for once I was in my own space, surrounded by what was all mine.

Since nights sleeping in the minivan were invariably short ones, I felt comfortable parking most anywhere, occasionally in a rest area parking lot on interstates but more often in a truck stop. Even a vacant lot might do. Usually I woke before sunrise and was back on the road—a full day ahead, more of the routine. A touring musician friend once suggested I try motel parking lots because they'd be safer, and I did once in Syracuse. Just past dawn, I woke to nearly a dozen adults within thirty yards of me, all walking dogs as I popped out of the van, buckling my belt as I hustled to the nearby Denny's to use a bathroom. When I did sleep in the van, I preferred no one see me, which was usually the case, and why I've never slept in my van in another motel parking lot. Who knew when there might be another big dog show in town.

When I did park in motel lots, it was as a paying customer, and when I began this touring, I favored Motel 6. Usually I avoided chains, but what I liked about Motel 6, even more than their budget rates, was their consistency. Every room in every motel, I was met with the exact off-white wall, the exact carpet and bedspread. I could depend there would be nothing extra: no clock, no piece of art on the wall, no shampoo. Just a table, a chair, a dresser with TV on top, a counter with a sink just outside the bathroom, a toilet and shower inside the bathroom, a room that was clean enough, and where I felt safe parked with a vehicle full of boxes that would mean nothing to anyone else but was everything to me. There was a time for change—and most days were full of change—and there was a time for routine. Whether I was in Nashville, Oklahoma City, Pocatello, Eureka, Eugene, in a Motel 6 I could wake up and feel comfortable, that at least I knew where I was, and I'd been there before, even if I hadn't. Sometimes, when I needed extended time to spread out papers or take care of one aspect of business or another, I happily chose the motel over a spare room at a friend's.

Still, Motel 6 was not everywhere, and as I grew into the touring I enjoyed the variety of a Day's Inn, a Super 8, or an independent motel, where I could be happily surprised, like at the O'Haire Motor Inn in Great Falls, or fear for my safety, like at the Budget Motel in Statesboro. Always, though, when I had a choice, I traveled economically. And when presenters paid for a room at a bed and breakfast, or a more upscale hotel, that was reason to wish I'd brought along a date. Sometimes at conferences I paid to stay in such places myself, sharing with a pal.

I stayed with old friends, new friends, rich friends, poor friends, friends who were good for a night at most, friends who encouraged me not only to stay for a week or two, or even longer, but to bring my work inside, all of it, no matter how messy it might get. That was rare. Isabel had been like that. Sarah had been like that. And there were others.

Outside Washington D.C., I stayed with Russell and Alane. We'd originally met at Folk Alliance in Cleveland, which they were attending because they'd started an internet radio station, Hober.com. When I sent my first CD, they loved it and played it, and a year later loved the second one just as much. Before long, they'd offered to sell my CDs and books on the station website. If you're ever near D.C., they said, we have a big house on a lake. You might need time off from the road.

As we spent time each successive year at Folk Alliance, I learned more and more about them. Russell (his radio alias was Gregor, which was how he'd first introduced himself) had done a stint in prison, run a nightclub where he'd helped start Michelle Shocked's career, been married, been divorced, and raised a daughter. He met Alane when they were both migrant fruit pickers. Russell had an aptitude for technology, as had Alane. Embracing the internet, they got involved in web design, managed to win a first major client, who liked the work, and referred them elsewhere. The next years they contracted with clients such as *National Geographic*, and others, billing what that market demanded. They owned one house in Takoma Park, and another which they lived in, on the lake near Frederick, where I eventually came to visit.

I liked that they were not only interested fans who understood the business but were interested enough to suggest all manner of opportunities for what they saw as an intriguing case study: The Alaskan Fiddling Poet. They knew people who presented shows and who I might want to contact. They wondered: had I thought about having a movie made of me? Alane was even learning to play fiddle: maybe I should make an instruction tape.

There I was introduced to all manner of blogs, to the Daily Show (which they'd recorded on TiVo), and to Russell's political theories, which could sometimes be chilling. For decades he'd been in and around D.C., watching policy unfold. The corruption, he claimed, was so deep, it would take a generation to make things right. That is, he warned, if we started now, remained vigilant, and caught a few breaks.

My second time visiting, I house-sat for the weekend while they drove to New England to see family. Downstairs, before leaving, giving me a final tour of the house, Russell opened a drawer, showed me the gas masks. I know you won't need them, he said, but then reminded me the nearby military base, Fort Dietrich, was less than ten miles away and contained the largest cache of chemical weapons in the world.

There were more places I stayed prior to the visit at Sarah's. Many more. And there have been many since.

Near Albuquerque, I stayed at my writer friend Lisa's house. I've known Lisa almost twenty years, since Fairbanks. There was the one marriage there, and a second that lasted from a Peace Corps stint in Eastern Europe through school in New York and a job in Michigan. Now she teaches in the city, lives in the mountains, has a house on a gravel road that could almost be Alaska, and juggles a complicated love life. In Taos, I slept on the floor of a condominium owned by an entrepreneurial poet speculating in real estate. In San Antonio, I stayed with a true friend of the arts, a bon vivant lawyer in a funky old house with chickens in the back.

In South Florida, I stayed with a family of musicians who wondered what I was doing, sitting in an easy chair addressing envelopes for two full days, my entire time visiting. In a small community near Gainesville, I spent a night at a house owned by the town's Democratic former mayor, who'd lost her position in a feud with a Jeb Bush functionary, and claimed George W. was a shoo-in to repeat in 2004, while Jeb was primed for 2008. In Tallahassee, I spent a night in the house of a violinmaker who hosted a concert in his home, who was grateful to be alive after suffering a long illness that had partially destroyed his lungs.

In Alabama, I stayed two nights with an elderly couple I'd met when they vacationed in Alaska. A retired teacher, she'd donated money so I could visit the school where she used to teach. However, what seemed more crucial to her was that I take Christ into my life. One breakfast, I tore into a piece of toast before we prayed, and realized that in this house I'd just committed a grievous offense.

In Lafayette, Louisiana, I stayed in the storage room of a music store and gift shop, where to use the bathroom was to run an obstacle course in the dark around several CD racks. In rural Tennessee, I spent two nights in the house of a beautiful banjo player, who was getting near hourly phone calls, 7 a.m. to 11 p.m., from a new boyfriend several states away. In the North Carolina Piedmont, after a show in Winston-Salem, I stayed with an old friend, a musician who had toured all over the world, and pronounced me, the fiddling poet, a success for doing this like I had. In West Virginia, and again in Virginia, I stayed in homes where I got to converse with fellow fiddling poets.

Near Charlottesville, I stayed in a house with a big map of Alaska on the wall. Invited to go into the refrigerator and forage, I was asked whether I had food preferences. I shook my head no, saying I'd eat most anything. So, I was told, you're one of those opportunivores.

In Elkins, West Virginia I spent a hot summer week in an attic of a historic downtown house that was also a restaurant, and which had fed and sheltered other artists. Eastern Long Island, I spent two nights—one on the couch of a bass-playing, songwriting chef, the other visiting an old tennis teaching buddy, now the father of three precocious kids. North of Hartford, I slept one night in a stone house that felt like a mini-castle. South of Burlington, Vermont, in the midst of a three-month tour, I spent a few days catching up with an old Alaska musician friend. Near Ithaca, I stayed in an old farmhouse, which somehow always transported me back twenty years. In Bloomington, Indiana, I spent the night in the home of a radio disc jockey, my most talkative host. In Chicago, I visited my pal who lived in a Polish neighborhood on the north side, where I could spend my day speaking and reading Polish, if only I could, and where I once visited for almost four months, my all-time record. Across to St. Louis, I stayed in the cozy spare room inside a loft at an artist's co-op. In Iowa City, I left dirty clothes in the bathroom of a French professor and had them forwarded. In Cheyenne, I spent a few nights downstairs, put up by a writer who worked for the state as he raised a family. In Great Falls, I not only stayed at the O'Haire Motor Inn, home of the legendary Sip 'n Dip, but at the home of yet another fiddling poet, this one with a collection of yardsticks, globes, and books written in Latin. In Pendleton, Oregon I spent a night on the basement sofa—a novice fiddler had invited me and my accompanist home after attending a show sixty miles away.

In Seattle, I always had choices: the house of a hospice nurse and sometimes shaman; the house of a couple where the wife is my oldest Seattle friend and for years was the only person I let cut my hair; the house of the woman who repairs guitars when not indulging an impossible appetite for sweets; the house of the couple with the handsome boys and the car that runs on used vegetable oil; the principal's office in the old Lake City neighborhood school, a building that's been converted to artist housing, where Andrea and Mark live; the upstairs guestroom in Anita's house, the same space where I once paid rent. Then there were the years my friend, Jamie, had his boat, which I slept on once or twice. Now he's married, living in Santa Fe, and I'll likely spend a night my next time in the region.

Near mile zero of the Alcan Highway, I spent three nights in the home of a wheelchair-bound teacher who was away on a trip. And, further north, after a lit summer night drinking shots in a roadhouse across from a distant gas station that sold my CDs, I spent a few odd hours passed out on a ratty couch while the rest of the bored group continued drinking. Even further north, Whitehorse, I spent nights visiting my vaudevillian Yukon cousin, Marty Waldman, who rumor has it now lives in Victoria and goes by Marti, after the sex-change.

In Juneau, I stayed in one of the yet-to-be-renovated rooms of The Conn, Fiddling Jim's home, a century-old boarding house, where hospitality was unsurpassed, and I could depend on homemade bread, plenty of pasta and sauce, slices of fruit and cheese. In Haines, I stayed with my activist pal who whipped me in Scrabble, or else with the concertina-playing doctor who's remarried and begun a third family. In Fairbanks, I could count on Cindy, who I met my first week in the state, a writer and teacher who had a horse now, owned a house up Chena Ridge with her partner, Mike, and where I'd roll up my shirt sleeves to start washing dishes. One summer, though, making a CD, I spent a few nights at Charlie and Nancy's cabin when they were gone, and once on the floor of Pat and Robin's recording studio, when at 2 a.m. I couldn't find the key to Charlie and Nancy's. In Palmer, I stayed with Deb and Paul, one a writer, the other an artist and teacher, who had one home there on the side of a mountain, a second off the grid in Fairbanks. In Anchorage, I'd stay at David's, where we concocted fiddling poet schemes, and also at Pam's, whose life work was to save the Arctic National Wildlife Refuge from drilling, and where we yearned for Fairbanks and commiserated about the debt we carried and our relentless workload. In Kenai, I stayed with Alise, where we'd drink and flirt while her three children slept. In Homer, finally, end of the road, I stayed in Matt and Nancy's studio—he was a musician, she a painter—a few steps away from the house that bordered a wildlife preserve, where you were apt to spot moose, maybe even bear; and once I spent a week at a cabin with a spectacular view of Kachemak Bay—I was visiting a woman I'd once dated. But that one's been sold, so I'll never be back.

I'd stay. I'd leave. Sarah might have consulted her cards one more time and proclaim that as I traveled onward I took something of the spirit of each place with me. If I did, I was unaware, at least in those terms. How can the elusiveness of spirit be measured? Unless spirit could be measured in the lives I witnessed, the stories I gained, which only accumulated as I traveled more miles.

Always there was somewhere else to go.

4
Logistics / Technology / Whatnot

September 11, 2001
Austin

This is no poem
about planes hijacked and flown
into New York City buildings,
cameras catching the surreal, endless
snippets—some edited, some not—
of towers on fire awhile,
then suddenly collapsing, the heap
a mix of concrete, dark
smoke, bodies, ash, everywhere
the rubble—and that ignores
a third plane hijacked and flown
into the Pentagon, a fourth
plowing into a Pennsylvania field,
the thousands dead. That's the poem
television writes. Underneath is another—
strange world of good and evil,
love and hate, great anger
and even greater faith.
Nothing ever changes. Everything has.
We'll need friends, family, music.
A language that transcends.

Early June 2001, I stood outside Coffee Roasters on Geist Road in Fairbanks. The night before I'd been out late, celebrating the release of my second CD, *Burnt Down House*, which I'd recorded in town six months earlier. After the regularly scheduled tourist show, I'd played a set in Ester at the Malemute Saloon, and then we'd had a jam session. We'd gone until almost 3 a.m., long past dusk, and ended the evening driving home in the quiet late-night daylight. It was one of things I loved about Fairbanks, how the summer light turned time upside-down. Another was this scene at Coffee Roasters, dawdling before getting on the road, in no hurry because, though I really did have to get back to Anchorage where I had so much to do the next two weeks packing up my apartment before leaving it for good and going on tour, hurrying didn't matter. In June there was always plenty of time. My pal Cindy was there. And so, unexpectedly, was Mattie, whom I'd always liked but who had also always lived in Juneau with a boyfriend. Somehow she was working on Mike's little farm. This was the third time I'd run into her in three days. Each time had made me happy.

That was also what I liked about the state and especially about Fairbanks. In certain circles, everybody and everything related. Mike was a fiddler, had even played on one of the cuts on the CD. He'd been by last night, but had left early, since this was the busy season. A native New Englander, Mike used to work for the park service in the Brooks Range. Now he grew flowers, had a dog team, was building a house, had recently gotten married. The privileged poor, he'd once called us, explaining the choices we'd made, and how it was we'd come to this stage in our lives—a pair of guys in their forties, free to follow dreams, work nonstop, skirt financial ruin, be the envy of certain friends.

Cindy was one of the few people I let worry about me, and she was worrying now. She knew I was nearly broke and couldn't understand why, instead of saving up to apply for a teaching job somewhere, I'd put my money into making CDs— indeed, was planning on recording another in Fairbanks this winter and was going to drive out of state with no plan other than to somehow go from job to job. I can't even get hold of you, she complained.

Of course you can, I said.

No, I can't. You don't even have e-mail.

So what? I said. You can write me a letter. It'll get forwarded, and I'll write you back. You can call my voice mail; I check messages all the time, and I'll call you back.

No, she said. If I needed to get hold of you, I couldn't.

We hugged, and I watched her pull out of the parking space. Then I turned to Mattie, who was still standing beside me.

Did you hear all that? I asked.

She nodded.

Am I crazy? Am I? Doesn't a phone count as a way to get hold of someone? What about writing letters?

Mattie shrugged her shoulders. People are funny, she said. I don't have e-mail either, but people who do just act funny sometimes. She smiled. I understood what you meant.

You did?

She nodded.

So, hypothetically, if I were to invite you to join me on this tour, and you wanted to, you'd be able to find me, no matter what.

Mattie smiled. Oh, I'd be able to find you.

I went into my back pocket. Just to be sure, here's my latest card. I found a pen, scrawled a phone number. Where are you going to be in the fall?

Mattie continued smiling. I'd been inviting her places, hypothetically and not, ever since we'd met. I bet she had no idea where she'd be but knew it wasn't going to be on tour with the fiddling poet. Still, I'd always liked Mattie. I liked all kinds of women, never felt I had a single type. But if I did, it would have been like Mattie. Smart, pretty, earthy, with a sense of humor. Long blonde hair. Pretty blue eyes. Like my first girlfriend, Frannie. It never hurt to let her know I liked her, I thought, as I gave her a hug, turned to get in my car.

For a year now, ever since my first CD had been released and I'd begun using the internet to look up information, I'd been mulling opening an e-mail account. Cindy was only one of a myriad of friends who'd converted to communicating almost wholly online. And though I'd had fair luck on the phone, I'd begun meeting club owners and presenters who refused phone calls and conducted all business electronically.

There were reasons to get an account, I knew. Of course there were those who rolled their eyes, who I imagined hissed *Luddite* when I said I didn't use e-mail, or who'd say, You of all people, doing what you do, you need e-mail more than anyone I know. But there were others who'd cheer me on, who'd say, Good for you, e-mail takes up all your time, and once you start you can't go back—hold off as long as you can.

So I held off, and continued with the system that I had.

It was a rickety system, granted, but one that had naturally evolved. In Juneau, where I had a post office box, when I traveled for weeks, I depended on my friend, Jan, who lived next door to the post office. I gave her a spare key. When I was on my longer trips, every several days she'd walk next door with her little boy, Riley, let him put the key in the box, and turn. She'd put the mail in an envelope, and forward it to where I'd be the following week. Back in Juneau some weeks later, I'd stop by to visit, maybe play a few fiddle tunes with her husband, Tom, and reimburse her for the postage.

In Anchorage, even before I'd decided to rent the basement apartment close to downtown, I understood I needed not only a permanent address but one where I wouldn't have to depend on friends. Everywhere there are businesses whose service is to provide an address for a fee and, for an additional fee, will forward mail. I simply found one that was well-established in Anchorage. Summers when I was in town, it was a pleasurable part of my day to ride the two miles one way to my mailbox, pedaling uphill along a section of the Chester Creek bike trail, then up another trail toward West High and Romig Junior High. On the sidewalk then, across Northern Lights and Benson, across Minnesota and Spenard, I'd hop the occasional curb to 36th and Arctic. My box was less than a half-block from the corner. Winters, I drove. And when I was out of town for more than two weeks so needed mail forwarded, I could call anytime between 8 a.m. and 7 p.m. Alaska time. It was a matter of calculating not only where I'd be in a week or ten days, but also figuring a place which felt safe to have something sent. Over the years, the folks working there had gotten to know me well. I'd call, leave an address, then would forget about it until I rolled into wherever I'd thought to have my mail forwarded. Invariably, a packet was awaiting me, and I learned most times it would take three or four days to reach the destination

In all these years, the only time the system has gone even slightly awry was recently when I had almost three weeks worth of mail sent directly to a house I was subletting and had to wait more than a week. After almost two weeks, I contacted both the local post office and my mail service, checking too to see if the forwarded mail had somehow been lost or misplaced. Already I'd called to have a second pack mailed, which had already arrived, three days after mailing. Checking the postmarks from this second pack, I had proof there were indeed three weeks unaccounted for. Afraid the first packet of mail might never appear, I began contacting people I'd been expecting checks from, letting them know I had a problem.

One afternoon the following week, there was a knock on the door. An elderly neighbor handed me the packet, which he said had been delivered to his house instead of the one I was in. Several times I'd seen the man working in his yard the previous week. I could only wonder why he hadn't returned the misdelivered mail to the carrier or why he'd taken so long to bring it over. He'd likely had it almost two weeks. Though the packet didn't contain the two larger checks I'd been expecting, there was still over $800 worth that needed depositing, as well as other pressing business.

I learned to attend to all my business on the road. Banking was easy: simply sign the checks, stick them in an envelope, and send them to my Anchorage credit union. I always had stamps handy. I not only knew the due dates for all six credit cards, but knew when my phone bill was due, when my semi-annual car insurance bill was due, when my AAA service bill was due. I always paid on time, whether I had the bill in my hands or not, though I did run into trouble two or three times when the bills weren't credited correctly, and I had to explain the errors.

Because I didn't use e-mail, I'd grown especially dependent on the phone. When I first started my business in Juneau, even before I had my own place, I bought a voice mail account so there was a number to reach me. When I moved into the studio, I kept that number—kept it until I moved to Anchorage—plus had my own phone line. Home, I'd spend full days making calls. Traveling, I started buying phone cards, which I'd use to check my message phone number or else to call people directly.

As the technology has changed, so has my system. Though I found phone cards with cheaper and cheaper rates—and the phone card choices can be dizzying —they've become harder to use in public. Just a few years ago, pay phones were plentiful, and certain phone cards could be an excellent deal. But because of the proliferation of cell phones, the few pay phones you can still find now charge a connection fee that has risen to up to a dollar per call. There was a time that I'd make fifteen or twenty phone calls at once, leaving quick messages, sometimes even reaching someone. That's no longer economical on pay phones, though I'll still do it on motel or private phone lines since the dollar connection fee doesn't apply there. Many mornings in a Motel 6, I'd race to make cheap phone card calls before the noon checkout, when I'd hurry out the door at 11:58, lugging my music instruments and overnight bag to the front desk, where I'd drop off the key and head to the minivan to begin the day's drive.

Until fairly recently, the cell phone option was the one that always seemed impractically expensive. Sketchy service areas, huge roaming charges, and for what benefit? I wondered. Pay phones used to be fine. And even when those rates soared, as long as I had access to a motel phone, or was staying with somebody who didn't mind if I tied up the line, the phone cards worked. To reach me quickly, I have my Anchorage voice mail number, which I plan to keep indefinitely. The number is on every piece of promotional material, even my CDs, and I check at least once daily. To contact me cheaply, and at length, there's the postal service. For years now, I've been corresponding that way with my Denver poetry buddy, Bob. We keep faith in what is slower and steady.

Saturday, September 8, 2001, I was attending a conference in the Texas hill country west of Austin. The national Folk Alliance conferences in February had grown so large that most regions now held more intimate regional conferences in the fall. I'd been wanting to play more in Texas, and had a friend, Jerry, who I'd originally met as a correspondent. He was co-editor of a poetry journal I'd published in, *Nerve Cowboy*. An excellent clawhammer banjo player with a style similar to Andrea's, he was a friend of Fiddling Wolf, whom I'd known for years. Jerry and I began playing music whenever we had the opportunity and performed together several times. In December, I'd be recording my next CD up in Fairbanks and Andrea had indicated she didn't want to commit. Jerry was happy to. Here, at the Folk Alliance regional, we were even showcasing on the main stage. Also attending the conference was Marilyn, a pretty singer-songwriter who'd been flirting with me.

I missed arranging a roommate at the conference, which cost me an extra

$35/night for three nights, but which allowed me to invite Marilyn to stop by after my showcase to play music, talk, share a beer. I'd been attracted to her the first time we'd met, a year earlier. The way she'd been flirting, the attraction was obviously mutual. We tried playing one of her songs, but had hardly started before we put down our instruments, began kissing and cuddling. I got up to close the door.

Sunday afternoon, I followed her back to Austin, where she lived. Her apartment was south of downtown. I'd be staying several miles north, with Jerry and his family. One more sexy hug and we made a date for the next night.

I can hardly wait, I said.

Neither can I, she said, kissing me deeply.

Past midnight Monday, after a couple of beers, more wonderful conversation, Marilyn asked me to walk her to her car. Come in for a minute, she said. We hadn't even settled before we started cuddling across the front seat, Marilyn burrowing closer. She didn't know what to do: get a room at this late hour or go home and figure it out tomorrow. Being with me, she said, was clarifying things for her. She'd told me her life was complicated. I knew she'd recently been in a long relationship, and was still sharing an apartment with him. What I hadn't known was he was threatening to kill himself if she left, so she felt she had to be careful. But she wanted to be with me, could see driving off with me in a few weeks. A few weeks, that was all it would take. She needed to get out of Austin. Besides, touring had been a dream for her. She clung to me even closer.

I let her cling. If she wanted to get a room, I was all for it. If she wanted to wait, I could wait. I knew I wanted her. I'd make space in the car, buy something bigger, do what seemed best. Marilyn wasn't part of any immediate plan, but she sure could be. Mattie up in Alaska was never going to call me. I kissed Marilyn, and let my fingers slide downward. She kissed me back. We could buy a room now, we supposed, but no, we thought. She had to be careful. I didn't want to push. We were here in Austin, not out of town in the hill country.

The next morning I woke at Jerry's, and his wife Megan was watching the news. In New York City, a plane had crashed into one of the World Trade Centers and the building was on fire. We watched live as what looked at first like a little commuter plane improbably circled and then hit the second tower. We sat transfixed most of the day. When I called Marilyn, she picked up the phone, said she couldn't talk to me, but whispered she'd call Jerry's and leave a cell number, and she hoped to see me at my Wednesday night concert at the Cactus Cafe. Though our club date went on as scheduled—one I only felt able to do since the day of the attacks I'd written a poem about September 11 and could integrate it into the show—it was poorly attended. Marilyn was one of the no-shows. Of course, who could predict anything during that extraordinary week? Earlier Wednesday, Jerry and I had been looking forward to appearing on a popular University of Texas public radio station interview program. After the terrorism, our guest slot had been cancelled.

That weekend I was leading workshops in San Antonio, and then I had two more weeks before heading to West Texas, my next gig. A few days earlier Marilyn was considering coming with me; now, with the tumult of 9/11 and her complicated relationship with her ex, she was nearly impossible to reach. Once that next week we went out for dinner. Once for drinks. I couldn't write her, couldn't call, except on the cell when it was safe. You should e-mail me, she said.

This isn't as much fun now, is it, I said, sitting in her car again, the night we'd eaten dinner together. Though we still kissed and hugged, I heard her say now that this was going to take awhile. She hadn't said that before. Her ex was going through hard times, she said. He needed her.

What about me needing you? I said.

She shook her head. I'm sorry. 9/11 made everything weird. Or maybe I just shouldn't have gone home that night, and just gone gotten a room with you. She shook her head, then buried it in my chest. Now you're just going to have to be very very patient with me, I'm afraid.

I'm afraid we don't have a lot of time, I answered, putting a hand in her hair and starting to tousle. I didn't know exactly how Andrea and Mark began a relationship that withstood distance for so many months, but I knew it hadn't been like this.

Later that week, Jerry helped me open a Hotmail account. The next day, at the downtown Austin library, I spent half my hour on the computer trying to figure out my pass code and the other half staring at the screen, thinking of Marilyn. I ran out of time before I could type a quarter of what I'd wanted to say. The next day, back again, the process was quicker. At least most of what needed saying got written. I pressed the send button, and assumed the words would reach her. And the day after, having received a note back from Marilyn, I guessed this was how it worked, so wrote her another. Beginning early October, I had jobs west. Thanksgiving, I'd be flying north from Seattle. Probably I'd be back through Austin in January, but only for a few days, and it seemed our time was now, in person. But the time was passing. I'd be leaving alone, and that would be it. Typical, I thought, how it took a doomed relationship to induce me to begin using e-mail. I saw Marilyn one more time while I was in Austin. She couldn't leave her ex-boyfriend now, she said. We were back in her car, her right hand on my knee, fingers probing. You'll just have to understand, she said.

What followed was exactly as I suspected. Writing Marilyn, and waiting to hear from her, spurred me for awhile. But from the beginning she responded erratically, then barely at all. Gradually, I let work contacts know I could be reached electronically, which obliged me to continue checking daily. As I traveled west towards California, and then north into Oregon and Washington, I found myself imperceptibly changing my routine, incorporating a daily visit to my e-mail account. At first, since I received few messages, I didn't have to do much. Still, one of my concerns was the difficulty in finding computers. Phones were everywhere, I reasoned; computers were not. And if I was going to do this, I wanted to do this right, which meant going on-line daily.

It was easier than I thought. When I stayed with friends, if they were wired, as most of them were, they were quick to offer me time on their computer. I also found I could use internet cafes, which were fairly economical or, in a pinch, a copy shop, which often rented time for $10 or $12 (or more) per hour. My favorite way to check e-mail, though, was by going to libraries, sometimes on college campuses when I had work there but especially public libraries.

After all these years using e-mail now, I've found it is better—and worse—than I imagined. As my business endured, it was more essential than ever to stay current. Any day, anything could happen: an invitation to perform somewhere, a presenter or band mate checking in about an upcoming gig, news about a conference. For me, receiving messages meant replying promptly. And while it would have been convenient to have had internet access on the laptop I carried, the laptop was older, and I used it only for word processing. Being dependent on e-mail like this meant my first stop in a community now—and sometimes a stop in the midst of a long 500-mile-day drive—was the public library, where I could get on a computer.

As a result, I've become experienced in the ways of public libraries, and their computer stations.

In my old hometown library, Anchorage, most computers were accessible only through typing in the numbers on a library card, which meant only residents were eligible. There was a strict one-hour limit per day; the computer shut down when your time was up (first giving the appropriate five-minute, then the two-minute warning, asking you whether you'd like to save your work). Six computers, however, were set up for all comers, whether resident or not. I've found if I need to get as much work done as I can, I arrive early, sign up for one of those, and, after my hour is up, go on to the resident-only flank of machines.

The rest of the country, I found, was a variation of the Anchorage system. In Seattle, you had to have a library card. If not, you could get on a computer only if one was available and you asked politely at the reference desk. The reference librarian would then walk you to a computer, punch in a code, and let you get to work. In Albuquerque and Buffalo, non-residents needed to buy library cards that enabled you to log on and both places had a one-hour limit. (In Albuquerque, you had to put the card in a slot to start the computer; not used to the system, I left the card in and lost it, so my next time in town I'll have to buy another.)

In New Orleans, which also had a one-hour limit, you were assigned a name and a password, which, when typed into a central computer, assigned you a computer. When your computer was immediately available, the process worked well: just type your name, enter your password, and follow the instructions about which computer to begin using. The trick here was that if you had to wait, once your turn came up, you only had five minutes to log on, and the turn was announced only on the computer screen. At busy times, there was always a group huddled by the central reservation computer, checking the approximate wait times.

Approximate, that was the key word, which I learned the hard way. One morning, waiting for a computer at the downtown library, I resigned myself to more than an hour wait, as my name was far down the list. I busied myself with the current magazines. Forty minutes had passed when I went back to the central computer, and found the line had passed quickly, and my turn had come and gone. I now faced a 90-minute wait. I left the building, shaking my head and grumbling.

New Orleans, though, had one of my favorite branch libraries anywhere, a converted mansion on St. Charles Street, uptown, not far from Tulane. Early September 2002, I spent a few weeks nearby. Part of my routine was to bike to this library and be waiting at the front when the doors opened at 10 a.m., to be first in line for the computers. (One of the tricks for getting on computers at popular places is to be there when the place opens for the day). By 11 a.m., I was done, and most people were facing more than an hour wait for one of the five computers at that branch.

On a drive from Elkins, West Virginia to Glenville, where I was to perform at the college there, I stopped in the town of Weston, found another library housed in a mansion.

Excellent.

In Tuscaloosa, two minutes before the hour-time limit runs out, if you were lucky, you'd get this message: Presently, there is no waiting list for computers. Press enter for an extra hour of computer time. Again, excellent (though if you pressed enter you'd lose whatever you were currently working on).

In Newberry, South Carolina, you were allowed a half-hour, once a day, no exceptions.

In Peachtree Corners, a suburb of Atlanta, you were also allowed a half-hour, but since the system wasn't managed by computers, you were free to stay on as long as you needed, until a librarian announced there were people waiting, which always set off a mad scramble. If you did have to get off, you were allowed back on once the computers freed up again.

In Hattiesburg, Mississippi, and Opelousas, Louisiana, the libraries opened at 8 a.m. on weekdays. It must be a Deep South thing, the promise the day might get off to such an early start. In Lafayette, Louisiana, though, the library opened at 9 a.m. What was unique there: the hour sign-up started and ended on the hour. If you logged on, say, at 9:20, you were only guaranteed 40 minutes.

In Las Vegas, the libraries opened at 10 a.m. on Sunday mornings and the computers had a two-hour limit, which felt luxurious.

In Boulder, it was first-come, first-serve, stay-on-as-long-as-you-wanted, though the computers, two rows in the library foyer, were set up so you could only use them while standing, which made for a kind of survival of the fittest.

In Hagerstown, Maryland, the computers were assigned by a single reference librarian, so while there was usually a wait to get on, the computers could be empty for 10 or 15 minutes while the librarian was helping someone on a reference task.

In Mobile, Alabama, and Roswell, Georgia, Hotmail accounts could not be accessed. In Council Bluffs, Iowa, where I spent a weekend prior to performances in Omaha, as long as there was no one waiting, you could stay on as long as you wanted—and it was a beautiful new library too.

In Eugene, Oregon if you were a fiddling poet and had a friend who worked at the library (and who also played music), you could say hello and receive an invitation to use your friend's office computer.

In Weaverville, North Carolina, if you used the library's computers everyday for a week, you were well-known by the staff, greeted by name, and, though there was a one-hour limit per day, encouraged to hop on any computer that was not being used.

Early May, 2002, New York City, nearly eleven months on tour, I now faced the 5,000 mile drive to Anchorage, only a single small gig en route—a performing space in Prince George, B.C. One long day out of Manhattan, sleeping for a few hours in the back of the van, and I made it to Minneapolis where I holed up two days reading poetry in a motel, doing my job judging a South Carolina state arts council fellowship. Another marathon drive and I was west of Havre. Turning north, I spent two days in Banff, two more in Prince George, then an overnight in Whitehorse. The travel routine on this trip was similar, and different, than others. It was always similar, I reflected, coping with the long days behind the wheel, a cassette in the tape deck, the need to reach a fixed destination. It was always different though; there were always new towns, new landscapes, the possibilities of a surprise. Canada was always a pleasure, invariably cleaner than the States, and smarter somehow. In Banff, the internet cafe was packed, and incredibly cheap. My second day there, I drove uphill to the performing arts center, where I met the manager, handed him a CD, and immediately began scheming how I might make it back through sometime with Andrea, who I knew would love to play in the Canadian Rockies.

I arrived in Anchorage ready to promote my new book from Fairbanks to Homer, and finish mixing my third CD. Also, David McCormick had made headway on the plan for a website. Working at his music store was a teenager who assured him he could put www.kenwaldman.com on the web. What was best, David assured me, was that he'd do it cheap so we could oversee and make sure it was done right at a fraction of what it would cost professionally.

We paid for a server, and chose the one affiliated with the internet record store, CDBaby. This server specialized in working with musicians and had a prime advantage: once it was set up, I could update both my calendar and news pages without having to learn code or pay a webmaster (and I understand it's now even possible to design a simple site that allows you to go in and handle everything yourself). We still had to deal with the technical issues, so we arranged a meeting —or tried to arrange a meeting—with our young web designer, Brinton. Eighteen years old, he could have been my son. We asked, we demanded, we pleaded, we cajoled, we wheedled. One week, he was studying what the job entailed. One week, his computer was down. One week, he was ill. One week, he didn't show up at work and didn't return phone calls. Finally, late June, one week before I was to begin driving south, we met at Brinton's house. A recent high school graduate, he was still living at home, sharing a room with his brother. Checkbook in hand, feeling slightly disreputable, I watched from the side as Brinton sat in front of his computer, scanning in photos, typing in text. David, who had an eye for color and layout, stood at his shoulder, whispering instruction. During a four-hour session, the website began taking shape. One more meeting, two at most, and we'd be done, ready to post online.

But Brinton was busy, David was busy, and I had a gig in Whitehorse on July 4th, then shows in Skagway, Haines, and Juneau. This year I'd take the ferry to Prince Rupert and drive south through Prince George. Though Brinton promised to meet with David and finish the website, he failed to return my phone calls. Three weeks later, I entreated my pal Woody, in Colorado, someone who knew his way around computers, to look into the problem. It took him most of a day—all he had to do was figure what exactly Brinton had done—to go into the nearly-complete design and finish it. By the time I arrived at Clifftop the following week, Woody called to tell me I should go find a computer somewhere; he'd posted the website so I should have a look.

By then, I had no doubts that having a website was a good thing. But even so, I hadn't expected it to be as useful as it was, even from the start. October, I was to be back in Colorado, performing at a library. My contact there was trying to arrange school visits. She asked teachers and administrators to view the website, which led to three schools booking me for a total of four assemblies, and an extra $1300.

What I loved about this life was that even when a half dozen plans failed, a dozen plans failed, two dozen plans failed, as long as I had my wits, I could pick up the phone, or type an e-mail, and make one more plan which might well fail, but, who knows, might even succeed.

When the third CD, *Music Party*, was released in late 2002, I thought it would lead to a number of summer festival invitations around the country. I applied to dozens of festivals from Yellowknife and Dawson City to Chattanooga and Birmingham—many I discovered online—and as I toured the first two months of 2003, driving from Seattle south through California into Arizona, West Texas, Louisiana, Tennessee, North Carolina, and Maryland, I waited to hear back. Recording and releasing three CDs in two and a half years had been exciting. I'd received radio airplay. I'd been featured in newspapers, and recently in a highly-regarded folk and world music magazine, *Dirty Linen*. I'd received good reviews. I wondered where I'd be invited this summer.

March, I realized wherever I might be other than Clifftop, it would have nothing to do with festivals. That's when I called Patrice in New Orleans. When I saw her in January, she told me she'd received a writing residency in New Mexico and she'd be needing to make arrangements for her house and dog. I wondered then, as we talked, if she still needed someone to house-sit and watch her dog.

I was getting ready to take care of that, she said. Good thing you called.

And so that became my plan: to stay in one place and write. I had an Alaska memoir that had been demanding attention. Once people heard about my plane crash, they always wanted to hear more. Well, I'd tell them all right, make the plane wreck the central episode of my life from 1985, when I arrived in Fairbanks, to 1998, when I moved to Anchorage. Writing about every aspect of the wreck in depth, I'd flash back to my graduate school days in Fairbanks, my year in Juneau, my year in Sitka, and most of all to my two years in Nome, when I lived in the region.

I arrived in New Orleans prepared to write. I plugged in my computer and my printer, an Apple ink-jet no longer being made. The printer, I found, had somehow gotten broken. It was a small part, but to replace or fix it, I soon discovered, would take ingenuity. Eventually I decided what would be quickest, easiest, and cheapest was to buy another printer on e-bay and immediately purchased one (incidentally, my first, and, so far, only e-bay purchase) . While I waited for the printer to arrive, instead of beginning the manuscript, I had an idea. Patrice had a home computer with internet access and she'd invited me to use it as much as I needed. I imagined what it would be like to work more deeply, not being constrained by the half-hour or hour time limit I ordinarily found at libraries. Already I'd learned to research all manner of material on the internet. I'd started with folk music disc jockeys. Since then, with varying success, I've become much more knowledgeable about literary agents, book publishers, club owners, concert promoters, newspaper calendar editors, music writers, and more. With a little digging, I learned, you can discover almost anything.

At Patrice's, I tried an experiment. Late March 2004, the AWP Conference would be held in Chicago. I thought, Why not try to find work in colleges and universities in Wisconsin? Referring to a book I owned that listed colleges state-by-state nationwide, I went down the list in Wisconsin, clicked to each school's English Department website, figured out who taught the Creative Writing classes, and queried. My letter, I thought, was a reasonable one, and included credentials that might likely pique interest: book publications, journal publications, other appearances, the fact that I could play fiddle as well as read poems. Reviewing schools, and the particular writers teaching on the campuses, intrigued me. Receiving several replies encouraged me to keep at it.

One year before, May 2002, beginning that long drive from New York to Anchorage, I worried how I could afford continuing. I was working, but not enough. Expenses were too high. Maybe this wasn't to be, I reflected. The plane wreck settlement money was long gone. I spent the money on making CDs, on books, on marketing, on getting from place to place. I'd done the best I could and failed. The Monday morning after Mother's Day, at a pay phone in Shelby, Montana, I was checking messages and heard I'd been invited to spend a week in Louisiana where I'd work in schools in two communities and perform one evening show, the total fee the equivalent of the minimum I tried to earn each month. If I needed a sign, I'd received one, so stopped worrying. Now, house-sitting at Patrice's, I was again feeling poor and again in doubt. No one in Wisconsin was hiring me, but the cold query had at least warranted a few responses. I read the e-mail letter again, the one I was sending out. Hell, it sounded pretty good, I thought. I decided I'd try another state. Illinois was just too big. I started going down the list of colleges in Iowa.

Quickly, but maybe not quickly enough, I realized what I'd committed myself to. I thought of my friends Mike and Tania, musicians who split time between Puget Sound and Ireland, who'd been performing far longer than I had. They'd managed to cobble together a life out of this. They weren't famous; they were just excellent, fun, professional. The trouble, Tania once told me, was once you started on this path, you found you got good leads everyday everywhere, and while all the leads looked equal, at least at first, only two out of ten would even come close to panning out. And you never knew which two they were, so you were bound to follow all ten to conclusion.

Sure, the process was interesting for Wisconsin, then Iowa, I thought, as I sat in front of Patrice's computer. But did I really want to look up every college in California, in New York, in Massachusetts? Already I was finding every college website was different. Some schools I already knew the faculty I'd want to contact. Some, once I saw the department list, I'd say to myself, Oh, so that's where they teach. Some, the department website described what each faculty member taught, which made it easy. And some, some were designed as if to thwart me at this stage, so I thought more deeply, and learned to go into the registrar's site to see who

108

taught Creative Writing or Poetry the preceding semester, or would be teaching the upcoming semester. And for some schools, to get the name I was looking for, I had to maneuver even more deftly.

Did I want to do this?

I thought of my latest credit card bills, and the few events I'd lined up for 2003-2004. Small shows in North Carolina and Virginia for the fall. A concert series in Florida in January. Despite the new CD that had come out the past year, it looked grim. Patrice's computer was in front of me, and I had all May, June, and early July to use it all day and night if I wanted. The novel hadn't sold. Why did I think a memoir would? It was one thing if it was well underway, but here I was, still waiting on a printer in the mail. At least if I queried every college in the United States, I'd get a few jobs. I'd have to. How could I not? I had two books, three CDs. The past year I'd played at the Dodge Poetry Festival in New Jersey and the Kennedy Center in Washington D.C. The past year I'd been a visiting writer at University of Tennessee in Knoxville, at the College of Charleston, at SUNY Plattsburgh, and at more than a half dozen other colleges and community colleges. Since 1989, I'd had close to 400 poems published in excellent journals all over the country.

Ohio. Lots of schools in Ohio, I thought. I'll start looking up Ohio.

5

Two Gigs and a Tour

April 11, 2002
Minneapolis

Last night I drove from Milwaukee,
napping once in a church parking lot
past Baraboo, again in a travel stop
near Menomonie. The past two weeks:
Galesburg, Chicago, Ann Arbor, Detroit,
Cleveland, Buffalo. Palestinian suicide
bombers terrorize that region. Afghanistan
remains incomprehensible, as does our
national government. This morning I'll appear
on Minneapolis community radio, the weekly
literary show where I'll fiddle and talk, read
a few poems. This afternoon, rehearsal. Evening,
the performance. Don't quit your day job,
I say to everybody who claims
my life romantic. And point to erratic
schedule and pay, occasional audience,
the lack of a love live. It's the latter
that's the killer, I think, as I walk
a half-dozen blocks in the rain, grateful
today I have the freedom and resources
to complain only of this.

The first week of December 2002, I flew a Tuesday night red-eye from Anchorage to Indianapolis. Arriving, I was met by a former Indiana State University English professor, a man who had run at least three miles every day for years. He'd run on streets, trails, beaches, indoor and outdoor tracks. He'd run in the woods. For two weeks on a cruise, he'd run the hallways and decks. His goal was to run in all 50 states, and he'd bagged 49. Only Alaska remained. Driving to Terre Haute, he grilled me about my home.

Two Gigs and A Tour

After stopping at the English Department office, I was taken to a bed and breakfast several blocks from campus. I had two responsibilities before being returned to Indianapolis for my Saturday flight north. Thursday evening, I was to give a forty-five minute talk as part of the Joseph S. Schick Lectures in Language, Literature, and Lexicography. I could say anything I wanted as long as at least some of the material was based in the nineteenth century, or earlier, and pertained to the title I'd submitted, "The Frontier Writer's Mind: Journeys On and Beyond Land." Friday afternoon, I was to perform for a half-hour as part of the Hoosier Folklore Conference that ran concurrently with the lecture series. My title for that set was "Fiddling Poet Music: Where Alaska and Appalachia meet." My remuneration was food, lodging, airfare, and $2000.

Friday would be easy, and I looked forward to performing for a roomful of folklorists. My concern was the Thursday evening talk. Though I'd worked at numerous universities, this particular event was more academic than my usual jobs. Even the title of the event made me uneasy. I knew what language and literature were. But lexicography? I had to look that word up. The writing or compiling of dictionaries, I learned, which wasn't going to help me. Plus, I had visions of stumbling over the nineteenth century provision and having my paycheck withheld. Many of the fiddle tunes I played had been popular in the 1800's, and earlier, but I hadn't studied the folklore and wasn't prepared to talk about them other than to say, Here's an old favorite from near Civil War time.

Several months earlier, I'd been smart to have chosen a title that mentioned frontier, land, and writers, and worded it in a way that allowed me to be literal or metaphoric, which gave me wiggle room. I also remembered that in graduate school, I'd written two papers on Walt Whitman, both of which I'd stuck in a bottom of a box that had been lugged on my various moves for fifteen years now and was most recently buried in a friend's Anchorage closet. Before leaving for Terre Haute, I rooted the papers out—a B+ and an A, I saw, scanning—and packed them with me. Worst case scenario, I could read about Whitman for a few minutes, play a few 19th century fiddle tunes, and proclaim there had been a migration west through North America. Once I had my Americans crossing the Rockies, I could play the K.C. Kartchner Arizona fiddle tune I knew, then talk about the settling of Alaska. Then I was really home free. I could mention how some people still lived up north without running water, still played music without amplification. I'd always thought Fairbanks was one-part 1950, one-part 2020. Now I'd just restate the idea, exaggerating 1950, extending it back to 1895. And then I'd read the poem about washing dishes without running water, then the one about my old Fairbanks cabin, then a few about playing music. These were poems I read everywhere. Here, for this lecture series, they just needed a new context.

I mentioned my concerns to my host, who assured me I'd do fine, but not before mentioning a prior year when a folksinger had not sufficiently woven the 1800's into her presentation, and later been rebuked by one of the members of the Schick committee.

She still got her check though, I asked.

My host nodded, smiling.

I smiled back. Still, I'd be taking no chances here. $2000 was a fair bit of money. I didn't want to risk reprimand. I only wanted everybody to know how much I appreciated the invitation.

Spending three days meeting wonderful people, enjoying exquisite hospitality, performing briefly—despite the trepidation, my visit to the nineteenth century came off without issue—was easy. Flying from Anchorage to Indianapolis was almost as easy. The challenge for this job, as usual, was in landing it. No one on the Schick Committee thought to call the Alaskan Fiddling Poet. Only one person there had barely heard of me when I first made contact with the committee. And when I made that contact, it was not because of an English Department Lecture Series. I had no idea. I'd only been given a name.

I was invited to Terre Haute, first because I made that first CD, *A Week in Eek*, which I mailed to disc jockeys I thought might be interested. From the beginning, Mike Kelsey at WFHB in Bloomington was one of the most enthusiastic, playing several cuts through the summer. When I sent him *Burnt Down House* the following spring, he was just as enthusiastic, which gave me an idea. Since I'd be driving to Clifftop, and Bloomington was almost exactly en route, I called to inquire whether he'd be interested in hosting a concert for me. No concert, he said. But he could invite me to his radio show, and if I ever came through the last Saturday of the month, the whole two-hour program was a live studio jam. In any case, he said, whenever I did come through, he and his wife could put me up for a night or two. Their son was in college and they had a spare room.

This wasn't what I had in mind, but at least it was a solid invitation. I left Portland, then drove across to Idaho, then Colorado. I left Denver Thursday morning, and after two long days of driving pulled into Bloomington Friday evening. It was easy to accompany Mike to the studio Saturday morning. His show was fine, the music rough and fun. In the band was a terrific young fiddler, Deb, who I shared lunch with before heading out in the afternoon. We exchanged addresses, and a month later I received a letter from her. She was finishing up an education degree at Indiana State University in Terre Haute, where she was also interning for a folklorist in the English Department, an Irish pennywhistle player named Nan. In fact, she'd traveled with Nan to the British Isles to help with her research. Deb wrote that I should contact Nan, because Deb had mentioned my name to her and Nan had a lot of money to bring people to campus.

When I called Nan, she couldn't place me at first, and laughed when I mentioned Deb had told me she had money to bring people in. No, she said, she was only on a committee, and while it was a good gig, it was fairly competitive. She did say that what I did sounded like a fit, and that if I was interested, I should send one of my CDs, my book, and a vita.

That was how it started, a phone call after I'd been given a name. Over the next nine months, I'd occasionally call or write Nan, sometimes by regular mail and sometimes by e-mail once I started an account. When my second book was published in early 2002, I let Nan know and sent her a copy on request. Late spring I learned I was to be invited, and another of the committee members asked me for the title of the lecture and a current publicity packet, which I was happy to supply.

A fairly substantial job, the process was straightforward. Once I was invited, all I had to do was show up, and remember to keep the Thursday evening lecture somewhat inside the nineteenth century. The highlight, I think, was the Friday night dinner party at a good local restaurant. Everybody involved in the series was invited, including most of the English Department faculty. There was an open bar, plenty of appetizers, a choice of entrées, choice of dessert, unlimited wine with the meal—all compliments of the late Dr. Schick.

Are you happy? one of the faculty members, a folklorist, seated to my right, asked me every so often. Dr. Schick wants you to be very, very happy, and he'd like it very much if you had some of the wine. Then he raised the bottle, and topped off my glass with a little more of the cabernet.

A year and a half later, I appeared at the 11th annual Border Voices Poetry festival, a day-long program of poetry readings and workshops on the campus of San Diego State University. The celebration was sponsored in part by The *San Diego Union-Tribune*, where the festival director, Jack Webb, worked as an editor. Amidst numerous award ceremonies for teachers and students, there were four featured poets for the 2004 event: Robert Creeley, Adrienne Rich, Sandra Cisneros, and me, Ken Waldman. If you don't read contemporary American literature and have no interest in the culture surrounding it, all four names will likely mean nothing. But if you've ever studied modern poetry, you'd be quick to spot the one that didn't belong.

Robert Creeley was in his mid 70's, had written more than 60 books, many published by New Directions. Celebrated for a distinctive minimalist style, he'd lived all over the country, had been not only a prolific writer but a prolific correspondent, and had been a central figure in various poetry subcultures: from Black Mountain to Bolinas, from LANGUAGE to the Beats. He'd won an NEA fellowship, a Guggenheim Foundation fellowship, a Lannan Lifetime Achievement Award, the Bollinger Prize, and numerous others.

Adrienne Rich, a contemporary of Creeley, had published nearly 20 volumes of poems and several non-fiction books, most recently with W.W. Norton. She'd won many of the same prizes and fellowships as Creeley, and in addition had won a National Book Award as well as a MacArthur Foundation "genius" grant. Like Creeley, her poetry had been selected for inclusion in virtually every comprehensive anthology of contemporary American poetry.

Sandra Cisneros was my age. Of her four poetry collections, the most recent had been published by Alfred Knopf. In addition, she'd published two novels, a story collection, a children's book, and had won an NEA fellowship, a MacArthur Foundation "genius" grant, as well as an American Book Award. She also happened to be the most widely read Latina writer in the world.

And Ken Waldman. He'd written two books that hardly anyone knew. He'd released three obscure CDs. Ken Waldman. How'd he get invited? you ask.

That story began six years earlier, outside Portland, the annual AWP conference. There I met Mike, the literary programs director for the Wyoming Arts Council. Intrigued by my mix of literature and music, he promised that if I was coming through the region, he'd forward contacts for me to use as I could. Planning to come through Denver in the fall, I took him at his word and called, which led directly to school visits in Cheyenne and a show in Casper. Those first successful dates led to another round of school jobs in Cheyenne the following fall and a date at the community college.

The contact Mike had given me at the community college, Leaf, was a poet, one of the English department professors there. After my evening performance, Leaf jotted the names of three friends from his graduate program, who all currently taught in two-year schools: one in Michigan, one in Minnesota, one in California. Leaf suggested I contact them, mentioning that he'd given me their name. Scott was the professor in California, and after I told him what I did, he said that while he was interested in having me, it wasn't his decision to make: I'd need to contact the dean, a woman named Pat.

I contacted Pat, sent her my first book when it came out, then my CD. She said she was interested, but her budget was limited—I should let her know if I'd be nearby. Fall 2000, I contacted her again to let her know that February 2001 I had a job in Los Angeles, another in Yuma, and could swing through San Diego. I received an invitation, and one evening gave two presentations in a large classroom, mostly in front of writing students, Scott's as well as others. But Pat had also shown up and had enjoyed the program. If I was back in the area in two or three years, she said, I should contact her about returning.

October 2003, I'd set up jobs in Las Vegas and Los Angeles, and tried reaching Pat, leaving her messages by phone and e-mail. I had two days between jobs, and could easily swing through San Diego if she was still interested in having me. The past two and a half years I'd had a new book out, and two new CDs, so certainly there was justification in having me back if that was a question.

Trying once more, I talked to Pat's secretary. I learned Pat still had her office for now and still came in once a week, but she was retiring, was officially retired in fact, and was staying on only to facilitate the change in administration. This fall David would be the one making the decisions for events like mine—and Pat had let David know of my availability.

I waited a week, then called and e-mailed David, then Scott, then Pat. I talked to Pat's secretary one more time. August, I heard there was a good chance an event would take place. The beginning of October, four weeks before the probable date, I checked phone messages in Emporia, Kansas, the midst of a long day driving between Peru, Nebraska and Oklahoma City. David had called and wanted me to call back. I did and managed to find him in. We confirmed the date.

For this, I sent out my usual publicity, a press packet to arts and entertainment editors as well as the calendar editors at daily and weekly newspapers. I handwrote the name and address on the envelope, used distinctive stationery, and, if I felt the justification, would include one of my CDs, or even a book, in the packet. It was a crap shoot. Just like you never know which of the hundreds of job queries would succeed, you never knew which packet to which editor would translate into a photo in the weekend calendar section or a half-page or longer feature story. In Winston-Salem, I landed an extended feature story in the daily paper because I'd sent a packet three months in advance and called to follow-up. In Columbia, South Carolina, I landed one for a packet I feared was past deadline. You just never knew.

Less than four weeks to the date of the show, I mailed out the packets. I also sent a note to a woman, Celia, inviting her to the show. All I knew about Celia was what I learned in those long hours of research months earlier while house-sitting in New Orleans. She taught at San Diego State University and was involved with a poetry event there. Then I forgot about the date, except for an e-mail note a week before the event from an editor at the *San Diego Union-Tribune*, asking why my name was familiar—had we met in Alaska? he wondered. I e-mailed back to say no, we hadn't met there, but I recognized his name because I'd probably queried about doing something for the poetry event he put on. There was so much going on that month, dates in Durango, Telluride, back to Colorado Springs then Greeley, Rock Springs, Pocatello, a job in Utah, then onto Las Vegas and Los Angeles.

A ridiculous amount of driving that month, I reflected as I drove from San Fernando to San Diego on the day of the evening performance, aware that the important work for that particular day was to arrive in San Diego on time. I always tried to avoid city traffic from 7 a.m. to 9 a.m. and 2 p.m. to 6 p.m., and Southern California always seemed especially daunting. I stopped for lunch in Carlsbad, feeling fortunate my first time through since I not only happily found the public library a few blocks off I-5 but also a reasonable Thai restaurant nearby. I arrived just north of San Diego well before rush hour, found a Motel 6, and was mindful not to get too comfortable. I wasn't there yet. I remembered my previous visit to the community college. A dark February night, I'd gotten lost, and the parking had been horrific.

After checking for messages from my motel room with my phone card, I stayed on the phone and returned a half-dozen calls. Then I got back in the car. The college was approximately ten miles south. According to the map, if I could find my way to a main arterial, Genessee, which appeared close, I could reach campus without using a freeway. It would take longer, but at least if I left now I'd be assured of arriving early. Entering the freeway, I'd be risking a rush-hour jam.

As happens, after all that, the event itself felt anti-climactic. I made it to the campus without incident, with plenty of time to get settled. For the presentation, I did what I invariably did: I read poems, I played fiddle, I talked. It wasn't my finest hour; it was far from my worst. People laughed when they were supposed to, applauded all the fiddle tunes and even a good number of the poems. Perhaps a hundred and ten people were in the classroom. Pat was there, as was David. Scott had a conflict, so I only saw him briefly after the show. Afterwards, in addition to talking with several students, I also met a woman who had been sitting attentively in the front row. She introduced herself as Celia and thanked me for the invitation. Though she'd lived in San Diego for years, it was the first time she'd been on this community college campus.

Of course, I knew who she was then. She waited until the students had departed and then we chatted amiably awhile. If she'd like, I said, she could take the book and CD of her choice. When she asked if I thought I could do what I'd just done on a bigger stage, I said, Of course, this is what I do.

The Border Voices committee was meeting again next week, she continued. No promises just yet, but Jack Webb would probably be in touch afterwards. You can be reached through your website?

I nodded, assuring her my e-mail address and message phone number were both on the contact page.

Six months later, I was back in San Diego, courtesy of Border Voices. It was an enthusiastic gathering. The pay and hospitality were both first-rate, and everybody seemed to enjoy my main stage performance with Jordan Ruyle, a friend from Long Beach who drove down to play banjo and clog. Two memories stand out: spending one fretful half-hour on a panel with Robert Creeley and Adrienne Rich (Sandra Cisneros had already been whisked away since she was to appear later that same day at the *Los Angeles Times* Festival of Books), taking notes like a madman graduate student so as to be careful not to say something eminently stupid each time it was my turn to speak; and arriving at the hotel, spotting the big color festival poster for the first time, the photos of three famous writers and me.

I took several of the posters home with me, asked Jack Webb for a reference letter, which he was kind enough to write. I made color copies of that poster and quoted Jack Webb. And like that I carried my Border Voices experience with me, transforming it into a sheet I could mail out to help land the next job. For a music event, that sheet was virtually meaningless. But for a writers' conference, or a literary festival, or for a performing arts center considering a multidisciplinary program, it had real worth. My thinking was it might make people curious enough to want to know more about my books and CDs.

I learned to tailor each packet to the needs of a particular presenter. For people who knew contemporary poetry, I'd send that Border Voices sheet, add a book review or two, and probably the feature in the *2004 Poet's Market* (a long-established—and hefty—resource guide for poets, each year's edition includes several interviews, and being included offered certain validation of my work); for music festivals or club owners, I'd most likely send the 2002 feature story about me in *Dirty Linen*. To that, I'd add clips about other festivals and club dates and probably stick in a CD. For public libraries, who sometimes were also active presenters, I had another packet, which included details from previous library shows. For college English Department reading series, I'd focus on the writing and my experience as a visiting workshop leader; for college student activity offices, I'd emphasize the music and include articles from college newspapers and a few alternative weeklies. For younger students, in addition to a general sheet that outlined what I could offer in particular settings, I especially liked using reference letters from teachers. Depending on the specific job possibility, I could quote elementary-school teachers, middle-school teachers, high-school teachers.

I began lining up my spring 2005 dates a year ahead of time. The tour lasted fourteen weeks, beginning with a reading at the University of Alabama Birmingham's Creative Writing program and ending in northern Montana, where I was in residence for four days as part of a storytelling festival set each year in Cut Bank. In between I worked in thirteen states, driving as far east as Boston, north to Montreal, west to Seattle, and flying up to Alaska for two weeks of jobs. From Thursday, March 3 to Monday, March 14, I was in South Dakota. One South Dakota presenter I worked with, Doug, was astounded that I'd not only booked so many dates in the state, but that I'd be grossing close to $5,000, just me, a solo artist.

How'd you do it? he wanted to know.

I'd had no intention of playing anywhere in South Dakota, but I'd had no intention of not playing there either. Here's what I knew. For years, I'd committed to attending the AWP conference, and in 2005 it was to be held in Vancouver the end of March. So there was that, and a large arts council job conveniently fell my way in Alaska for the week after Vancouver. So far so good.

Folk Alliance was going to be in Montreal in late February. That was the other side of the continent, I knew, but enough time to drive across if I wanted to attend. And I was planning to attend. By April 2004, I had solid commitments for attractive late January jobs in Birmingham and a few hours away in Carrollton, Georgia. The next weeks, I received an invitation for a job in Boston for mid February, a week before the Montreal conference, and then an invitation for

119

a college reading series in Ohio, between Cleveland and Columbus, the Monday following Montreal. I'd also been in touch with a library in Jackson, Wyoming, and by late May, knowing I'd be driving west the following March, had received an invitation to perform on St. Patrick's Day.

The longer I've been involved in the process, the better I've come to understand the rhythms in coordinating these sweeping cross-country arcs to make for an efficient tour. It was the same work confirming a $3,000 job as a $300 job or even a $50 job. The larger budget jobs usually required far greater lead time, but the actual work of contacting the presenter, traveling to the job, and performing was the same. In fact, the better-paying jobs were often easier. There was more pressure perhaps to make sure everything was perfect but the facilities were invariably first-class, the personal treatment respectful.

So the task became finding higher-paying jobs—or adequately-paying jobs that offered prestige—to commit to. Once committed, there was a psychology to the business, I discovered. A presenter might not be interested, not at first, but when you mentioned you were performing within two- or three-hundred miles— here, it would help to name a venue or an organization that was known—and would be, or could be, driving right by, then there might be interest. And once I was already in an area, I could afford to commit to smaller, interesting jobs that only made sense when I was near. The few times I've prematurely committed to a smaller job, I've regretted it.

Late April 2003, I'd been invited to play in North Georgia at a small monthly concert series that I understood usually drew 50-70 people, no matter the artist, with a $10 cover. With eight months lead time, I thought, Sure, no problem, I'll find a few other jobs in the region. But I'd gotten busy, and what phone calls and e-mails I'd made had yielded nothing. Weeks before the show, I was especially sorry I'd originally taken it. My New Orleans house-sitting time was just begin-ning. To play the date—and of course I needed to honor the commitment—I'd have to drive ten hours up and ten hours back. I liked performing. And usually I liked driving. But only when there was a real sense of purpose to the activity. Worse, for this one, there was no guarantee, just a percentage of the door, which for my show came to virtually nothing. It seemed attendance had been dwindling the past three months and the trend had continued. We drew ten people. What kept the date from being a complete waste was the opening act, an Athens singer-songwriter who brought an accompanist, a fiddler and guitar player named Amanda. With the slim turnout, I thought I might as well ask Amanda to join me too. We had fun playing, and our partnership worked so well that Amanda has accompanied me my past two trips in the state, all manner of shows. Still, if I booked too many shows like that North Georgia one, I wouldn't be long for the business.

I recalled all this as I planned my 2005 tour.

By May of 2004, I knew I'd be waking up in north central Ohio on Tuesday morning March 1 and would be needing to arrive in Jackson, Wyoming by Wednesday evening March 16. Two free weeks and, for the right job, I was willing to work anywhere in Ohio, southern Michigan, northern Kentucky, Indiana, Illinois, Missouri, Iowa, Kansas, Nebraska, South Dakota, Colorado, Montana, Wyoming. There was even the possibility of a reasonably well-paying job in North Dakota I'd been pursuing. I made a few calls, sent out e-mails. What seems easy isn't. People don't necessarily return those calls or e-mails. And I just didn't have time or resources to follow up further.

Late May, I drove to Alaska and worked a few jobs. June, I recorded a CD in Fairbanks and took care of Alaska business. July, I drove back south and east, a dozen jobs en route, traveling with a music pal from Chicago, Jordan. After another visit to Clifftop, I had free time from mid August to mid September, and spent it in Lafayette, Louisiana, subletting a little apartment near downtown. There, because there was no phone, I signed up for my first cell phone plan. And because I had the time those weeks, I hand-addressed several hundred envelopes, stuffed packets, sent them off, one with a CD to Canton, South Dakota. I'd been looking up festivals in the back of a pair of magazines—*Dirty Linen* and *Sing Out!*—and both listed one in early August in Sioux Falls, organized by the Friends of Traditional Music, the Canton address. Old-time bands I knew from Seattle and Portland had been invited this past year, which was good enough for me. If someone in South Dakota liked my friends, they might like me. In the midst of a mailing, thinking of South Dakota anyway, I sent it out.

A month later, back on tour, a free Sunday evening in a motel in Nashville,

I'd been thinking of making a few phone calls. The first two weeks in March hadn't yet been booked, and I thought to follow up with the South Dakota folks, whoever they were. There was no name on the Friends of Traditional Music website, just a phone number. It was a feeling, an intuition I should make this call, and not one of a hundred others. First try, I reached Gaynor, who was happy to hear from me, and we talked awhile. He'd first read about me in the feature story in *Dirty Linen* two years earlier. So when the packet came, he was disposed to listen. He liked it a lot, he said, and in fact had been playing it on his radio show the past couple of weeks.

When I mentioned I'd be driving through South Dakota in five months, he asked when exactly, because the organization occasionally presented smaller shows throughout the year and even sponsored two school residencies. He'd have to have my visit approved by the board, but that was a formality in this case. It was his decision to make. If I could make it to Sioux Falls the first Friday of March, he said, I could visit a school for the day and do a show sometime that weekend. He also knew another venue 60 miles away that might also be interested. If I sent him another packet with a CD, he'd see what he could do.

The next day I mailed him my other two CDs for his radio show, and an extra to pass along to the other presenter. Then I waited. Meanwhile, sure I'd be in Sioux Falls on Friday, March 4, I contacted Brian, a writer I knew in Vermillion, just sixty miles away, who taught at the University of South Dakota and edited the literary journal there, the *South Dakota Review*. We'd met several years before at an AWP conference. His publication, which often featured writing set in the West, had been among the first to accept my poems. I'd asked him once about visiting campus sometime but we'd never gotten specific. It was understood there was not much of a budget—$500 or less—so it only made sense for me to pursue that opportunity if I was already close, which had never before happened.

I called, found him in, let him know my situation, and learned the week following my tentative date in Sioux Falls was the university's spring break week. But if I could arrive on Thursday, March 3, he'd likely be able to make something work.

I also contacted a writer, Kent, who taught across the state at the university in Spearfish. We'd first been in touch a year earlier, when I'd written to creative writers at universities across the country. He was interested then, and was interested now, but warned he had no budget, so suggested I contact the faculty advisor for student activities, where there was still money available. I wrote the advisor, as well as other student activity advisors. In addition, I found a site that listed local arts councils, with contact names, for the whole state. Once my dates in Sioux Falls and Vermillion were confirmed, I e-mailed each arts council on the list to let them know I could be available from Saturday March 5 through Monday March 14.

Early December, I received a phone message from a student in Spearfish who was a member of the student activity team that presented concerts. She'd viewed my website and wanted to know if I still had a free weekday night to perform. We played phone tag for several days, eventually agreeing on Monday, March 14. Once that date was confirmed, I called an arts center in Sturgis, twenty-five miles from Spearfish, that had no budget but had e-mailed me that they were interested in having me lead both a fiddle workshop and a writing workshop and do a solo show as long as I understood I'd only be paid a percentage of the proceeds from the events. Now that I was in the area, and had been given permission by the college to do other work nearby, I arranged to be in Sturgis on Saturday and Sunday, March 12 and 13. Meanwhile, Gaynor, my contact from the Friends of Traditional Music, called to let me know Doug and Judi, filmmakers who ran a monthly series in an old general store they'd converted to a music hall in a small town near Yankton, were happy to have me play there on Saturday night, March 5. If I needed to, Gaynor said, I was also invited to stay a few extra days at their place in Wakonda.

Mid January, now beginning my long tour, due to arrive in South Dakota in six weeks, I'd landed those jobs, plus a show at a college in Mt. Vernon, Iowa on Wednesday March 2, and another in Sheridan, Wyoming on Tuesday, March 15. I still had a full week free, Monday through Friday, March 7-11, when I'd be in South Dakota. For months, I'd been hoping to hear from a presenter in southwestern Minnesota, an hour east of Sioux Falls, someone I'd actually met at a conference, and who wanted to see me in the community's schools. But so far I'd had no luck there. I'd also corresponded the previous month with a staffer from the South Dakota state arts council, mentioning my confirmed jobs in-state, and querying whether he could recommend arts councils worth making an additional effort to contact because they were especially active or still had unused money.

I never did hear from the Minnesota contact. The arts council staffer apologized for being slow to respond, sent the same list I'd seen on the website—organizations I'd already e-mailed—but had checked several he thought might be the best prospects.

Late January, stopped for gas a half hour outside Chapel Hill, North Carolina, I took out my new cell phone, called one of those names the staffer had checked, the director of the arts council in Pierre, the state capital. When she answered the phone, I introduced myself, and explained that I was going to be in the state, had days free, and would be happy to share my talents in her community. She sounded interested, and, yes, they had money. She envisioned a two-day residency, shows in senior centers, a library, one of the Native learning centers. If I could send her a packet, she'd be in better position to tell me.

Twenty-five minutes later, I had that packet in the mail.

A few days later, I called another name on the list, who was also in, and I introduced myself again. The head of a small town arts council a hundred miles northeast of Pierre, she said, yes, she thought there likely might be interest in having me to the school there, and they did have a budget, but first could I send a packet.

Happy to, I said.

The first week of February, I'd confirmed both jobs: a two-day residency in Pierre on Wednesday and Thursday, the school visit in Faulkton on Friday. A week later, when Doug, the filmmaker (his Kerouac documentary, *Go Moan for Man*, was twenty years in the making) who ran a music hall, contacted me about sending him promotional materials, I told him I'd already mailed materials to newspapers in Yankton, Vermillion, and the bigger regional paper in Sioux Falls.

What? he said and I could hear the wonderment in his voice. No one's ever done that for one of my shows. You're good, he said. Really good.

If he could have seen me on the phone, I was shaking my head. I wasn't that good, I told him. I'd performed at venues where presenters hadn't thought to promote the shows, and people hadn't come. I was only trying to help bring a few more folks to the event, help us all survive.

I was reminded of an episode two years earlier, a prestigious venue that wanted to change the date of my show six weeks prior to the performance. The presenter had looked at my website, and thought it would be easy to move the date up two nights, when nothing was on my schedule. I explained the dilemma. While I would have honored his request if I could, his show was one of many on that particular tour. Though he'd seen my website, and assumed I was free two nights prior, I wasn't, having just received confirmation for an event that I'd set in motion six months before and, besides, was attending a conference—also not listed on the website—so had a commitment earlier the same day. I also reminded him I was bringing an accompanist, who, in this case, had already arranged to drive several hours each way and take two days off of work. While I could talk to the accompanist about the possible change, I wondered if it was really necessary. After all, I reminded the presenter, we'd been talking about the date for nine months now, and thought it was firm. No contract, I know, I said, because he hadn't sent one despite repeated requests. If he felt he had to change the date, legally he could do it, I supposed, but I just wanted to let him know my position.

I didn't know you had it so tightly wound, the presenter said, sounding surprised. How about we just keep the original date for now?

Tightly wound? I wondered what he meant. Didn't everybody strive to arrange tours efficiently? How else to survive in this business? Was I being viewed as stubborn and inflexible for doing my job as best I could?

6
The Dark Side: Show-Biz

Adrift

Now I understand. Having lost child
and wife, hometown and house,
I love my life like I love the gray
northern sea I know nothing of.

An eider speaks to me in my dreams.
So does a spruce. Last night the ghost
bird honked: Swim. The ghost tree
groaned: Buy a sailboat and learn.

I woke knowing I must trust wind
and water. I'm selling everything.
A friend has a craft I can live on.
The icy depths will teach.

The anecdotes are endless. Every job, every tour is a story, though not all are
created equal. Take the prestigious venue, where six weeks prior to the gig, the
presenter called to ask to change the date.

Not much of a story there and nothing dark—yet. Telling this story, it helps to
know the venue was the Kennedy Center in Washington D.C. Like many gigs, the
invitation was part luck, part circumstance, part hard work. In 2002, I'd been to the
national Folk Alliance conference in Jacksonville. Musicians who attend will play
sets virtually anywhere in order to be seen and heard. You never know who might be
listening. Midnight, then, I read a few poems, played a few fiddle tunes, and talked
a little about the poetry and the music as I sat in a chair in my hotel room. It wasn't
so much a showcase as a kind of surreal conversation since only one person was
there to watch, and when I asked him who he was, he gestured for me to continue.
I did and he sat politely for several more minutes, then rose as I finished playing a
tune. When I thanked him for coming, he reached over to hand me a card, and we

talked briefly. He worked at the Kennedy Center, he told me, and booked events for the Millennium Stage, a free show 6 p.m. every night of the year in the foyer of the building. As he left, I thanked him once more for coming.

I waited two months and called his office, found him in. I'll be in Baltimore, I said, late February 2003, so I'll be nearby. He mentioned Monday nights he often brought in songwriters. A fiddling poet would be different, yet would fit, he thought. We penciled in a date, meaning it looked good for both of us, but were not bound by contract. Over the next six months, we talked twice more. He said it was too early for a contract, but I should assume the date would hold. He liked the idea of an accompanist. October, I sent him a note, letting him know who'd be coming to play with me. I assumed that this being the Kennedy Center, they had their own timeline of contracts; these people were professionals.

When the presenter called in January to ask to switch the date, what had taken me aback wasn't so much that he'd been truly surprised I'd scheduled my tour so tightly—again, I wondered, wasn't it standard to at least try to arrange things that efficiently?—but he'd reached me by calling me directly in Austin, Texas. Only a few dozen people knew or cared I was in Austin, and no one knew where I was staying. He could have left a phone message at my Anchorage number. How'd you reach me at my friend Jerry's house? I asked before getting off the phone. Later, I imagined he must have been smiling across the wires at the question. He *had* left a phone message, he said. But he needed to try to switch dates quickly here; something had come up. So, he said, he'd looked at my website. It mentioned a show in Texas and that I was playing with Jerry Hagins, whose telephone number was listed in information. He said he didn't know I was there, but guessed I might be, and he'd guessed right.

Listening, I understood this was what it was like working with professionals.

And that's what set me off a month later in Chapel Hill, North Carolina, at my friend Isabel's. Friday, I received both a phone message and an e-mail from one of the Millennium Stage staffers, asking me to confirm I'd still be appearing in Washington, a week from Monday. I answered both immediately. The next day, a packet of mail arrived for me, the past two week's, from Anchorage. Included, at last, was the Kennedy Center contract.

As I started reading, I got angry, and the more I read, the angrier I became. Four weeks prior to the date—six weeks was preferred—I was to send a comprehensive press packet with photos to the publicity department for them to promote the show locally. Ten days prior to the date was the deadline to let staff know what products I'd be selling. There was more, but I couldn't concentrate. My first ever appearance in D.C, I'd already sent materials to newspapers and radio, including several NPR editors, and had been happy to do so; I'd have been happier if I'd have had the opportunity to have my efforts supplemented by the Kennedy Center staff, who it seemed would have, if they'd received such materials, if only I'd known the right name of the staffer to direct the materials to, as listed on the contract. And I'd have been happy to let staff know that I did expect to sell books and CDs.

I understood these were minor points. After all, I was still performing there.

But then I got even angrier. It was no wonder that they'd had to call and e-mail just to be sure I'd be coming. Maybe I was being labeled one more lazy and disorganized artist, someone who couldn't be bothered signing a contract and sticking it in the mail. And then I started wondering how it was I could be found by the presenter while I was in Austin, where no one knew where I was, though the same presenter didn't have the courtesy to send a contract on time so I could make best use of the organization's in-place infrastructure, not to mention fulfill the legalities of the document. Not only that, but running late, he allowed it to be sent to Anchorage where I couldn't possibly have been—as a glance at the schedule on my website would have verified—and which meant I'd been fortunate to even have received it when I did, just nine days prior to the show. The contract had been meaningless. Why even bother?

I stewed for a day, then spent several hours Sunday writing as diplomatic a letter as I could to the presenter, wondering why he'd treated me so—and the word that came was—disrespectfully. Did he treat other artists similarly? I didn't know, but doubted it, and patiently explained who I was, why I persisted, and what made the work worthwhile. I told him I'd have thought the Kennedy Center, at least, would have been more professional here. He was, after all, a representative of the Kennedy Center, and by treating me rudely, he'd forced me to question once more why I bothered doing this work. I bothered, I told him, because ultimately I believed in what I was doing: making poetry accessible to people who otherwise had no idea, doing the same with traditional fiddle music, and with Alaska. I enjoyed teaching, I said, and when I performed I was teaching poetry, teaching about fiddling, teaching about Alaska. I looked forward to coming to Washington D.C., where I expected to have a fine show. I ended by apologizing for having to write such a letter.

The show? That's the easiest part, though like the one at the community college in San Diego, and like so many others, it sometimes felt anti-climactic. After my accompanist, Doug, rolled in from West Virginia, we played a few tunes in the afternoon to warm up. At 6 p.m. we were introduced onstage, and a tune led to a poem which led to another poem, a story, a tune, and the hour sped past. The show was similar to many others I'd done, but different, because no two were ever alike. I was grateful for the opportunity, which to this day allows me to casually say, sure, I played at the Kennedy Center. For some people, it's impressive to hear, and I let them believe it—it's part of my work, marketing the illusion that by playing the Kennedy Center's Millennium Stage, I'm somehow more fit to come to their own community. For them, stuffing packets, I include a copy of that evening's program, which I've combined with a classy review of one of my books.

Regardless, I don't expect to be returning to the Kennedy Center Millennium Stage any time soon. I don't need to.

The Kennedy Center show was unusual in that I was treated disrespectfully *after* I'd been invited. Normally, once you're invited to a venue of that caliber, that's when the fun begins. I've been fortunate to have met so many great people, from office to technical staff, who enjoy their jobs, which in part is to make every part of every show go as smoothly as possible. The challenge, at least for someone in my category, is to nudge that invitation.

September 2001, the month I was in Texas, I heard from someone reliable that the director of a prestigious music club in the upper Midwest was interested in what I did. The timing couldn't have been better since I'd already committed to be in the region the following April, and had plenty of flexibility for dates. I called several times, left messages, and found him in briefly before the end of the month. We spoke for thirty seconds before he had to take a more pressing call. I'm interested, he confirmed. You're around early April? Call me early November.

Early November, I left a message, then called almost daily, running down pay phones from California to Washington, trying to catch him in. Thanksgiving Eve, he answered his phone, we talked a few minutes, and I was told to try again in two weeks, when he'd know more how the days I still had free were shaping up. Mid December to mid January, I once more called virtually every day, leaving messages, letting him know how one day, then another, were no longer available because I'd be working elsewhere. Finally, miraculously, I caught him in, and the only possible day he could book me I still had available. We quickly confirmed. He thanked me for being so persistent, which he said had been necessary in this case.

The event? I had a three-piece band, with a guest fiddler joining me for a few tunes. Good show, slim turnout, little money, but the experience was enjoyable. I loved playing the hall. Though the director had hoped for at least double the audience, he'd stayed for the whole show, and told me afterwards he'd like to try it again. But will he? At least he's still in the same job, and I've been mailing him updates once or twice a year. I'm not Bob Dylan, I tell presenters, my shorthand for letting them know I can't promise an audience, can only do what I can, and hope for the best.

You're on a faith trip, one artist told me several years ago, when I mentioned I never sent out contracts, didn't feel like I needed them, because for the most part the money was so small, and if someone wanted to do you wrong, a contract wasn't going to stop them. And if they felt the need for a contract, they'd send me one. And if ever I needed proof that the legalities wouldn't make much difference, there was the Kennedy Center. They'd have been free to ignore any contract I sent, while waiting for theirs, which they'd send when they felt like. But faith? No, it didn't feel like faith, just common sense.

Now that the money has gotten bigger, and I'm dealing with presenters who expect me to send contracts, I'll do so more and more. But I often open with a personal statement before I list the details to agree upon for a particular show.

I simply ask that presenters treat me as they'd wish to be treated themselves: with honesty and respect. I've found as long as that happens, everything else falls into place. Just like I return phone calls and e-mails, I'd ask the presenters do the same. As long as there's interest and communication, events inevitably come off without a hitch. Further, I like it when I can offer my services in such a way that folks in a community will collaborate— and sometimes what I do allows an opportunity for folks to collaborate who've been talking about it for years, but never quite had that opportunity previously. This makes for a win/win/win situation for the presenter, for the audience, and for me.

Perhaps if I *had* mailed such a contract, I'd have avoided the awkwardness I experienced with one long-running summer festival. I sent a packet one August and was happily surprised to get a prompt reply. They'd like to hire me, the director said in the e-mail, and mentioned the fee they could pay, and the expectation that I'd do a concert set and several workshops.

Fine, I e-mailed back, sending them a letter by regular mail. Then I sat back. Perhaps I should have sent a formal contract, or phoned them, but the other summer festivals I was in contact with were all scheduling their acts in January or later. I was busy. And they were a long-running festival, who I assumed knew their business.

In January, I received a brief form letter e-mail from the festival, the director's name on the bottom, thanking me for my interest in the festival, and regretting there was not space for the many wonderful acts applying to play. When I wrote back, the director was quick to point I had no contract. I replied to ask why hadn't they worded the prior invitation, *We're considering hiring you; keep our festival weekend free if you can until we decide in early January,* or something equally accurate. Then I questioned why the form letter dismissal, not even a personal note, after we'd personally corresponded. She said she was sorry, perhaps next year, or maybe they could even fit me in this year if I was in the area. Well, I'd been planning to be in the area this year, I said, which didn't seem unreasonable. After all, I'd counted on the festival gig. Do you have other jobs in the area? she asked. Not yet, I said, then mentioned I'd let nearby festivals and clubs know I'd been invited, and was now waiting to hear, and had been told it wouldn't be until February or March. Well, let us know if you're in the area, she said. I said I could be in the area, I reminded, and around we went on the impasse.

So they'd changed their mind about having me to the festival, and without the contract, they could do what they wanted. At that point, all I could do was write the festival director a letter, replay the story, and say what was worse about this incident, for me, was that I'd let other organizations know I'd received an invitation, which was true; at least it had been the preceding August. Now, these other organizations might believe I'd merely been grasping for an invitation or was a liar, which wasn't going to do much good for someone like me, who was building a reputation.

When I saw the director a month later at a conference, I was told that yes, my letter had been received, and if I was in the area, I should let the festival know. I already said I'd committed to being in the area, so yes, I'll be in the area, I responded. Well, if you're in the area, do let us know, said the director pleasantly, and took leave.

And we'd somehow taken our impasse to the next step.

A faith trip? I've learned that always there are infinite possible jobs, and for each there are infinite ways it can go right or go wrong. Who's to say what would have happened if the invitation had actually come through and I appeared at the festival. Based on my dealings, I bet I would have been treated shabbily. But who ever knows? In any case, instead of playing at the summer festival, I spent that weekend in New Orleans, deep in my research project, shooting e-mails to college professors and others all over the country, and felt like I was being productive.

Regardless, I strive to act transparently, honestly, and assume people will treat me well in return. Now I even say that in a contract. But a contract can't guarantee it, nor can it even guarantee you'll get paid. At best, all it can do is say what needs saying, which varies for every date, as might a poem. A poetry trip, maybe, is what I'm on, which means looking for meaning in whatever happens, no matter how bizarre.

I recall setting up a September show at a Seattle coffeehouse that occasionally presented concerts. Still living in Anchorage, late May I met the woman, Maya, in charge of bookings, and arranged a date. July, back in town, I reconfirmed. August, I sent flyers to the coffeehouse. A few weeks before the show, I sent out several hundred cards, my complete Seattle mailing list, and the next week, at the Bumbershoot book fair in Seattle, invited hundreds more in person. In retrospect, I must have known the show was somehow primed for disaster. The afternoon of the show, having just finished a gig at an outdoor market in Portland, I was preparing to drive three hours north to Seattle. I called the coffeehouse just to make sure everything was in place for this evening. The manager was in, happy to hear from me. It's you, he began. I was wondering if you'd ever clue us in. Oh, we had a few calls, I think, but we told them it was cancelled. It wasn't on the books.

But I arranged it with Maya, I groaned. I stopped by and talked with her twice.

Maya's no longer working for us.

But I . . .

And she took the schedule book with her. You're the third person who's had this problem. We've been trying to get Maya on the phone to straighten this out.

Wait, I said. I have people coming.

No one's working tonight. It's short notice.

But I have people coming and I set this up three and a half months ago.

I'm sorry, he said, hanging up.

I called him back a minute later with an idea. What if I do a show in your parking lot? I said.

What?

Look, I have to show up anyway, and let people know this wasn't my fault.

We'll put up a sign.

You can put up a sign, but I'll show up anyway. It's the right thing to do. So I'm asking. Since people will be there anyway, and I'm going to be there anyway, do I have permission to do a show in your parking lot?

Just don't tell anybody, he said, and hung up on me again.

The show that night, which went off in the dark in a little alleyway beside the parking lot, reminded me of everything that used to go wrong with such regularity in rural Alaska. I told different stories than usual, read different kinds of poems, played fiddle tunes I usually never played publicly. It wasn't a huge crowd, but it was an engaged one, and, serendipitously, equaled the exact number of chairs we'd managed to scrounge up. At the end of the evening, the last of the concert-goers strolling off, the coffee shop owner happened by, parked his car, and asked what he thought we'd been doing.

I shrugged my shoulders, told him I was sorry he'd missed it—it had been a nice little show—but he could talk to his manager, who could tell him what I'd been doing there.

Like Tania and Mike once told me: two out of ten job leads might come through, and the trouble is you never know which two. And you also never know why those other eight don't. You call and call. Mostly, people are in meetings, or are otherwise inaccessible. You e-mail and e-mail, and never hear anything in return. You send press kit after press kit and never know if they're even received. People are busy, I know. This is all part of the job, I know. But still.

Ignoring me is far easier than scanning a page or two or picking up the phone to ask what it is I actually do and what I can offer so they might have real information before genuinely saying, No, we're sorry.

At least that might have stopped one arts council in North Carolina from turning down my application to work in the schools in part because "it was not clear what I did was curriculum-based." This in response to a packet of materials which included a description of my school programs and several reference letters from teachers, librarians, and even students lauding successful writing residencies. It was one thing to reject me because they didn't know me personally, but how could they question that the work wasn't curriculum-based? What wasn't clear? I wondered. The exact same packet had gotten me hired elsewhere. I'd looked at their website, read the mission statement, seen the names of other artists they'd brought in. Maybe writing had stopped being part of this county's educational curriculum. Who knew what was going on there? Of course, they were going through difficult times financially, so maybe that was part of it. And, of course, there was the increase in state-mandated testing. What rankled me most was that this particular county had even charged a hefty application fee for artists who wanted to visit. Mostly, I was sorry I'd bothered applying in the first place.

I couldn't tell if that was better or worse than the presenter who sputtered one day on the phone how I was wasting everybody's time because they never booked solo acts for residencies, and how their series needed unique artists who could interest a university community that had so many business majors. When I wrote this one back, I highlighted what was already clear on my materials: that while I still performed solo on occasion, I joined with accompanists for concert series and festivals. And added that as an undergraduate at Duke University, I received my B.A. in Management Sciences, so maybe there was a fit here.

The Dark Side: Show-Biz

Though I was continuing to accumulate a wide resume, sometimes it felt like I was back in Barrow, late April 1997, listening to that former elementary school principal summarily dismiss me. But I persisted there and ended up working at that very school the next four years. That experience allowed me to ignore the presenter from an arts center near Boston, who told me on the phone that he thought my mix of fiddle music and poetry would "confuse their patrons," this from someone who regularly programmed both acoustic music and poetry, from mainstream to cutting edge. And I could ignore another presenter, who told me, We already have fiddlers in our town, we already have poets—we're not interested.

I let the remark slide. Why present anything? I might have answered, if I'd have been a little quicker there, and wanted to fight. But I didn't need one more fight. It was easier to just go down the list and call somebody else.

I continue to learn how best to work around the rudeness and small-mindedness. People are busy and most are doing the best they can. Some are more competent; others, less. We all have good days and bad. Anyway, it was like I'd told my pal Woody several years before: performing has never been my dream—it's been more accident than anything else. No, performing has just been a way of staying busy until I could get my books published.

You want darkness. The book business, now that's dark.

7

The Darker Side: Publishing

After Hearing John Haines Read

Poet to whom all others are measured
who write of Alaska, he appears tough
as his work, an honest line, gruff
and lean, an honest being indentured
to land. His speaking voice, long-weathered
by six-month subsistence winters, is rough
and smooth at once, as if wide enough
to embrace both poles. Think rock pressured
by ice and light. Think immensities
mated with silence. Think centuries
of fox, bear, marten, beaver, owl. Picture him
silver as snow gathering on birch limb,
gold as some wolves. Or building a fire
in forty below night. Someplace farther.

If I'd needed a sign for my place in the book industry, I found it the first week
of May 2002 in New York City, where I attended BookExpo, the annual gathering
for everything related to books and publishing. Forty thousand people, I heard,
and the exhibit halls were filled with the very largest publishing houses to the very
small. Some years my publisher, John Crawford of West End Press, attended, but
he wasn't this year, which was too bad. My second collection had just come out,
and since I *could* attend—meaning I was within several hundred miles and had the
dates free—I *would* attend, and made certain of it two months prior by landing a
small gig at The Knitting Factory for the Sunday evening following the convention.
The Knitting Factory was a well-known New York City club. Since I'd be in the city
anyway, I had no excuses.

Nearly five years earlier, I'd completed a novel which I couldn't get published.
Maybe attending BookExpo would help me in some slight way understand this

process. I hadn't dedicated my entire life to getting the book published, but I'd put in time. I'd read books about finding agents, and queried a dozen who seemed like a fit, including in the query what each agent demanded, usually a one-page letter, perhaps 10 or 20 pages of the manuscript, a self-addressed stamped envelope. Of that initial group, most quickly rejected me, and a few I never heard back from, though one strung me along for more than a year before reluctantly turning me down, saying the book was good, and someone would likely take it on, but whoever did would have a tough road of it, finding a publisher. By the time I received that appraisal, I'd been rejected by a second dozen, a third dozen, then a fourth dozen. Mostly, these were form letters, though one well-established agent in that first group took me to task for describing the four sections as "novella-length." Novellas, he said, didn't sell. I shook my head, upon receipt of the note, wanted to shoot a letter back saying I was describing length, and, anyway, wasn't *The Sound and the Fury* a novel of four novella-length sections? Instead, I took the criticism, however unjustified it seemed, as a window into how a successful agent might think, and revised the second round of letters to say the book was made up of "four sections, approximately 20,000-25,000 words each."

Maybe this was reasonable, sending a fresh batch of queries each season. Maybe it wasn't. Should I send more queries? Send less? Just before moving to Anchorage, summer of 1998, almost a year after finishing the book, I attended an event near Seattle where hundreds of writers—mostly with mainstream projects— met with agents and editors who also mostly trafficked in the same. My novel, a contemporary relationship story, a plain old literary novel set in Fairbanks, Juneau, and Nome, sparked no interest, nor should it have with the kind of industry people attending. The two agents who asked to see the first long section speedily turned it down. Another read the first five pages and said it didn't start quickly enough. God, I thought, rereading the same pages. I had to start it somewhere, and in this the main character had just moved to Alaska after a divorce, met several musicians his first night in Fairbanks, and already was sleeping with one of them there, a pretty fiddler with boyfriends stashed throughout the state. I guess I should have included a murder, I thought to tell this agent, but imagined him replying, *Yes, now you're talking.* The whole three-day conference depressed me, making me feel more desperate than I'd ever felt about my writing. Where the AWP Conference at least in part celebrated the making of literature, this gathering was about shoving to be first in line to sell a concept.

After moving to Anchorage, I sent out another dozen queries and also wrote a dozen editors at major publishing houses. Why not at least contact some of the decision-makers directly? I thought. Just like I'd found agents' names, I found editors' names in appropriate directories and in *Publisher Weekly* articles.

And a few weeks later, I received my first surprise. The exact query that still elicited little interest from agents—in that whole first year, only two ever asked to see the complete manuscript, and only a few more asked for even the whole first section—somehow intrigued the same editors who, supposedly, agents presumed utter disinterest. An editor at Little, Brown asked to see the whole manuscript, as did one at Grove Atlantic, and another at Algonquin. Several others asked to see the first hundred pages. Only two or three wrote to say they were not interested, or did not read unsolicited material.

I sent the manuscripts out and waited. Of course, in retrospect, I shouldn't have been surprised agents still were not interested in even looking at the manuscript. Meanwhile, senior editors were passing, though saying nice things about the writing and the book, and regretting they had no idea how they would sell it. I couldn't tell if they meant the kind words, or were just being polite. Still, almost a decade later now, I recall the letter from the intern at Grove Atlantic who'd been assigned to read the manuscript. She couldn't put it down, she wrote me, continuing ... *but here at Grove Atlantic we publish more literary works, so as much as I enjoyed reading* Now Entering Alaska Time, *I could not recommend your popular fiction to the editor.*

After that burst, over the next few years I'd occasionally send the novel out if I had reason. Summer 2000, once my first poetry collection and first CD were both released, I discovered websites where I came across the names of a whole new set of agents. These, too, I queried. One was interested enough to ask where I'd sent the manuscript previously. Mentioning my experience, she scolded me, saying I should have known not to have contacted publishing houses directly; now I'd ruined it, she added. I didn't hear from her again, though was curious how exactly "I'd ruined it." As I meandered through this process, following my nose, making what time I could, it became apparent that all it ever took was one agent, one editor, just one person in the business with enough clout—or sometimes even just enthusiasm—to shepherd a project through to completion. I wondered what the agent was talking about, and decided she was one more person to work around.

That fall for the first time I even had an agent reject me twice. Attending the Pacific Northwest Booksellers Association tradeshow in Portland, I saw an Alaska friend, who had recently published a non-fiction book. Greeting me, she introduced me to her agent, who asked who I was and what I was doing at the event. I mentioned I was there because a poetry collection was out, but also because I'd finished a novel. A novel? The agent was curious.

It's set in Alaska, I explained. Fairbanks, Juneau, and Nome. Contemporary relationship story. Literary.

Send it along, the agent said.

Well, I said, I already did. I queried right when I finished it.

Send it again, the agent said. Be sure and write *solicited* on the bottom left-hand front corner of the envelope. That way, it'll be sure to be routed to me.

Several weeks later, the agent rejected me again, though that second time I do like to think the agent actually looked at it.

Prior to BookExpo, the past year on tour, I'd had no time to chase further leads. But that didn't mean I hadn't continued thinking about it. I carried it with me in the van, along with a short story collection that I also thought was publishable but which had never found a home. If I needed to send either book somewhere, I could do it immediately. And when I doubted the worth of the novel, I could remember what my music partner Andrea had said her first time in Alaska. Unable to find any fiction but genre mysteries, she grudgingly accepted when I offered the manuscript. Quickly, though, she became engrossed. Her response upon finishing: What is it with your country that you can't get this published? A few other friends had reacted just as positively, and in 2001 I'd run across a writer from Washington State who led a workshop at a gathering I attended in 1990 and read the first section of it there, not long after it had been completed. After I reintroduced myself, he put a hand to his chin, said, Yes, surprisingly, after more than ten years he remembered the story. If the rest had turned out as well as that part, I should keep at it. I told him that, Yes, I thought it had gotten better as it went along, but I'd had an impossible time getting it published. He said even though he'd had success with three novels and a book of non-fiction, he had quite a few hard luck stories in that regard himself.

So. A sign. I said I'd received a sign in New York City at BookExpo.

Because I had two CDs out and a second book newly published, I'd written to the group managing the event, querying whether there might be a place to perform on site. There were showcases, it was explained, and, sure, for $500 I could participate in one at a nearby conference hotel that might be a good fit. Someone would be singing. Somebody else would be reading with a flutist accompanying. Did I want to sign up? Upon quick review, it was easy to see spending money beyond a three-day conference pass was to throw it away, especially this first time through. I had one last question before pre-registering. I had two books out with West End Press, both distributed by University of New Mexico Press, I was quick to add. But neither West End Press nor University of New Mexico Press were attending this year. Still, for my name badge, should I use one of those organization titles, or the one for my record label, Nomadic Press. After all, I said, the CDs have poetry on them.

We'll put you under Nomadic Press, I was told.

Weeks later, picking up my tag, I read: *Ken Waldman, Nomadic Press, Anchorage AK, Non-Industry Visitor.*

I can joke about the tag now, and joked about it then. Talk about a sign. And it's true: unless you're published by a major house and sell plenty of books, it's easy to be marginalized. Non-industry visitor? That's right, if you've written poetry collections.

Before I ever began touring, I'd have assumed bookstores were poets' friends. And even when I made my first trips out of Juneau, and then Anchorage, chapbooks and fiddle in hand, good independent bookstores were occasionally willing to have me read: Village Books in Bellingham, Elliott Bay Book Company in Seattle, Eagle Harbor Books on Bainbridge Island, Powell's in Portland. But I should have been listening more closely. My first time in Montana, one independent bookstore was happy to host me, but let me know that they'd promote me as a fiddling storyteller. Regardless how accomplished the poetry was, they said, their bookstore clientele would be suspicious.

The Darker Side: Publishing

Though a number of bookstores continued to be supportive once my first then my second poetry collection came out, I learned it was not only just as difficult getting gigs at bookstores—often, you had to schedule dates four months, or longer, in advance—but chasing them would doom me. Without an opportunity for a cover charge, or to negotiate a guarantee, all I could reasonably expect was space to read and an opportunity to sell and promote books. In some cases, that was enough—and it was never something to be taken for granted—but it was no way to make a living in my case, and I'd make the decision to pursue such a gig as I'd make the decision to go after any other that paid little: I'd consider going into a bookstore only if I was already in an area.

Sadly, I found when I did pursue such a gig—and I'd send promotional materials with the same care I'd send to any other venue—a number of bookstores had a strict policy: poetry doesn't sell—no; or, poetry doesn't sell—we do one night a month so, perhaps, if you're in town that night we'll feature you; or, poetry doesn't sell—though we do occasional nights where we'll bring in ten poets who will each read two poems, so, perhaps, if you're in town that night you can come and read with the others, though you'll need to send a packet now to our poetry coordinator.

I tried to explain that I wasn't like other poets since I played fiddle (and the poems I read were good, too, I'd add), and across town, or maybe an hour away, possibly 50 or 100 folks would show up to see me, sometimes paying as much as a $15 cover. Also, I often got written about in the newspaper, which meant free advertising for them, so likely people would indeed show up and they'd sell books, whether mine, or others that the people coming to my event would purchase as they browsed.

I said all that and still heard: no, poetry doesn't sell.

Perhaps one of the most unsupportive was located in a western town where there was a college I'd performed at several times, a radio station that played my CDs, residents that liked what I did, where I had friends. The small independent bookstore downtown there occasionally hosted events, though never one of mine, despite previous queries. Spring 2004, I inquired again because I'd be driving through in the summer and had already arranged a children's show through the library and a house concert for an environmental organization.

I'm sorry, the bookstore's event manager said to me over the phone when I called to follow up. It makes no sense to come to the store when you've obviously saturated the market.

Wait, I said. I'm not sure you're understanding what I'm trying to say. I'm getting paid to do a free show for what will probably be 150-200 children, and then I'm doing a house concert with a $10 cover charge a few miles out of town. Don't you think a free reading downtown would complement the other two activities?

No, I don't, said the manager. And besides your books have never sold very well here.

How could they, I shot back, when they've never been stocked? Could you check and see if they've ever been in stock?

I don't believe they've sold well, she repeated.

Are you serious? I asked. Are you familiar with what I do? I sent you a packet. I'm just calling to follow up.

I'm sorry, she said. It looks like you already have things well-planned in our community. Do stop by and say hello while you're in town.

Still, that exchange was an improvement over the one I had in January 2003 with the Borders Bookstore in Anchorage. I'd called because the current issue of *Book Magazine* had just come out, one of its last issues. There was a big picture of Alice Sebold on the front, and the cover advertised articles about Toni Morrison, Hunter S. Thompson, Annie Proulx, Andrew Weil. Inside were pages and pages of book news, including a lone poetry review, which was of my recent collection. I called Borders to alert them.

Maybe you'll want to order a few books and make a display? I'll be happy to send the article, I said after I introduced myself and explained my situation. But since I know you stock the magazine, maybe you'll figure something out. Certainly it should help sell a few copies, anyway.

What are you talking about? the woman asked.

You said this was Borders. Right?

Yes.

I'm calling since I'm a writer, and I live in Anchorage, and well, I already said all that.

142

Yes, you did, the woman said.

So.

All decisions come from Ann Arbor.

Can't I talk to the store manager, then?

You have to talk to Ann Arbor.

Are you serious?

Here's the number, the woman said. She repeated it twice, then said good-bye and hung up.

Sitting on the bed in my room in a Motel 6 in Vallejo, California, I just stared at the receiver. The day before, I'd picked up a copy of the magazine in a Berkeley newsstand, read the review, then bought two more. The issue had just come out. More than twenty years earlier, I'd worked in a bookstore in Chapel Hill and I thought I knew what bookstores were supposed to do. It just seemed to make sense to call someone in Anchorage. But who? The independent bookstore downtown had been supportive of my work to a point, but wouldn't deal with this, I knew. The Barnes & Noble in town had always seemed a little dense when I tried dealing with them. The book had been out for months and they'd yet to order it. So I tried Borders, even if it was a chain. Now I didn't know. I had a number in Ann Arbor that I didn't want to call, but that the bookstore in Anchorage had given me. The first Monday in 2003, I thought. Why not? This is a new year. So I phoned Ann Arbor.

When the man answered, saying *Borders,* I launched into my spiel, that the bookstore in Anchorage had said I should call, and that I had a book out.

Whoa, he said. Slow down. What are you talking about?

What do you mean?

Are you suggesting a promotion? Do you want Borders to promote this book?

Well, it's your store. I'm a writer in Anchorage who has a small review in a national magazine, and I thought if I let somebody there know, it might help your company sell a few more books. But now I'm talking to somebody in Ann Arbor.

Anyway, he said, if you want, I can give you the number for someone in promotions. I'm not somebody who can help you. Today I'm supposed to be installing lights bulbs.

Light bulbs?

Yeah, I help out in the central office where I can.

This time, I hung up.

A year later, I told this story to a woman I was sitting next to in an Anchorage bar after she told me she worked at that Borders. She was sorry, she said, but it hadn't surprised her. The good news for me is that she still works there, so at least I have someone to contact. And when I do stop in the store now, I see they have my books and have even stocked them as I suggested: a few in poetry, a few in the Alaska Literature section. It was better than Barnes & Noble, where more than three years after publication, I was still waiting for them to stock that second book.

Despite the misadventures with both chain and independent bookstores, I'm aware I'm one of the fortunate ones who've at least had books published, and for now have six poetry collections with national distribution, and now have this book of prose. When people ask how I managed to get that first book done, I tell them I had poems published in literary journals for years, finished a draft of what would be the first book in early 1994, and then at a conference in 1996 met John Crawford, who asked to see it. He kept it for a year and a half before rejecting it, but with an invitation to resubmit if I made the changes he suggested. Ten days later, I resubmitted. A year later, he accepted the manuscript, and the book came out a year and half after that. And that was neither fast nor slow. It was the way of publishing, which could be glacial, and which you had to come to peace with if you were seriously looking for publication.

There is a shortcut, however, through book contests.

Theoretically, book contests are a great idea. A press publicizes a poetry competition, hires a judge, and publishes the winning manuscript. Requirements vary: it might be for a first book only, a second book only, for writers under the age of forty, for writers over the age of fifty. What was certain was an application fee, which might be as little as $10, as much as $30. And if you entered enough of them, it wasn't cheap. My poet pal Bob, in Denver, estimated he'd spent nearly $10,000 on competitions the past decade—enough, he moaned, that he could have started a press, published his own as well as others, instead of flushing it in the toilet.

But at least you're helping subsidize all the books that do get published, I pointed out.

Bunch of crooks. It's rigged. And what are you talking about, you know how this game works as well as I do, he said.

I nodded. It was a variation of Tania and Mike's two of ten rule. The contests may not have been rigged per se, but depending on the aesthetics—and scruples—of the judge, entering a contest was as useful as dumping money and poems down a rain gutter.

A few years ago, I was a visiting writer at a two-year college, where my host mentioned she was a preliminary reader at a book contest administered by a university press in her home state. I should enter the contest, she said, because my work was good, and she could promise that at least I'd be assured a fair reading.

But I saw who the final judge was, I told her, and I didn't think anything I could possibly send would have a chance. A whole different taste.

Nodding, my host said I was right, and apologized for even suggesting. Bad idea, she added.

No, not necessarily, I said. If I had an extra $25 maybe I'd do it, because you just never know. And then I told her a story I'd heard from a writer I knew who'd won one of the National Poetry Series contests. A year after he won, I saw him, and asked about it. Funny story, he said, because I'm not one of those writers who ever wins contests.

So what happened? I asked.

Well, he said. You know how that contest goes. Five books get published—five judges each pick a winner. The judges were supposed to be picking from a pool of twenty or thirty finalists. But one poet last year was a little different. This one said, Don't give me the finalists; send me every manuscript that was originally submitted. So they sent them along, and the poet considered every single one, which was how I got chosen. And, of course, the way this story goes, since mine wasn't in the original finalist batch, I'd have never had a chance, except this judge insisted on seeing every last manuscript.

Interesting, I told him.

No, what got really interesting was this contest flew all five winners to New

York to receive our awards, he said. While I was there, I thought I'd read the other four contest selections. One winning book made absolutely no sense to me on any level, just felt like spectacularly bad writing, but had been chosen by one of the writer's former teachers. Another winning book made sense at least, but was very predictable, very dull, also chosen by a former teacher of the writer. A third book was very very good and also had been chosen by a former teacher. And there was one other winning poet, besides me, wondering what we were doing there.

So, that was one contest story, I told my host poet, and if I had $25 to burn, I'd send it along to the one you're reading for. An awful bet, sure, but you never knew. Maybe the judge dies, or gets sick, and somebody who'd like my stuff ends up deciding. Or maybe this year's judge improbably takes a real shine to one of my poems, reads the manuscript a little differently because of it, pronounces it accomplished, and, upon reading the other finalists and finding nothing quite as good, decides to choose mine even if it didn't fully satisfy. What is the chance though: one in ten thousand, one in a million? Only thing certain was unless you entered, there was no possible way to win.

I was reminded, too, of an interview I'd read in a journal I once subscribed to, *The Chiron Review*. The poems, and occasional short fiction, were often uneven, but the good ones could be truly eye-opening, as was the interview with a poet I always enjoyed, Charles Harper Webb. A professor in Southern California, and also a therapist, Webb had published hundreds of fun, energetic, accomplished poems for years—I'd seen his poems *everywhere*—but had been unable to get a book published. The interview, as I remember, explained part of his process and how Webb had sought a mentor, who he hoped would tell him he was wonderful and that it was the system and the poetry establishment to blame. He did eventually find the mentor he sought, who told him, Yes, he was wonderful, but also told him in the next breath that being wonderful wasn't going to be enough. Without connections, he explained, Webb needed to be perfect, and as wonderful as he was, no, he wasn't yet perfect. Ultimately, Webb needed to strengthen the poems, because in the end, if the poems were good enough, the books would get published, even without connections. Many years later, I was happy to see Webb had a half-dozen full-length collections with excellent presses, and undoubtedly had more books on the way.

The Darker Side: Publishing

That was probably why the following year, when I found a website that listed numerous agents I'd never previously encountered and who accepted e-mail queries, I thought to act. I composed a new, and, I thought, better query letter for the novel, emphasizing that my two books of poetry were both in second printings, that my three CDs had received widespread airplay, that my past three years of non-stop touring included an appearance at the Kennedy Center Millennium Stage and co-billing at a festival with Sandra Cisneros, Adrienne Rich, and Robert Creeley. I offered a link to my website, and a three-line synopsis of the Alaska-set book, mentioning I'd been writing fiction long before I'd ever written poetry.

A half dozen of the fifty agents I wrote asked for thirty to fifty pages, though none were later interested in seeing more. Another dozen politely declined the invitation. The others, I assumed, were just too busy. Despite my added credentials, I still had no connections, still felt like I was wearing my BookExpo tag: Non-Industry Visitor. Maybe I'd have to return to that encounter with the agent near Seattle, the one who read five pages and thought the novel started too slowly. There was something to learn from the criticism. My query this time may well have been similarly flawed. Next time, maybe I'll refer to Alaska as Armageddon. Then I might even have reason to return to the long-finished manuscript, make it biblical, a titanic struggle of good and evil, instead of something as mundane as some guy in Fairbanks trying to find his way, some woman in Juneau trying to find her way, who meet, become lovers, and spend a difficult winter together in Nome.

It's been a dark business, getting books published. But as long as I'm still trying, there's a chance. And then there is this: it makes show-biz seem easy.

8
Mr. Small Businessman, Your Goods Are Odd

Buster Keaton, Romancer

> Half stone face, half sourpuss, the dour
> young suitor, dismissed by his beloved,
> tumbles from the porch, a miffed glance above
> as he takes his pratfall in the flowers,
> his dark eyes part rage, part pout, part glower,
> a huffy scowl slowly easing as he's moved
> to sniff the garden's roses. *By Jove*
> rolls on-screen to signify the whiff. Our
> hero lifts himself from the dirt, brushes
> clung soil off his trousers, stoops to pick
> a few fine long-stemmed petals, then rushes
> up the steps. His girl warily accepts, sticks
> the bouquet in a vase. Six words appear:
> *Thus starts the lover's promising career.*

Publicist, self-promoter, negotiator, consultant, CEO, financial officer, salesman, chauffeur, navigator, travel agent, mover, typist, graphic designer, tech writer, editor, researcher, professor, teacher, shipping clerk, book rep, bill collector, record producer, and, oh yeah, occasional artist—poet, fiddler, band leader, tunesmith, novelist, performer. It's a good thing I perform, I sometimes joke, or else I'd never have time to play fiddle.

Don't quit your day job; you have no idea what it takes, I'll say, when writers, teachers, or musicians suggest they might like to do what I do. But I could just as easily say, Sure, quit your job; go right ahead as long as you are motivated and are prepared to work all day every day. There are plenty of opportunities out there, though you might never find them.

Typical day? There *is* no typical day. It's boring work sometimes, stuffing several hundred envelopes, later waiting in line at the post office. Dispiriting work sometimes, making fifty phone calls, then fifty more, just like the day before, and finding no one in, no one getting back to you. But it is never routine, and often quite energizing in unexpected ways. An e-mail might come from out of nowhere— someone you didn't know writes to say you've inspired them. A presenter finally calls back and offers you $2,800 for a job that fits perfectly inside a tour. The check arrives in the mail, enough to pay for the CD you're mastering next week.

Sometimes the work is easy. The easiest days, actually, are the ones where I actually have to be somewhere, get up at a certain time, use the alarm clock, a day I'm earning money for doing something in public, or else driving several hundred miles. The days I'm doing something demonstrable. The hours are filled, and there is no choice; you're on schedule or else. If the mind happens to wander, there's nothing like performing in front of a couple of hundred people to focus you, especially if they're second or third-graders. On those days, depending on the schedule, maybe there's time to make a few phone calls, do fifteen minutes of e-mail, run a few errands. Or maybe it's all travel and performance. The time might be spent getting to the venue, and then leaving afterwards in order to get to the next place on time.

Sometimes the work is hard. Most often, strangely, those are the days when I'm not working publicly or traveling far. That's when the real work occurs: when I have to go revisit my lists and priorities. The choices are always infinite. Should I send publicity to newspapers for all upcoming shows, or wait until the following week, the next time I'll have space to really spread out? Any deadlines coming up for conferences, for grant applications, or for book submissions? Should I make calls or send e-mails to fill last-minute dates for a tour three months away? Or how about the tour six months away? Or how about the tour a year or year and a half away? And what about the follow-up from that last mailing I did because if I don't get to it soon, who's to say they'll remember me when I do call, if indeed they remember me right now if I do decide to call this very moment? What do I feel like doing today? Who do I want to call? Are there people I promised to call? Do I need to find a post office? A library? A copy center? Is there someone local I should call to possibly drop in and see since I'm in the area? And what about my bills? (Twelve years I've stayed up-to-date paying my credit card bills.) Or is this one of those days that I have to go spend the afternoon hauling everything out of my van, take inventory, then repack and rearrange so I don't have to shudder every time I go in the back to try to dig something out?

Sundays are a little easier since I have a few less options, but they aren't that much easier. I can't call people who work in offices. I can't buy stamps. Still, there is always plenty to do, and I'm doing it all myself.

An agent would help, I know, but I've also learned it can't be just any agent, but the right one. I've yet to find an agent for my writing. In 2001, I found one for booking performances. We'd met the preceding autumn at a conference where I was showcasing and she was representing one of her acts, a Canadian music group. She liked my set, enjoyed the CD I passed along, invited me to join her small roster. I was to be an experiment: her only American artist, the only act under a $5,000 fee. What she told me: people will like what you do; the challenge will be finding presenters who will take the time to see and hear what you do, so they'll give you a chance. We worked together close to a year; she never found me a job. Finally, what I did was too different, she explained; she couldn't sell it without more help. Perhaps if I were to make a video, she suggested gently, knowing I'd have to spend a couple of thousand dollars to make one that might not make a whit of difference. Maybe if I'd have had my website running, that would have given her what she needed. We'll never know. I do know that if I'd had another agent, one who specialized in educational shows, maybe, or one who had other small unusual acts on their roster, so knew more people who'd more readily respond to my eclectic mix, that might likely have helped. Or maybe one who concentrated on traditional music acts. But I'd queried, and had no luck. In some cases, I believe it was because I didn't quite make enough money to interest them. In some cases, their rosters were already full. In some cases, I could have pursued more aggressively. Finding an agent is one more job, one that's about finding the right fit. For now, I stay busy making personal contacts, then sending along CDs, books, newspaper articles, all manner of paraphernalia. When I have time, I make follow-up phone calls, send personal e-mail reminders, handwrite letters. Did I say I work all the time?

Maybe it was at one of my conferences or festivals—or more likely driving on the way to one, thinking—when I realized attending a conference was supposed to be work. I paid fees, committed travel and time. But in return, not only was

150

I meeting with people in my field who I had lots in common with, but people I naturally enjoyed socializing with: fellow musicians, writers, teachers. Work had become my social life. Likewise, attending a festival was supposed to be play. I paid my admission (or was paid to attend), committed travel and time. In return, I not only met people I enjoyed socializing with—fellow musicians, usually—but also met people who might play with me on future jobs or might even be in position to hire me themselves sometimes. My social life had become my work. Maybe I do work all the time, but that also includes attending some terrific parties and knowing some incredibly talented people.

Somewhere along the way I realized I better carry business cards with me all the time, maybe have a CD or book handy. There was Tania and Mike's rule again: two of ten good leads might turn into jobs. But as you got into the field more deeply, you learned not only that you never knew where the next lead might come from, but sometimes what even constituted a lead.

I had a friend in Anchorage, Duke, a painter and performance artist. He was the first Alaskan I'd ever met, camped beside me in a campground at Lake Louise, Alberta, in September 1984. He was on a bike trip with his girlfriend, Marie, and two other friends, Alan and Wade. More than twenty years later, I remember how their van with seven bikes on a roof rack pulled up beside my white Chevy van, my 10-speed red Schwinn clunker on a rack out front. Later that night after we shared a meal, and were drinking by the campfire, Wade said to me, If you enjoyed talking to us, you're going to end up in Alaska someday. Alaska had been the last place I'd ever considered, but that trip west I'd been looking for a home, and, there, I'd been given a sign. Or maybe not. I ended up moving to Seattle. But after having a relationship fail and then writing a story that told me, yes, I was now a writer, I moved to Fairbanks, a little more than ten months later. Thirteen years later still, I moved to Anchorage, and occasionally would see Duke. One night he told me he rarely sold paintings to friends, or other people he'd expected would more readily buy; rather, it was the expectation that there were people who should be buying that set the whole process in motion—someone would talk, something might show up in a newspaper, somebody would show up in a gallery, and Duke would sell another piece to someone he wouldn't have expected to buy.

It was true for me too. I drove ten hours to play in Georgia in front of ten people, but found a suitable accompanist for shows in 250-seat performing arts centers. I attended a conference to meet over 200 presenters who I hoped would hire me, and a fellow artist gave me the name of someone I might want to call, who ended up hiring me when I did. I followed a path that distanced me from a family I was already estranged from and in the process made peace with my father, or, more accurately, his ghost.

My father was a businessman. The last time I had any contact with him was fall of 2000. I was in Anchorage, the year my first book had been published and my first CD released. A disc jockey in South Florida had played my CD, and my father must have been listening. I was not sure how else he might have known, or how he'd have heard. He left me a message on the phone, saying he'd heard my music, and wished me luck in my new career.

I don't know if it's a career, I wrote him back in a letter. It's what I'm doing now, I said, and for now I'm enjoying it.

My father liked the telephone. I disliked his occasional calls; there was never anything to say, nothing to do but listen impatiently to the same advice he always gave—unless I changed the subject to sports, which would sidetrack him until he wandered back to the same unasked for spiel, that I should prosper, be happy, enjoy my life, and bury the unpleasantnesses. Bury the unpleasantnesses. There was never anything to say unless I wanted to start an argument that could never be won. My father had always been a bully. That was his way, at least his way inside the family. I'd occasionally write him, which allowed me a more comfortable position, though usually I followed his phone lead, saying nothing save a few pleasantries. He's never been a letter-writer, and, approaching 80, he's not going to start. Since that call in 2000, though, he's never called, and I've had no reason to call him or to write again.

I don't miss him, but I do think about him sometimes, and certainly understand him better now. His father, my grandfather, established a small family printing business, Waldman Printing, that my father expanded into Consolidated Drake Press. He found partners, added employees, bought bigger machines, moved into a larger space, took the train from Philadelphia to Manhattan to hustle more business. Head salesman, he took clients golfing, or to lunch, or to pro sports events. He took work home.

With the help of a friend in Juneau, in 1995 I made that first chapbook and named my business Nomadic Press. Over a dozen years later, I'm still at it, with lots of employees—all of them named me!—and hustling my business across the continent, meeting associates in conference halls, music clubs, festival campgrounds. But where my father made real money, enough to afford a comfortable upper-middle class life, I scrape by, shaving expenses everywhere I can. The privileged poor, my friend Mike called it. My father never drove a car with 285,000 miles on the odometer. My father never stayed in bargain lodging. My father never lived without health insurance.

Do you pay taxes? someone asked.

Of course, I said.

In that, I'm like my father, a taxpayer—though my father never paid taxes like I've learned to. Give me a couple of days off in late March or early April, and I'll find a Motel 6 or Super 8 near, say, Buffalo, Chicago, or Athens, Ohio. I'll spread out every credit card statement from the past year, spread out my checkbooks, spread out my past tax returns, and do my annual accounting: all the motel rooms, the gasoline, the stamps, the copying, the conference fees, what I paid for CDs and books, fiddle strings and magazine purchases. I make money each year—though no matter how much I make, it is about the same as what I spend. Supportive friends say one of these years I'll be earning so much that I'll need an all-star accountant.

Hasn't happened yet, I answer. I'm more apt to need a fancy bankruptcy lawyer. For now, I joke, I do taxes as I used to do high school chemistry lab. I don't follow the rules exactly, but close enough so I'm sure I'll pass. If the IRS ever came after me, they'd shake their heads. A waste of time investigating him, they'd assert. And a ridiculous way for a man to conduct business. He made money. He spent money. He stayed busy. And what does he have to show for it? A few books? A few CDs? More on the way? And, what, owing $80,000 spread out over six credit cards? You call this prosperity? You call this a life?

Still, my debt is a triumph, I figure, since there is no other way I could continue and make all this happen, and I was raised not to be this way. I grew up in a house where talking about money was taboo, but every expense was counted and recounted, and we never bought what we couldn't afford, whatever that might be. Meanwhile, I graduated from Duke, majored in Management Sciences, and haven't balanced my checkbook in twenty-five years.

You want a business plan? I have no business plan other than to return all calls and e-mails, to contact others when I have the time, and to trust my intuition above all else. To climb out of debt, all it takes is what it always takes: one huge grant, several very good months of near-everyday work, some luck. It's the same thing I've been saying for years. And one of these seasons, it'll turn. It has to. I believe it's turning as I write.

To tour like I have, it takes lots of money, or lots of friends.

And I've been grateful for my many friends.

For money, God knows how many grants and fellowships I've applied for: Guggenheim, Hodder, NEA, Rasmuson. I've sold books and CDs, and written books I could have been selling if only someone published them. I've performed from Barrow to Boston.

So far, it hasn't been enough to keep me out of debt.

I'm no fan of Bank of America, Chase, and the other banks that raise their credit card rates midway through, change the rules, make my slippery slope a few degrees steeper, even though I'm fulfilling the terms, always paying on time, the minimum or above. But I've read the fine print. It's a vicious game, a rigged deck. Still, I couldn't have done what I've done otherwise.

I'm always heartened rereading the essay my publisher, John Crawford, wrote for his West End Press catalog as he celebrated twenty-five years in the business of publishing books. "We are still not non-profit," he said at one point, "due to my own paranoia, laziness, stubbornness, and even the kind of populism that cherishes freedom of action."

Yes, I say, freedom of action. As long as even a little of my money holds out, and I continue with equal parts energy and ingenuity, I am free to act as I'd like to.

But still, how am I to find a girlfriend?

Sometimes I wonder: maybe if I just treated the whole dating process like I was doing no more, but no less, than finding an excellent gig somewhere, then I'd find someone. The first time I had the notion, I recoiled. The last thing I wanted was to reduce a woman to a job search. But then I wondered further: I've put so much time into my work; if only I put that much time, or, God, half that much time into nurturing a relationship, then maybe I'll be in luck. But then I thought about how much of my life I'd invested in my work. I didn't want to give that up for just anyone. Best would be to find another artist maybe, or, better, someone who had room in their life to join some aspect of my work with some aspect of theirs. A banjo player would be nice. Or a guitarist. Or maybe a writer. Or maybe I could meet an agent, or a festival producer, or an editor, or even a masseuse. Ideally, she could combine two or three of these talents with a willingness to tour. I'm joking, but only a little. Maybe I've been alone too long and am too set in my ways; maybe I'm too narcissistic, and need someone just like me.

Or maybe I just need to attend a few more conferences, or play more shows. Occasionally I do meet someone when I'm traveling, and we immediately click, and it turns sexy. When it happens, it's assumed I'm like this everywhere, and that I have groupies.

Groupies? I ask, amazed.

Granted, my fiddling poet persona allows me to act a little bigger and brasher than usual. But then what? Afterwards, I might stay in contact, or my partner decides to stay in contact, and the affair runs its natural course. The result reminded me of an encounter I had my first full summer in Fairbanks, where I met a woman from Anchorage at a party. I'd been powerfully attracted, and after talking deep into the long-lit evening, she rode with me to my cabin. The next morning, propped on an elbow beside me in bed, she said, Yes, it was obvious I'd been attracted. My non-verbal communication was perfectly in order, she assured me, for I'd been wondering—though what swayed her to come back with me was that I lived almost four hundred miles from her, so this would be safe, nothing too complicated.

We're not going to see each other again? I asked.

No way, she said smiling. If I'd have thought there was a chance of that, I wouldn't be here now in the first place.

Wait, I said. You're here because you know you're not going to be here again?

So why are you here in the first place?

I'm here because *I instinctively liked you*, she corrected. And you don't live in the same town I do so I'm not going to be with you again.

What if I drove down to Anchorage? I asked.

I'd be busy with my boyfriend, she said.

I didn't know that. You didn't tell me you had a boyfriend.

Well, I didn't, did I?

Why not?

I wanted to see what would happen—and it was great fun, wasn't it? She pushed herself up over me and off the futon, and I slapped her rump on the way.

And so it went. It wasn't until that winter in Fairbanks when a woman I knew told me the only sure way a man up north can get together with a woman he really likes is to find a couple almost but not quite in trouble, then be the one to add a little bit of that extra trouble.

Isn't that kind of harsh? I said.

It's why you'll probably be alone up here, she said.

Maybe as the fiddling poet, I might help give a push to an already-tippy relationship if the mood struck me. But it couldn't just be any mood and any already-tippy relationship; I'd have to really want it more than anything. Otherwise, what was the point of starting a relationship with those kinds of complications? Though the fiddling poet is a good bit of who I am, I'm not that exact person I portray in public. You think I live my life onstage? Offstage, I might hole up for weeks and months—after all, how else could I write like I have?

One friend assumed that as a touring artist I lived like a sailor, with a girl-friend in every port.

I have friends who are women, I corrected. They're pals. Sisters. For years, the women I felt attracted to, who I could sense were attracted to me, were all married or just as unavailable. Was it bad luck? Circumstance? Fate? I'd been in Fairbanks a year, just a month after I'd met and slept with the woman from Anchorage, when I heard one woman sigh—it was August and she had to decide who she'd be with that winter. It was in Fairbanks I heard one man complain that up north, winter being as it was, the women being who they were, he'd never once met a single

woman he really wanted to be with. Up here, he said, you end up settling for someone you don't necessarily want to be with. He repeated the line, emphasizing the
word *settling*, and bemoaned that women were always the ones getting to choose.
The odds were good, but the goods were odd. For that bachelor, it meant leaving
Alaska, returning to New York City where he grew up, and spending a couple of
years sleeping with every woman he could, and according to him there was never
a shortage.

One friend in Seattle likened me to a monk, with my devotion to work, and
my inclination to celibacy. I've never been single by choice, I responded, ticking
off the stages: living in rural Alaskan where there were virtually no opportunities
to meet women; illness and convalescence time; plane wreck time; poverty; near-
ceaseless touring so I was never in one place long enough. I mentioned how one
Nome friend explained his relationship history: he stayed busy with his projects,
he said, waiting in line until it was once again his turn. An attractive man, he'd been
alone for years between long-term relationships. I mentioned how in twenty years
in Alaska I'd learned of only one proven way of attracting women: inviting to fly
them somewhere spectacular in your airplane.

There you have it, my Seattle friend said.

What's that?

You chose Alaska, and the women who choose Alaska aren't going to choose
somebody like you first. You're an artist. You're a city and town guy.

I shrugged my shoulders, thought of what David told me. In his thirties,
when he was an editor at the newspaper, he dated lots. In his forties, teaching
music, he was meeting no one. A former girlfriend of his had visited from San
Francisco. Her response, he said, was she'd never met more interesting, obviously
available, single guys in one place in her life.

Maybe my friend was right. I deserved being single; I'd chosen Alaska. But
I also recalled an insight I had once I started touring more and writing less. The
MFA program I attended in Fairbanks may have had its flaws, but it had been a
terrific place for me to write out of for three years and it set me on a path. I'd come
up from Seattle, where I'd spent nine busy months. Upon first moving there, I'd
almost immediately written a story—one I'd been thinking about for years. And

then, having written it, I started job-hunting. There I was, just turned 29, trying to break into advertising as a copywriter. Maybe I was going to write another story, but I was busy interviewing at ad agencies, going out to hear music, exploring a new city.

Suddenly, it all changed. I met a woman, Ruth Ann, at a dance, a woman I liked and who liked me. We went out later that week, and the next night I dreamed of Ruth Ann in her seventies, an old woman, and I looked into her eyes and was still in love with her, as I'd been all along. As we got to know one another in Seattle, she wanted something casual and slow, at least at first, and me, I couldn't stop dreaming about her. Desperate to slow down the pace, wanting to do what I could to make Ruth Ann comfortable and give the burgeoning relationship a chance, I saw a flyer at a bookstore for a writers' group and called. It was just something to keep me busy. We met on a Tuesday. The following Tuesday, I'd written a story unlike anything I'd previously written, something that flowed, and had real life to it. I understood something had shifted within me, and if I wanted to write more stories like it, I could.

I didn't go to the next meeting of the writing group, in fact, never went again. Instead, I drove to California to visit friends, and to stay away from Ruth Ann, who I adored, but who needed space. I returned to Seattle to a message on my phone: Ruth Ann wanted to see me—she'd been thinking of me. We went out again. She liked touching me, being friendly, but every time she put a hand on my shoulder, or on my arm, I had to restrain myself from telling her what I was feeling.

The next morning, I drove to her house to surprise her. She was just out of the shower, running late, hurrying to get dressed and see a friend, and certainly didn't want to see me, surprise or no surprise. Our break-up was dramatic enough that I felt I better go see a therapist. In retrospect, maybe Ruth Ann and I never had a chance. But I'd had that first dream and the others. What was I to make of them all? As we talked, my therapist and I, it was there, in my second session, I mentioned I'd been thinking about applying to graduate school in Alaska—and was that a crazy idea? Was I actually crazy? Maybe you're crazy and maybe you're not, the therapist answered. But you can apply to the program and decide to go, or not go, at a later date.

Mr. Small Businessman: Your Goods Are Odd

I applied, was accepted, and less than six months later was living in Fairbanks. The insight? Though I'd written that story in Seattle, understood then that I was indeed a writer, if I'd remained in Seattle, I wouldn't have written like I had in Alaska. I might have written an occasional story, maybe. More likely I'd have bounced from one dramatic relationship to another for awhile, somehow found my entry level job in advertising, eventually gotten married to someone interesting and wonderful, would probably have written little outside of work copy, and would always have been vaguely unhappy about it, would always have wondered what I should have done differently.

Or maybe it wouldn't have been like that all.

Regardless, I'd chosen Alaska. And, yes, I wrote lots and remained single. I never planned for my life to turn out like this. But that oversimplifies it. When I first arrived in Fairbanks, I thought I'd be in the writing program for three years, and then I'd be back in Seattle. I had a novel I wanted to write that was set in a prison, about a Native man coming into his true power because of his incarceration. In jail, at last in touch with himself, he becomes a deeper self, and exerts major changes on everyone he comes in contact with. Everybody's lives change: fellow inmates, his lawyer, prison guards, his wife and children, even his parents back in the village. Daily life in the village even shifts. The plot had come to me in a dream sometime during those weeks I'd been struggling with Ruth Ann not wanting to see me.

Eager to write it when I moved to Fairbanks, I made a few calls and met a few people. Within a month, I was leading creative writing workshops in the local penitentiary. I was on my way, I thought. But though I did graduate after three years, instead of the novel, I'd written a couple dozen stories, my first poems, numerous short essays and critical papers. I knew too that I wasn't ready to leave Alaska. It was too interesting of a place; I was enjoying what I was doing; I still had so much to learn. And I must not have been ready to write that particular novel.

As a graduate teaching assistant at the university for three years, I taught composition, and my best student my first semester was a young woman from rural Alaska. You should go teach in a village some day, she told me during a conference, sometime the latter weeks of the class. People would like you, and you'd do well, she said.

I don't know if that's for me, I answered, thinking it was the last thing I'd want to do.

Yet I remembered the line. Eventually I applied for a number of jobs that would have me teach in rural Alaska. Nome turned out to be one part village, one part town, the hub community in a region of fifteen Native villages that I occasionally visited. Remembering my student, I could say, No, I didn't go teach in a village, and yet I did. And remembering the plot to my novel, I ask myself what happened. More than twenty years after dreaming it, the novel remains unwritten—and I wonder if perhaps I metaphorically lived a major part of it instead of sitting myself down at the desk, getting to work.

I met Ruth Ann in a dancehall, the old G-Note Tavern on 85th Street in the Greenwood neighborhood, the north end of Seattle. A string band had been playing that night, and as was usually the case, the caller varied the sets, mostly choosing square dances, occasionally line dances—contradances, they were called. And plenty of dancers had shown up to fill eight or ten squares, or two reasonably long contra lines. I was just starting to dance then, and my last months in Seattle, and then up in Fairbanks, I went regularly. Most anywhere with an active traditional music community presented dances at least once or twice a month, though big cities supported more. In Seattle, you could choose between three or four regular dances each week that 100 people might attend; in Fairbanks, with a fraction of the population, there was only a dance or two a month, with maybe 50 or 60 regularly attending. No matter where though, for a number of years I enjoyed going not only for the music, which I played, but for the ever-changing dance partners: some to flirt with, occasionally someone to potentially date.

Somewhere along the way, initially at the fiddle camp in Port Townsend, then at dance weekends in Alaska, I got introduced to Cajun music, and the two-steps and waltzes that accompanied the playing. In 1998, when I visited New Orleans, I rented a car and drove to Lafayette, the hub community of Cajun country, and spent three days driving around the region. I found not only first-class Cajun music, but also wandered into a couple of zydeco clubs, one way out in the country. Everyone was dancing to accordion-driven rhythm and blues and I'd never seen anything like it: I thought I'd happened onto a movie set. I bought a can of beer and just watched, amazed at the music and the dancing. I started talking to a tall light-colored black man who asked where I was from as he waited for his drink order. Alaska, I said. Oh, that's nothing, he said. Last month during Mardi Gras he'd met people from England, France, Belgium, Germany, Australia, and Japan. This is Lent and it's slow! he shouted. You ought to come back when there's a real party going on! Then he was off, beer in hand, back towards the music and the dancing.

I didn't return immediately, but have gravitated that direction ever since. In Seattle, I began going to both Cajun and zydeco dances when Louisiana bands traveled through. I learned there was a thriving dance scene in the Bay Area and sometimes even rearranged my schedule to make one of the Friday night dances in Alameda. I've been to dances in Denver, Birmingham, Atlanta, and New York City. I've been to dances in West Virginia, Maryland, Pennsylvania, and Rhode Island. I didn't go out of my way to go dancing though, unless it meant returning to Louisiana. Now, if I was within a day's drive and I had ten days or more off in a row, I got in my van and aimed that way. Usually the first night or the next, I was at one of the clubs.

When I lived at Anita's house years ago in Seattle, we talked once about dancing. In addition to being a marvelous musician, she was a terrific dancer: contras and squares, English country, Scandinavian, swing, Cajun, zydeco. She did it all, and most weeks went out three or four times either to play or dance.

Why aren't you going out more? she wondered.

I was convalescing, I said, but also had to admit after having gotten sick, I'd also gotten picky. It wasn't really that much fun unless I liked the music, liked my partners, and liked the dancehall.

Well, you don't really like dancing then, do you? Anita said. No wonder you're not going out.

And she was right, as she usually was about these things.

Maybe that was my mother's influence. It seemed we'd made peace, my mother and I, as best we could. She no longer expects me to call or visit because she has come to understand I won't. For a long time, we had no contact at all, then the occasional letter, now an occasional e-mail in which one or the other will chat briefly about the weather. We're polite, reserved, and no matter how things are really going, we'll say all is well. I do remember, though, sitting in the living room of the house outside Philadelphia, back when I was in seventh grade. Another mother was phoning, asking mine about her son's interest in dance lessons. He certainly will not go dancing, my son, my mother huffed. He'll be right here at home, studying, right where he belongs.

You tell them, mother, I'd have chimed in now, whereas back then I just sat there, eavesdropping, wondering why she hadn't bothered to at least have asked me what I thought. It was funny now, my mother, our house growing up, more reminiscent of the Yup'ik village of Kipnuk. There, several years ago, when I jumped out of the small plane with my fiddle, an elder looked at me suspiciously, then grew indignant as he guessed what was in the case. We don't want any of that here, he said to me. No fiddle music. No dancing! Brings divorce!

LKSD, I said, I'm here with LKSD, articulating the acronym as if it were my shield, and it was, in a way, since I was there in Kipnuk under the aegis of the Lower Kuskokwim School District, and the school was the biggest building in the village. Don't worry. No dancing. Only playing a little. I put the fiddle down, put my right hand up, pointed with my index finger, and making it into a kind of pen, started writing the letters in the cold air. LKSD. I'm going to show the kids some writing. Don't worry! No dancing!

Louisiana was far far away from Kipnuk, from my mother, from Seattle even. I could depend on the music, the dance partners, and the clubs. As a single guy, I could lose myself in my work if I wanted, then show up any Friday, Saturday, Sunday, and feel like I had an active social life. Depending on the week, Monday, Tuesday, Wednesday, and Thursday weren't bad. Christmas Eve, no problem— some club would be hosting a terrific band. I met teachers, lawyers, laborers. People liked to dance and everyone knew how. When I asked a woman to waltz, she was ready.

Then again, she might have already asked me.

May 2002, in New York City during BookExpo week, I was staying on the Upper East Side at the apartment of my friend, Howard. Howard and I had known each other almost thirty years. We met teaching tennis together five summers at a camp near Boston, spent the year between summers three and four driving cross-country: a month in south Florida, two weeks in New Mexico and Colorado, a month in Arizona, three months in northern California, other days here and there. It was a heady mix of visiting friends, working temporary jobs, reading intense fiction (1978 was the year I was introduced to Knut Hamsun, Henry Miller, and Charles Bukowski), hitting the odd tennis ball. Now Howard was a physical therapist in Manhattan. Debating whether to go into practice for himself, he endorsed what I'd been doing.

Sure, stay for as long as you need to, he told me. No problem with your stuff.

Like neighborhoods where I've stayed in San Francisco, New Orleans, and Chicago, New York City was one of those places I couldn't risk leaving my van on the street while it was packed full. Fortunately, I found a spot less than a half block from his door. The one-bedroom that Howard shared with his dog, Dudley, started small; after I'd stacked a few dozen of my boxes where I could, piling them in what out-of-the-way places I could find in the living room, it felt much smaller.

Howard encouraged me to use his computer when he wasn't around. Before BookExpo started, I was happy to stay in all day at the desk in front of the screen, catching up. Thursday night, I returned late. Howard was up, sitting at the computer. I told him I'd been at a party earlier, met a woman I was excited about. She wasn't in the book business, I told him, but had a friend who was, which was how she'd come to the party. We started talking, I said, and one thing led to another. We ended up joining a bunch of people at a club, and then I took a subway back to her place, somewhere near Houston Street. She's a dancer, and knows someone I recently toured with.

What else, Ken? What else happened? Like me, Howard had been a lifelong bachelor. And like me, a student of relationships.

What else?

Did you kiss her?

Yeah, I said. Once good-night. And then once more after we hugged a little longer.

Not bad, Howard said. Do you have her numbers?

Yeah.

Her cell number?

I just have one number.

Her cell?

How should I know?

Not good. She should have given you two numbers. Or you should have asked for them.

I don't think she even has a cell phone.

She's a dancer in New York City? She has a cell phone. Howard looked at me incredulously.

She's not a dancer dancer, I said. She's someone who dances. Or used to dance, I think. Her day job though is administrative in some kind of theatre.

She has a cell phone, Howard said. And I bet you don't ever see her again.

She said she's coming to my show on Sunday.

Are you going to call her?

I'll call her tomorrow.

Good luck, Howard said. It's a jungle out there. By the way, I'd wait until Saturday to call her. Don't even think of calling tomorrow. You'll appear too desperate. He swiveled in the chair, to face the screen. He hit several keys. Now do you mind if I show you something?

Sure, go ahead.

Howard punched several more keys. You should try this, he said.

What's that?

One of the services I'm on. I'm dating a lot lately, Ken. A lot. Quality women. Better than hoping to meet someone at a party. Or getting set up by friends.

I shook my head. Howard lived here. I'm on the road, I told him.

All the more reason, Ken. All the more reason. He went onto another service where he had a membership, hit more keys. Women from Seattle appeared. He hit some more: women from Anchorage. As he scrolled down, I told him to stop. There was someone on there I knew.

And later in the week, Howard proved himself correct: I never did see the woman I'd met that one night, never talked to her again. A month later, I did receive an e-mail from one of her sisters, who was a writer in Wisconsin, and who the dancer in New York had tried to set me up with.

March 2003, I was back. I liked going through New York City at least once annually. Getting a gig meant an opportunity to send packets to *The New York Times*, *The New Yorker*, and other publications. And though it seemed useless, if I felt in the mood, I'd send notices to a few agents I recently queried, maybe an editor. I still had an open invitation to stay at Howard's, but didn't want to overdo the welcome in the city. This time, I spent a few nights north of town, at a friend's. Harry was a fiddler who made up tunes too and had lived for a long time in Brooklyn. He understood how these things went. It even worked to leave the car safe in his driveway for a few days, while I took the train into the city.

This time as soon as I was settled, Howard again invited me to try internet dating.

No way, I said.

Look, he said, as he sat at his desk, motioned me to watch over his shoulder as he scrolled through photos on the computer screen. Just look. There are all these women in the city here. Yo Ken, come over here. I'm showing you something. I stood behind him, shaking my head. Ken, tomorrow night you'll meet Susan. Eight months. We've been dating eight months.

The next night I went to dinner with Howard and Susan. Sweet, smart, pretty, she sat there in front of me, in real life. I was convinced.

What did you think? Howard asked later.

I told him I liked her.

I do too, Howard said. She's not perfect, you know. She has two young children and is always fighting about money with her ex, who's a jerk. And she's trying to lose ten pounds. But the thing is we get along so well. What screws it up is I'm just not fit to be a father.

Is she asking you to?

No, said Howard, relieved. But that doesn't mean I don't see what she needs. It's tough, Ken. The perfect woman isn't out there.

I know. Believe me, I know.

But, look, do you want to try to get on this service?

I nodded. I have no idea how, though.

I know how, Howard said. I'll get you on.

Maybe I shouldn't have been so reticent the year before. After all, I'd been reading personal ads for years, answered a few, had even received a response once or twice, and gone on a couple of dates. Twice I'd even tried submitting my own, most recently when I'd lived in Anchorage. After all, I thought, until I tried every last avenue I should never complain about my social life and this seemed like the end of the line in Alaska. I did meet a woman I liked, a single mother who lived two hours out of town and who turned into a friend.

And then there was a woman even further away who, when we first talked on the phone, asked if I minded if she was slightly overweight.

No, I said.

Would you mind then if I said I was five months pregnant? she asked.

Well, I said, it's like almost everything: it depends. Being pregnant is who you are right now. We've never met.

And really, I thought, what did I know? Unless I met her, she could be anybody. But when we did meet, she wasn't anybody, just a very sad plain-looking woman in a desperate situation. The best I could offer was to buy her dinner. I was only sorry I couldn't possibly offer more. I told my Anchorage pal David about my experiences, and he sighed, then mentioned he'd tried that route a couple of years earlier. If I'd only asked, he said, he could have told me what would happen, and saved me a little time.

Howard watched intently as I signed up for the service, offered to transport the photo from my website to the dating website so I had a photo to display, which he said was a necessity. Then he advised what I should say for my profile. Reviewing my draft a few minutes later, he shook his head. Not good, he said. You're saying too much. Most women will be intimidated. What you want is to get someone curious. Make it so they want more.

I'm not going to be interested in women who are intimidated by me saying what I do. And, besides, I'm saying up-front I'm willing to move anywhere to make a relationship work.

That's not how it works, Ken. You got to give it a chance. It's a game.

I'm giving it a chance. I've signed up. Besides, since I do what I do, they're going to find out sooner or later. I want to be with someone who thinks what I do is special, not a liability. I'm not into playing games.

But it is a game, Ken. And saying too much too soon is a sure way to lose.

I'm not saying all that much, Howard. Just a little about what I do and what I'm looking for. Besides, if there's interest, I can always direct them to my website.

You have a point, Howard said. The website could be helpful. Though I still think you're saying too much.

In New Orleans that summer, I met someone who contacted me first but didn't want to take off her sunglasses when we met, wasn't interested in seeing me again, and acted irritated when I later saw her on a street and politely said hello.

Later that summer in New Orleans, I met someone who was surprised I wasn't chubby, as she was. It seems I'd punched a key that changed the description of my body from normal to overweight.

In Atlanta, I met Sarah, who became my friend.

In Asheville, I met a woman who drove a hundred miles to meet me, a poet who praised my work.

In San Francisco, I met a naturopath who I liked, who liked me, but we agreed there was no chemistry.

In Chicago, I met a writer who intrigued me but who made it clear she wasn't interested romantically; though she offered to help me find an agent, she never did.

Near Sacramento, I met a writer I flirted with, who flirted back. I had to leave the next day. I wrote her but the letter was returned—her box was closed. I could have called her, or tried writing again, but never did.

In Durango, I met a woman from out-of-town who I flirted with, who flirted back. I could have called her, or written her, but never did.

Howard mentioned that before he met Susan, he'd developed a system to internet dating. One evening every month or two, he'd open a bottle of wine, spend several hours in front of the screen, summoning screenful after screenful of women, contacting ones he thought he'd like to meet. The next weeks, then, he'd follow through. Most didn't write back, but some did. With some, he'd correspond a few times. If it seemed appropriate, he'd begin phone calls. Some, he'd meet. It depended on where they were coming from, he said, and where he was at.

It's been several years now since Howard enrolled me, and I've remained signed up for the service, though I sometimes go months between logging on. But when I'm somewhere comfortable for a few hours, the right night, perhaps in Maryland at my friends' Russell and Alane's, maybe in Las Vegas at Jarret and Jennifer's, or even in New York City at Howard's, it could be both energizing and comforting to sit in a chair and click on all these women who were looking for men. I don't need wine but just sign in, perhaps to do a custom search. Women between 37-52; liberal or very liberal; artist maybe, or teacher or professor. I start there, punch in a zip code to start looking near—it could be the place I'm sitting then, or maybe where I'll be in a month—and I'm off.

Perhaps I add a few more job descriptors. Maybe they don't have to be an artist or an educator; maybe someone in medicine, or a service industry. Perhaps I narrow the field—slim redheads maybe, or blondes who like birds, just because I can.

The possibilities are endless, and by punching a few keys I can change the search. I can try looking by a keyword, typing in *banjo* or *MFA* or *journalist*, and see what happens. It isn't as much fun as going to a dancehall, or playing fiddle onstage. But it's better than complaining that life is unfair and no one will have me, or following-up on work e-mails at midnight because I want to stay caught up.

After an hour or two, I might only have written to two or three of the women, ones I can tell I'd really want to meet. Sometimes, mindful of what Howard told me, I'll write just a few words; sometimes I'll write something a little longer. I'll follow my mood. Regardless, these women I choose rarely write back.

What can I say? I'd been in Alaska a long time.

9
Driving North America:
The Contemplation of Home

Railroad Days
for Scott Sparling

In the Salt Lake rail yard
on what would be our lone trip,
Harp told me why he bummed
the country, criss-crossing
from Lansing to Pine Bluff,
Corvallis to Pensacola:
inside a locomotive, he died
nightly in his dreams,
and the end was like a free-
falling upward, a high dive
flight toward the stars—
and how one night he dreamed
he lay flat on the rails,
the Amtrak Empire Builder
approaching, its whistle
like something out of Genesis,
and it was that roaring
engine that called: *Harp, change
your life—heaven is everywhere
the next freight train goes.*

No two days of driving are ever quite alike. Some days, six, seven, eight
hundred miles click by simple as sight, and I drive well into the night, lights near
and far, feeling like I'm exactly where I'm supposed to be, my life unfolding in its
own perfect pattern; other days, half the same distances make the worst of slogs,
and I'll have to pull off the road to nap once or twice before finding a motel somewhere. I'm tired, I find myself saying aloud, and have come to learn when I start
talking to myself like that, I have about twenty miles to find a rest area, or truck

169

stop, to pull off. I'm tired, really tired now, I'm tired, I repeat, and then I have my five minute warning. If I need to then, I'll take the next exit, find a parking lot, or just some safe spot off the road, and turn the car off. I'll awaken ten or fifteen minutes later, startled. *Where the hell am I?*

Some nights after a gig, I'll drive two or three hours to a motel, or maybe it's one of those nights I prefer to find a safe spot to pull off, sleep in the back of the van, and save $45. Some nights, it's best just to stay in town. I've developed a sense of what I need, but even still, sometimes it's like everything else: I just never know until I get in the car and go.

My first sixteen years in Alaska, I never drove the length of the Alcan, from Dawson Creek to Tok. Since late June 2001, I've driven it three times, and once took an alternate route, the Cassiar Highway. The past seven years, I've crossed the United States nine times total, and from February 2002 through December 2007 have put 169,000 miles on my minivan. And the eight months before that, I probably put 20,000 on the Nissan Sentra. I've driven a few rentals too.

When I bought the minivan, the first thing that broke and needed replacing was the tape deck. That was in South Carolina en route to Louisiana. Arriving on the outskirts of New Orleans that next afternoon, I found a car stereo dealer, immediately bought another deck, and had it installed. In an hour, I was set. For years, I only listened to old-time fiddle music and had a reasonable collection, mostly on tape. I learn by listening, which, historically, is how this music gets passed along. I remembered hearing a story about an Alaska fiddler I knew, the one everybody thought of as the best in the state, as good as anyone anywhere. He makes his living as a biologist. For several summers, he worked in the field, and when he went out to rural Alaska didn't even bother taking a fiddle or banjo. Instead, he brought a reliable portable cassette player, batteries, and four or five tapes. But not just any tapes. He chose musicians he loved, playing tunes he wanted to learn. All summer then he'd listen so the tunes wore grooves inside him. Come September, back home, he had eight months to pick up the fiddle and play those seventy or eighty new ones he now had running through his head.

As I drive, I not only have my own favorite tapes I never tire of, but in December 2001 added three more. The last two weeks of the year, I was invited to an artist residency in Virginia, 20 miles north of Lynchburg. There to work on my novel, I flew from Anchorage to Seattle, then from Seattle to Washington D.C., where I took a bus the last eighty miles. I'd just begun my nonstop touring, and had spent the last six months driving cross-country and back, a month in Texas stung by a relationship, the past weeks in Alaska where I tried to find my bearings in a whir of social visits, work errands, a few school jobs, a new recording. Returning home to Anchorage this time had meant flying in to rent a car and juggle the same kinds of tasks I juggled elsewhere and staying with friends instead of my own space.

It seemed I spent most of my time in Virginia taking naps. I did write several poems, but barely touched the novel, which felt completed anyway. Mainly I couldn't keep away from the fiddle. The smartest thing I did for that residency was pack a tape player, just in case, and everyday when I'd pick up the fiddle, before too long I'd begin somehow to start playing something that not only I'd never played before but I suspected no one anywhere had ever played before. And then I'd be quick to play it into the tape recorder before I forgot. This wasn't just the occasional original I'd come up with before. Prior to the residency, I'd made up maybe twenty tunes total. After two weeks in Virginia, I left with thirty-five more.

A few days later, as I started driving around again, I popped one of those cassettes of new tunes in the car tape deck and kept it in for days. Then I did the same for the second. Then the third. And then I rotated back to the first. Once in a while, I'd go back to one of my other tapes, but before long I'd return to one of the originals for as long as two weeks at a time. Someday, I knew, I was going to make a CD of the best of these originals. But first I wanted to learn them so they were truly mine. It was one thing to make them up and another to hear them day after day so they felt familiar. And so I learned by listening to them for hours on interstates, in cities, everywhere I went. After nearly three years of listening, though I could only play a few of the tunes off the top of my head, the others all felt like old friends. When I finally had 10 weeks off in a row, I started listening to all those tunes a little differently, a little more closely, with fiddle in hand. The next three weeks I learned almost thirty, learned them well enough to teach them to others, well enough so we could record that CD I wanted to make, record it in a single weekend.

171

I rarely listen to the radio. A few years ago in Las Vegas, I lost the antenna to the minivan. Probably somebody took it—the only time somebody has done something to my vehicle—because one morning I went to the minivan and noticed it gone. Though I could no longer depend on reception anywhere outside a narrow listening area, I've never bothered replacing it since I barely listen anyway. I haven't missed it. When I'm in the car, if I'm not listening to fiddle tunes, I prefer silence. Books on tape? The one I tried I liked enough, but in truth I couldn't wait for it to end. Maybe it was the particular book, or my particular mood that day. I know: I ought to be more curious.

For many years now, I've been amazingly fortunate how well my vehicles have held up. Sure, I limped into Whitehorse the end of my second day on the road, and a few weeks later had to replace a fuel pump in Boulder. But except for the broken axle in San Francisco, the sedan ran fine. Ultimately, I got three and a half good years and close to twenty-five thousand miles out of a car I originally bought for $1,000. And I even ended up selling it for $500.

The minivan has been similarly problem-free, and when there's been a breakdown, it's always happened in a convenient spot. When my tire blew out on I-15 the October morning of my forty-eight birthday, driving south from Pocatello to a gig in rural Utah, I was just north of Brigham City, close to a rest area. I took out my bike, pedaled to a pay phone, and called AAA. Within an hour, I had a new tire and was back on the road. When my transmission failed three months later in North Carolina, it was late Sunday afternoon and sleeting. But luckily I was in a rest area, a pay phone a hundred yards away, and I was less than thirty miles from my destination, a conference I'd be attending. It was easy to get towed, pack out what I'd need for the next days, find a nearby motel, rent a car the next morning, return the rental car two days later, and pick up the minivan that now had a new transmission—even if it did cost me over $2,000. Then I headed off to Florida and Georgia for two weeks of gigs, enough to pay for the repair work, with another twenty-five hundred left over to help pay other bills.

March 2005, when my car shut down and rolled to a stop in suburban Boston, I was just early enough for my gig that I had time to call AAA and have them tow me thirty miles to the performance site with five minutes to spare before I was to go on stage. After the show, which went well, I called again to have them tow me one more time, thirty-five miles to a mechanic near my sister's, where I was staying the next three days. Again, the repair was made in time for me to retrieve the minivan and be off, this time to Worcester.

There was no sense getting upset when the car stopped running. I accepted it as the cost of doing business, because I knew I'd already done what I could, given my constraints. Every three thousand miles, I'd pull into a service station or quick lube shop to have the oil changed. Every nine months or so, I'd take a day or two, ask a repair shop I could trust—wherever I went, friends had their favorites—to do a full inspection, so at least I was forewarned if I didn't have the time or money to have the suggested work done. Nothing was guaranteed, and I realized my vehicle was old. But this was all the preventive maintenance I could do. My AAA Plus membership allowed me four free tows a year, up to 100 miles a tow.

What did upset me was running late, where I was in danger of missing a show. All of these years, and it's only happened once, outside San Francisco, when I trusted the presenter with the directions instead of my own map-reading skills. I entered the wrong freeway by mistake, got caught in a bumper-to-bumper jam fifteen miles from where I wanted to be, no quick way out, and ended up arriving almost a half-hour late for a children's show. That's when I needed a cell phone. When I finally extricated myself from the traffic, I not only was late, but made myself ten minutes later hunting down a pay phone to let the presenter know what had happened. But to be fair, in addition to needing a phone, I needed to find a bathroom even more—I thought I might pee in my pants I was so agitated, a crowd of three hundred waiting for me on a cloudy Saturday morning when, if I'd only looked at a map, I'd have been more than an hour early.

Many years after that gig, I'm still embarrassed.

Always, the challenge on the road has been to remain centered. And in doing, my own particular routine has evolved.

Since I'm in so many places, it always seems crucial to know just where exactly I am. Sure, I'm in Nashville, say. But until I read *The Tennessean*, or *The Scene*, I might as well be in Knoxville, or Louisville, or Memphis. Everywhere I go, I try to read both the daily newspaper and the weekly paper. Some less populated places, like West Virginia and Montana, have a state-wide monthly. If a place has two dailies, or a pair of weeklies, I skim both. In Las Vegas, which has three weeklies, I grab them all. It works two ways. Not only am I checking if my press kit has resulted in a clip worth keeping, but I learn what's going on in town. And having that sense of place allows me a glimpse into what is current. When I'm doing a show, there's invariably an opportunity to slide a reference to a local issue into one of my stories. How'd you know about that? people come up and ask afterwards. I don't know, I answer, shrugging, then add how I thought everybody around these parts just knew.

Summer 2003, house-sitting in New Orleans, I got in the habit of reading *The New York Times*, buying it daily from a newspaper box I passed as I walked the dog. Living in Alaska had politicized me, at least locally. But September 11 touched a global nerve. Sure, I'd written a poem that very day, but in good part because I was performing the following day, and if I wanted to perform I not only better have something to say, but it had better be at least somewhat crafted.

A month later, October 11, still dazed by the daily bold front-page head-lines—that week it was Afghanistan and anthrax—I decided anyone could write a September 11 poem, but who was going to write an October 11 poem? So I wrote one that morning in Boulder. November 11, visiting Victoria B.C., I wrote another. December 11, I drove back to Anchorage from a recording session in Fairbanks, and wrote another. January 11, I was driving between San Francisco and Flagstaff and wrote one more. I continued the sequence until September 11, 2002, in New Orleans, then added a coda late January 2003 back in Austin when it appeared war in Iraq was imminent, at least according to newspapers in Texas.

Imminent war—it was the same a few weeks later in North Carolina. When I visited Washington D.C. in early March, according to *The Washington Post*, the invasion was no longer imminent, but a foregone conclusion. Two weeks later in New York City, I followed the first days of the war in the pages of *The Times*. Sure, the paper's flawed, as is everything, but in a country of chain dailies that have shrunk their content and shrunk them again, at least there's the illusion of being comprehensive, and while sometimes the writing can come across as overly precious or pretentious, sometimes it's just gorgeous. Also, it's a rare day that I don't find at least one insightful letter to the editor. Just knowing there are so many discerning readers truly does hearten me when I'm driving around a big country, where everything's so different but so much the same.

A year prior to the 2004 presidential election, in Berkeley I picked up an *East Bay Express* and found an article warning about computerized voting machines and the dangers of widespread fraud in the counting. This was an issue I'd been keeping an eye on. Within a month, both in Eugene and Seattle I noticed weekly papers there were covering the same issue. Predictably perhaps, a few months after that I saw the same topic, much watered-down, on the Sunday front page of the *Atlanta Journal Constitution*. The truth spreads, I was learning, but slowly, and not always fully.

Traveling, I pick up a lot of information, talk to a lot of people, have time to think. A friend in Seattle introduced me to commondreams.org, a daily update of breaking stories and progressive commentary that barely appeared in the main-stream media. Links on the site propelled me further so that these days I always read Glenn Greenwald on the website *Salon*. That same Seattle friend wondered if I was scared touring in Florida—and couldn't imagine I'd find a friendly reception. A few months later, I found Florida like everywhere else: decent people working hard to make their communities into better places, though one couple there assured me it was common knowledge in those parts that the 2004 election was already rigged for George W. Bush. And Jeb Bush was a shoo-in for 2008, although the word was the family was not happy at the mess his brother was continuing to make, so Jeb might have to wait for 2012.

Republicans, an activist pal in Albuquerque said. You can't even say the word in polite company. Apologists for war and intolerance. You wait. Another few years it'll be as bad as calling people Nazis.

Another pal, a single woman I knew, talked about the men she'd consider dating. Sure, there were always going to be compromises, we agreed. Admitting to voting for George W. Bush, we also agreed, was a certain deal-breaker.

Earlier in my life, I'd been oblivious to current events. Growing up, I noticed my father turned to the sports page and the stock prices. We never talked politics,

175

but now I'm sure he was a Republican, and if not then, he's certainly one now. My mother, a lifelong Democrat, attacked the crossword puzzles. Through high school and college, and then the year traveling, the year in Boston, the years back in North Carolina, I didn't vote. A late-bloomer, I've called myself hundreds of times the past decade, though rarely now since the spring 2004 date at a Franciscan college in southern Michigan. There, prior to my performance, having dinner with the creative writer on campus and one of the English professors, Sister Dorothy, the sister took me to task for mentioning, for a second time, that I felt I was, indeed, a late-bloomer. Enough with that, she proclaimed. *At least you bloomed.*

Living in that house in Carrboro with Ned and James had planted a seed. Moving west to Seattle allowed the seed to take root. Moving north to Fairbanks allowed it to flower. Though I stayed busy with graduate school for three years, for the first time in my life I'd become aware, truly aware, of the moon, the sky, the light, the seasons. One summer—and there, too, I taught tennis, making me the furthest north tennis teacher in the United States—I had my first garden. Winter, I could have a car break down on the campus parking lot, and just shake my head, button the top buttons of my parka, wrap a scarf around my neck, slip back on my gloves, sling my daypack over a shoulder, and, already past 10 p.m., begin hiking six miles home in minus twenty chill. No need to complain or call for help. This was what you did. I was in a community where I felt I belonged.

Almost twenty years after leaving Fairbanks, now on tour, reading the papers, I'm not so sure this is a country where I really do belong. For most of my life, so much has passed me by. But four years in Juneau in the mid-late 90's awakened me. And now, here we are, an era that feels critical, and reading so many newspapers, so many blogs, the occasional magazine piece, driving North America, keeping my eyes and ears open, I try to take it all in. George W. Bush, Dick Cheney, Condoleezza Rice, Guantanamo Bay, Halliburton, Blackwater, The Patriot Act, our justice system, torture, foreclosures, the daily reports from Iraq—Baghdad and elsewhere. Now Iran. Or Pakistan. It never stops.

One day I sat down to write my own little essay about tax breaks and the economics that were going to allow all of us to prosper.

I began the piece by introducing myself and mentioning my credentials, which included academic degrees, many positive work experiences, and recent accomplishments—that I had two books in second printings, both with national distribution, and four more books recently out; and that I also had six CDs that had been widely and positively reviewed and had received wide radio airplay. The challenge, I wrote, was making it as a freelancer in the current environment. I was used to finding jobs in many places. But when an arts council contact I've cultivated for years says the budget has been cut in half, or zeroed out, that affects me. When a library contact says the budget has been cut—and hours shortened—that affects me. When a university English professor, or a college activities director, says the budget has been cut drastically, that affects me. When a school district official says not only has the budget been cut, but teachers have been laid off and the school year abbreviated, that affects me. When a festival, club, or coffeehouse says that in this economy they can only book established artists who are guaranteed draws, that affects me.

I wrote that though I still find jobs—after all, I have a track record and am resourceful—the going has gotten exceedingly tough. It almost goes without saying that I've been without health insurance since 1993, after an illness forced me to leave my assistant professorship in the University of Alaska system and that without credit cards, my decade-old business would fold tomorrow.

I've made choices, I wrote, and though I wish it were otherwise, here I am living the cliché of the struggling artist. For now, I have no choice but to accept that $10,000 of contracts for the coming autumn have recently disappeared because of failing institutional budgets. And as I get word that yet another job I've long angled for won't happen, at least not soon, I can't help thinking of the trickle-down theory I've read so much about. A typical day on phone and e-mail brings horror stories from contacts in California, Colorado, Kansas, Tennessee, Texas, North Carolina, Maryland, Ohio, New Jersey, New York. Another typical day, I can name ten others. A typical week and I might hear from virtually the whole United States. Always it's about money. Every place thinks that their problem is unique. No, I tell them. The problem is everywhere, and growing.

I wrote that I'm familiar with the argument that art shouldn't be subsidized— and what's really good will sell. Accordingly, the argument goes, if people aren't

177

buying, often aren't even returning calls, well, obviously the work isn't deserving.

Fiddling and poetry—who needs them?

Inspiration and dreams—who needs them?

Critical thinking and engaged students—who needs them?

I wrote that I don't have the grand credentials—I've won no Pulitzer, haven't won an NEA or cracked *The New Yorker*—but I have unusually good ones.

And I wrote that if I'm having to struggle so hard, what exactly does that say about this culture and this country?

Usually I read the papers sitting alone at lunch or dinner. That's my luxury, a paper or two spread in front of me as I eat out, though I think of eating out more as a necessity. I suppose I could have bought food at grocery stores, loading up on breads, cheeses, crackers, fruit, maybe deli salads. And once in a while I do that, and eat as I drive. But sitting down for a restaurant meal often feels like the only real break from work; just walking into a grocery store to shop sometimes feels like the task that puts me over the edge. So I've developed an eye for places to eat. Unless I'm somewhere really rural, I'm almost certain to find cheap, tasty, healthy food.

My rule is to avoid chains, the Taco Bells, Burger Kings, Pizza Huts. I've learned that anywhere with a crush of such eateries, the kind of strip that might adjoin a freeway exit or two in a community of any size, if I drive a little further toward town, I'll find the local Mexican, Thai, or Vietnamese place, or maybe the brewpub I'm seeking. Better yet, if there's a college nearby, I'll aim for it and be virtually assured of a good meal. Worst case scenario, usually if I look a little harder, somewhere near the chains I'll likely find a Chinese buffet, sometimes in a converted fast food house, sometimes in a modest, perhaps run-down, shopping center. And if I'm in a hurry, the buffets sometimes become my first choice. Not too expensive, especially at lunch, I can depend on a bowl of hot and sour soup to start, plates of vegetables and rice, maybe sushi or noodles, some fruit and a fortune cookie for dessert. On a bad driving day, lunch might be my highlight, and I'll cling to the thin slip of a fortune—*Your hard work soon pays off!*—as proof I'm still capable of prosperity.

After so many years on the road, I've found myself repeating drives, arriving in towns and cities where I've had a history, however scant, and know where to make myself feel at home beyond the usual visit to a library to check e-mail. For example, crossing the border south of Vancouver and back into the States, my first stop in Bellingham is invariably Village Books in the Fairhaven neighborhood, not far from the Alaska ferry terminal. I've performed there several times and am always happy to visit a store that actually displays my books and CDs, regards me as a slow and steady seller.

Seattle, I invariably head either to the Paper Zone or Arvey Paper, two big stationery stores within a mile of one another just south of downtown. I always like carrying distinctive cardstocks and envelopes—sending CDs in black envelopes with a handwritten address in white gel ink is a sure way to stand out at that stage of the process—and if I'm running low on supplies as I head back west, I'll gauge whether I have enough on hand to make it to Seattle. Afterwards, I'll likely aim for Fremont, near where I once lived. Dusty Strings is a terrific stringed music shop, and within a couple of blocks I can browse a good independent bookstore and an excellent newsstand, and choose from numerous cafes.

Portland, I'll try to arrive on Sunday night so I can head to The Moon and Sixpence, a bar off Sandy Boulevard, where a group I know, the Foghorn String Band, plays if they aren't gone on tour. I'll go either there or Artichoke Music, a fine music store on Hawthorne Avenue in Southeast Portland. In Eugene, I'll stop in Tsunami Books, a true community bookstore, one of the best in the country, and see how my friends David and Scott are doing. Further south, depending on my route, I'll stop in either Ashland or Arcata. Seven years now, occasionally passing through, and I've yet to perform in either town, though lord knows I've tried.

In the East Bay, I'll try to time a visit with a dance at the Alameda Eagles Hall or one at Ashkenaz, a club on San Pablo Boulevard. Otherwise, I'll stop in Berkeley to say hello to my friends at Poetry Flash and Freight & Salvage. I also think of Berkeley as the land of 3 cent copies, which is by far the best deal in the country. I always can find copying to do, so I'll park myself in front of a machine for two or three hours and congratulate myself for saving at least a hundred dollars.

If I'm anywhere near Nevada City, I like to stop, poke around, maybe drop in at KVMR, one of the best community radio stations in the country. If I'm driving to southern California, I'll stop in San Luis Obispo for something to eat, or else Santa Barbara. Los Angeles always seems so big and difficult, like fifty good-sized cities, one crowding another. It feels so hard to get around. Once, instead of spending three free days there—this was before I had friends to stay with—I drove four hours to Las Vegas because at least once I was there I could freely run my errands. There, I always head straight to the Clark County library on Flamingo. And I feel secure knowing there's plentiful cheap food available any hour, moderately priced motels everywhere, as long as a mammoth convention hasn't engulfed them all, which has happened.

Flagstaff, I'll drive downtown on route 66 and cross the railroad tracks towards Northern Arizona University. I'll be sure to head for Macy's, one of the homiest coffeehouses in the country. I'll wait in line for soup and salad or a slab of lasagna, then go back in line for a muffin or a piece of cobbler. In Albuquerque, several hundred miles east, I'll drive down Central Avenue across from University of New Mexico, find a parking spot, and order a burrito at The Frontier.

In El Paso, my friend Eddie Holland turned me on to the H & H Car Wash & Coffee Shop, which, as its name implies, is a cafe where you can get your car washed while you eat. Open only for breakfast and lunch, the mole I had on special there was the best I've ever eaten. Austin, I'll head to Bookpeople, where I once read; across the street is Whole Foods, a huge natural foods grocery with a gigantic deli.

New Orleans, if it's Thursday evening, I'll aim for Mid-City Rock 'n Bowl, a bowling alley/music hall that books great acts; Thursday, it's always zydeco. Otherwise, I'll just want to get out of the car, park somewhere safe—*safe*, now that's crucial in New Orleans—and get on my bike and ride. Daylight, it's my favorite city to be pedaling around in the country, or at least it used to be. I confess I haven't been back since Katrina, though I hear reports. Like everything, to really know I'll have to take time, see it myself.

Atlanta, I've managed pretty fair luck finding the Saturday night Cajun dances at the Knights of Columbus Hall on Buford Highway. Otherwise, I'll make a home for myself just north of the perimeter at the Peachtree Corners library, where I'll camp on the computers, get work done, secure I can spend a productive day with a post office next door and a Mexican restaurant a half block away. Suburban

Driving North America: The Contemplation of Home

Atlanta is the kind of place where I've had to break one of my rules: not to set foot in Wal-Mart. One day, needing a duplicate key, neglecting to first check the yellow pages for an address for a locksmith, I drove past several miles of strip malls, a seemingly endless string of groceries, dry cleaners, pizzerias, Chinese restaurants, fitness centers, convenience stores, big and small shops providing every imaginable service, but no small hardware store where I could reasonably expect to get a key made. Atlanta, then, where I learned to be a little more flexible.

In Asheville, the old-time music community is so strong it has its own phone book. There are jam sessions, dances, or parties virtually every night, and I try to time visits with the Wednesday open-stage at Jack of the Wood, a bar on Patton Avenue. Otherwise, I used to head to Battery Park Avenue, walk in the Flatiron Building, say hello to my friend Bob at the Poetry Alive office there. Then I'd walk downstairs—always the stairs, never the elevator—and duck in the Old Europe Coffee House, where their hazelnut praline napoleon is my favorite dessert in the country. But Poetry Alive has moved, as has the coffeehouse. These things happen.

In Chapel Hill, I'd stop by my old restaurant, The Pyewacket, that is until it went out of business and the space reopened under another name, serving nouveau Asian food. If I don't have time to walk by the house I shared on North Greensboro Street—and stop for a bite to eat on the corner at Weaver Street Market—I'll at least try to drive by. In Elkins, West Virginia, I'll stop at the Posten House, where my friend Alice lived with her kids. The past several years, I've only been in downtown Baltimore twice for conferences. But I couldn't help noticing how the parking meters were operative twenty-four hours a day, everyday, the only such place I've found in the country and which compared most unfavorably to River Falls, Wisconsin. There, I detoured briefly on the way to Minneapolis and smiled for days afterwards: fifteen minutes of street parking for a penny in the meter!

Philadelphia, where I was raised, at long last in early 2008, I finally worked for the first time. The past years, driving from D.C. to Manhattan, three times now I've gone to see the suburban house I grew up in. The trees were bigger. The house, smaller. It still felt sad. This last time, I circled the block twice, caught the attention of the little poodle on a chain in the yard. In New York City, oddly, after so many years in Alaska, I usually feel at home virtually everywhere, and when I have to move my car for street cleaning, I know where to go. Boston, my first time on Beacon Hill in twenty-six years, I walked the same streets as when I lived there, entered the same Charles Street 7-Eleven I once worked in, and shook my head. It has been a lifetime.

Ithaca, I'll stop in the Green Star market, and imagine how, if I had lived in town the past twenty years, I'd know everybody in the store. Buffalo, I'll say hello to Jonathan at Talking Leaves Books, then saunter up Main Street for a chicken shawarma omelet. Cleveland, I'll stop in Mac's Backs, the poetry-loving bookstore in Cleveland Heights, or else the Barking Spider Tavern, a music club only a few miles away on the Case Western Reserve campus.

Anywhere near Michigan, I'll try to find my way to Lansing, and Elderly Instruments, maybe the biggest music store in the country. Chicago, I'll just try to get to my pal Jordan's house without getting lost and remember to stay off Milwaukee or Elston, two of the long slow diagonal streets that defined stop-and-go. In St. Paul, I'll knock on Kent's door, and say hello to the other Nomadic Press. St. Louis, Wednesday night, I'll head to the late-night music session at the Cabin Bar next door to the City Museum, a private funhouse of a museum downtown that stays open until 1 a.m. on weekends. Denver, I'll never learn. But Boulder, I'll stop at Penny Lane, the first venue I ever performed with an accompanist, and order a smoothie. Before I leave town, I'll try to go to the bodywork studios near Broadway, where I'll arrive early for my appointment, take a sauna, then indulge in a massage.

Where else? Durango? Cheyenne? Sheridan? Great Falls? Missoula? Boise? Certainly Boise, where a former library director or some visionary on the board decided that on the outside of the building it ought to read *LIBRARY!*, just like that, capital letters and an exclamation mark. I'm always happy in Boise, driving a few blocks on Americana Boulevard, checking in at the library, saying hello to Paul and my friends at the Log Cabin Literary Center next door, then wandering downtown where I can order something delectable and healthy for lunch.

Years now of continuous travel—passing through Seattle at least a dozen times, Boise, Boulder, Denver, Durango, Austin, and so on; months in Lafayette,

Driving North America: The Contemplation of Home

New Orleans, Chicago; weeks in Asheville, Chapel Hill, New Market in Maryland, New York City, Ithaca, Cleveland, Athens in Georgia. Endless days on the road, sometimes the most gorgeous country, sometimes horrific city sprawl, thinking as I listen to solo fiddle tunes. I know this too: I've been in a long slow transition out of Alaska that could turn quick if I met someone who I was attracted to, who was attracted to me, and we caught that first spark. I'm looking for a sweetheart and a home.

But without that spark, then what? Maybe I'm still meant to stay in Alaska, I'll think. This is just a phase, a sabbatical. Like anywhere, there are countless stories of people who try to move but can't. Home is home, and you can't really leave, not really, not when it's in your blood. I lived in North Carolina for several years and when I left in 1984 to drive out west, most folks thought I'd be back in six months. It was fourteen years before I returned.

But I believe in signs, and I've been given a few. Early June 2004, back in Alaska after performing at that April poetry festival in San Diego, after two wonderful days working in a school in Dawson Creek, after selling $1,500 of books and CDs en route, I returned to Alaska to play a bar gig in Skagway with a friend from Haines. It was a little job for a little money, a place to stay, and dinner. Instead of playing tunes in a living room, we were going to play publicly, make it a nice informal homey time. If people wanted, I'd tell a few stories, recite a few poems. But mainly it was to have some fun. Still, I'd sent a dozen posters, and publicized it as I could. Skagway does big business with the cruise ships and accompanying foot traffic, but it's a little town. Was it accidental that the manager couldn't have been bothered to have anyone put the posters up throughout the community, though I suggested just that in my mailing? There wasn't even a poster in the window of his own establishment that faced the main street. Instead, the only one I found was taped to the wall by the urinals in the men's bathroom of the bar.

Welcome back home to Alaska, the manager was telling me.

Two weeks later, I received word a conference had selected me to showcase at their early autumn gathering in Pittsburgh. It was a fairly big deal. Besides artists and artists' agents and managers, most attendees represented arts councils, theaters, and performing arts centers from Maine to Louisiana, twenty-two states in all.

I'd been invited to show what I did with children in school residency settings so the talent buyers could see my presentation first-hand. It was certainly an opportunity, but one that also required an outlay of $700 for a booth fee, $400 for a showcase fee, as well as hotel costs, travel costs, food, and other miscellaneous expenses. I'd be spending approximately $1,600 to attend. Because I was still an Alaska resident, I stopped by the state arts council office in Anchorage, was told by one of the staffers that this was the kind of thing they might partially fund.

You mean in addition to travel? I asked.

Yes, I was told. If I filled the application, they might be able to help with the other fees.

Are you sure? I asked, since I was used to the state only funding a portion of travel and, given my history, I was expecting nothing from them.

The staffer nodded.

The next two weeks, I filled the paperwork, even getting a reference from the director of the Anchorage organization that presented major shows in town and knew the scope of this particular opportunity since for years she'd attended similar West Coast events. I was asking for $600.

The end of the month, I received a phone message from a second arts council staffer, saying that I might want to withdraw my application. Booth fees and showcase fees were clearly not allowable. If I was awarded the grant, I'd receive transportation only.

I reread the application: what was clear to the staffer was not clear to me. The next day I stopped in the council's office, where the staffer repeated that no, my request was definitely not allowable—it said clearly that tuition could not be funded; they did not fund educational opportunities.

I explained that I'd sent them a copy of the contract I had to sign in order to appear at the showcase, which said I had to buy a booth and pay a showcase fee. Booth and showcase fees were not tuition fees, I continued. I was attending this conference to try to get work. If those other kinds of fees were clearly not allowable, I said, that was fine, but you ought to rewrite your application to say that.

Look, said the staffer. I've already recommended to you that you withdraw your application. We only have so much money and you've made choices with your life. I'm sorry. That's just the way it is. I've talked to the director, who backs me on this. We don't fund this kind of thing. We've never funded this kind of thing.

I stomped out of the office, wondering why a state arts council had chosen to act as an adversary instead of an advocate. Of course I'd made choices with my life—I'd chosen to write, publish, play music, perform, invest in myself at higher and higher levels, which meant greater and greater expenses. Yes, I'd chosen to be a full-time working artist. At the time, I had two Alaska-set books, three Alaska-set CDs. I made my living driving around the country telling Alaska-set stories, sharing Alaska-set poetry, playing fiddle music I learned in Alaska cabins. I didn't begrudge the work—in one sense an unofficial, unpaid representative of things Alaskan. But this seemed wrong. $600 wasn't a lot of money. The arts council awarded grants of that size all the time. The opportunity was legitimate. The attitude of the staffer was condescending. Almost ten years after I'd been turned down by the arts-in-education roster, despite all I'd done in the meantime, I hadn't made much progress. Before, no one knew me and didn't believe I did what I claimed. Now, people knew me, maybe, but didn't believe I was doing work of value.

A month later, I was awarded the minimum grant of $100, which I accepted. I'd already filled the application and thought a half-line on my resume showing support in 2004 might someday be of use. Because of the conditions of the grant though, I could only receive support for travel from Nashville, where I'd been earlier in the week, to Pittsburgh. And I had to document travel receipts. Two tanks of gas got me there for $56.30. That would be all I was entitled to. After receiving my check, I wrote one back to the State of Alaska for $43.70.

There was one other condition. At the conference, I was supposed to advertise that I was there with the support of the Alaska State Council on the Arts. I decided to mention the grant to a fellow artist, who asked how much. When I told him, he said, They don't like you up there, do they? Mentioning it to another, I was told, A bit of an insult, eh? An administrator from another state arts council was curious, then incredulous when I said I'd received a grant for $100, but which, I explained, was actually for $56. He shook his head in amazement. It cost a whole lot more than that to administer one of those things—what were they thinking?

I shrugged. Oh, I had an idea what they'd been thinking all right, but I wasn't going to say.

There was one last condition to the grant: I was supposed to write about my experience at the conference and the impact of the grant. To comply, I thanked the state arts council for the two tanks of gas, which weren't unhelpful. I did mention, though, that during the conference I'd decided to stop letting people know that I'd been a recipient of a state grant. Artists and administrators, being naturally curious when it came to funding, hadn't been merely satisfied to hear that I'd gotten support. They wanted details. It wasn't in my interest or nature to act coy in this or to lie to new colleagues, I said, though in retrospect maybe I should have. Telling them the details—and the money involved—made me look less professional, so I stopped. I noted that never before had I been embarrassed to say I was from Alaska—until this grant process.

Touring, I had an opportunity to notice how other states and regions supported —or didn't support—their artists. Pennsylvania, I saw, offered huge support for its performing artists. Ohio, North Carolina, and Arizona also had generous programs. Minnesota offered several major grants for writers. In Louisiana, musicians received huge coverage at the many in-state festivals, which received increasing state support.

Seeking closure, I wrote about this grant experience to a member of the arts council board, who wrote back that in his experience the Alaska arts council had consistently done a better job than others he'd had dealings with.

Maybe, I wanted to say, but that didn't explain what happened in this case or his troubling comment that when he'd asked the director about rewriting the guidelines, the director had responded negatively, because doing so might limit the flexibility they now enjoyed.

What flexibility? I asked the board member. Why should the council be flexible only under certain conditions? Is it only for certain favored applicants?

The board member didn't reply to that one.

To be fair, it wasn't just the state arts council I had an issue with. Though I still worked occasionally in-state and in the region, more often I had experiences that left me puzzled. I'd graduated from an in-state university, had been a resident a long while, and had appropriate credentials, but when I queried about visiting one of the English Departments or Creative Writing programs, or to be on staff at one of the in-state writers' gatherings, I was bypassed, usually without explanation, only to notice that those who were actually invited sometimes had lesser qualifications. It was the same for most of the in-state arts councils and schools I contacted. And it was the same in Seattle. How odd was it, I thought, that the big music festival during Memorial Day weekend had a spot for me three years in a row, 1997-1999, but once I started making CDs, getting radio airplay, touring, I was rejected three out of four years? It was hard understanding when most of my friends were playing during those same years. I was also turned down without explanation for a month-long artist's residency sponsored by an organization whose programs I'd participated in for many years and who I thought would have been particularly receptive to my interdisciplinary focus.

As I drove the country, mulling all this, I understood there were fewer reasons to remain in, or even pursue working in, the Pacific Northwest. Why be where I wasn't welcome, where I still felt ignored professionally? Was I to blame somehow? After all, like most everyone, I like to think of myself as a decent person and I thought I'd been acting like one; but really, sure, like everyone, I can be a jerk and maybe it was finally becoming obvious. These people wanted nothing to do with me because I'd more than worn out a welcome. I was somehow loathsome. Objectionable.

Yet how did that explain that I had so many friends in Alaska, Seattle, and elsewhere?

When I mentioned this to Tom and Jan in Juneau, that maybe there were a lot of people out there that just didn't like me, Tom laughed and said, You're the last person in the world to have enemies. And Jan said, Yeah, who wouldn't like having you around? That's ridiculous.

And how did that explain what Meredith said? A radio disc jockey and consultant who'd been in the business for years, she once told me, Your problem, I think, will always be you're just too nice of a guy.

Or what a new friend told me upon hearing what I did? You need an agent, a bad guy to do your negotiating for you—your nature is to make things work. And people will take advantage.

Still, though I always tried getting along, maybe it *was* personality. Sometimes people misinterpreted what I did, or perhaps I was misinterpreting what others did. That could explain some of it. But it wouldn't have explained it all. If I was paranoid, I'd have thought conspiracy, or a boycott. But that seemed utterly ridiculous.

I wondered then: maybe, truly, the work I was doing was not very good. Once I'd gotten to Alaska, I'd always been confident about my work. Maybe I'd been confident to a fault, and if I went deeper into myself, I'd understand this was a severely misplaced confidence I'd been holding onto. The treatment in my own region, by people who supposedly knew me best, could only be considered as an indictment of the writing, the music, the teaching, the performance: none of it was worth supporting. Or maybe it had to do with something I'd been told by a musician I'd met in Seattle, Simon, who had grown up in Fairbanks. He said he'd had to learn not to mention where he was from. While lots of people might think Alaska was special, that wasn't so in Seattle. He found that people assumed if you were in Alaska, it was because you were only there because you couldn't make it somewhere else. Being from Alaska then meant you were inferior.

That reminded me of the performing arts agent from Manhattan who'd come up to Anchorage to consult. We met. When he heard my background, he shook his head, wondering how I'd gotten so lost. You went to Duke, he maintained, so how'd you ever end up way out here? I took his comments to mean any hard knocks I received, I thoroughly deserved, because I'd messed up—according to his view of the world, I should have somehow used my college connections and East Coast upbringing to be something more than a fiddling poet who was not respected by the art establishment in his own out-of-the-way state. What I wanted to ask him, but didn't, was how someone who'd spent all of two days in Anchorage and then ten minutes talking to me could judge what living in the state all these years had done? Some consultants might have been able to do it, but not this one. A charming man, he was just a little too smug, I thought, though a winter in Talkeetna or Haines might have cured him.

And then I recalled the year I taught in Sitka. Since I'd been writing poems for a few years, I'd begun devouring everything I could about poetics and was reading every contemporary collection and anthology that I could find in that isolated place. When I'd accumulated about eighty poems of my own, I printed them all out one night, arranged them in an order that I thought made sense. My first full-length collection. I contemplated sending it out. That winter, I traveled to rural Alaska to lead a writing workshop and met a fellow visiting professor, a poet who had published a full-length collection with a university press. When I asked if I might send my poems for a response, the poet said yes, it would be a pleasure.

A month later, the poems I sent had been returned, each page filled with bold lines of red ink, much small print, a shout of exclamation points, everywhere question marks. The poet introduced the commentary saying that ordinarily this response might have been excessive, but since I had a good heart, seemed willing to learn, it would be for the best if I was "blown out of the water here" because the poems were simply no good.

I admit: the reply did slow me for a week.

As happened, the following month, a poet was visiting Sitka for a month-long residency. This poet also had a book out with a university press, and, I thought, might as well, why not ask for another reading? I offered the poems with the preface that I'd just been told that the poems were deeply flawed. Within a week, I got the response that some poems were better than others, but there was nothing to indicate anything was extraordinarily off. About the earlier critique, the poet only said that for whatever reason I'd somehow touched a nerve and the poet was not responding to the poetry on the page.

All well and good, I thought, acknowledging the feedback, though ultimately it only meant a tie. Maybe the poems were truly awful, and maybe they weren't. I had no idea. Since it was all so new, I was more concerned with just continuing my reading and writing. After the school year ended, I remained in town for an annual symposium, which was led by several guest writers. That year the visiting poet was Robert Hass, who had consented to read participants' manuscripts. I sent him approximately twenty pages, all my poems with fiddle music references. When we met for a conference, I only had two questions: Were the pieces I'd sent even poems? And if so, was there anything in their favor?

He looked at me a second, and said, yes, they were poems, and he thought they were quite good too, but it might take people seven years or so to get it, so it might take awhile to get them published. That was all he said about the poetry before he handed the sheets back and we talked of other things.

I had my tie-breaker vote then, the summer of 1990—and was relieved that my poems were considered at least passable—though I had no idea how Robert Hass could come to the conclusion that it would take years for most of my work to find publication. As happened, except for my long illness time in 1992, I wrote plenty more and I sent poems to journals nearly continuously for more than a decade. In 1991, a half dozen poems got published. In 1992, a dozen. In 1993, about the same. In 1994, almost three dozen. Beginning in 1995, I started getting many more acceptances and continued to do so for as long as I submitted.

How did Robert Hass know it would take awhile? Maybe that's what makes someone a poet laureate.

Still, that was 1990. This was 2007 and I was driving around the country, ruminating. I couldn't get my novel published. Though I was landing more and more jobs, I still wasn't landing enough of the jobs I sought. Was I simply no good? It wasn't only the rejection, but the utter lack of courtesy from some people. That was what pointed to it. If I was any good, I thought, surely people wouldn't be treating me so shabbily; they must be assuming I'd never be in a position of any kind of power. They were busy, I knew, which could explain everything. But I was also busy, and I tried never to treat people as I was occasionally treated. Though I knew that sometimes there was never the 10 or 15 seconds necessary to humanize an exchange, that was rare. If someone wanted, they could always find 10 or 15 seconds. But they weren't finding it for me. Was I simply no good? But if I was truly awful, how to explain away the comment by Robert Hass? The one by Naomi Shihab Nye? The decisions by hundreds of journal editors to publish my poems? The decision of one publisher, John Crawford, to risk his money to publish my first two books, and the decision of another, Bryce Milligan, to risk his to publish my third? Then there was David Baratier, who published my fourth; Tom Hunley, who published my fifth; M.L. Liebler, who published my sixth. How to explain disc jockeys inundated by hundreds of unsolicited CDs choosing mine to play? How to explain presenters, inundated with hundreds of requests for dates, choosing to pay me well to come to their communities?

Was it only taste?

I recalled a woman I met in Seattle several years ago, before my first book came out, who adapted poetry and produced full-length plays. There were two poets I was considering working with, she said, you and Sherman Alexie. The problem, she said, is Sherman Alexie doesn't return my calls. And you, I can't get financing for.

Sherman Alexie was one of the writers and musicians I shadowed around the country. He'd be invited places; I'd be invited places. He'd draw a certain audience; I'd draw maybe half, maybe a quarter. He'd receive a certain stipend; I'd receive a quarter or a tenth of his. I saw him once, in Seattle. Probably I was envious, a large crowd hanging on every word. He read one piece the whole hour, told jokes, made the audience feel good. I was reminded of my friend David, in Wyoming, a writer and musician who said I should meet his friend, Paul. Paul told stories, played the didgeridoo, danced, and, as he saw it, toured as a professional Australian.

And you, he said, are a professional Alaskan.

And in the same way, through David's eyes, I saw Sherman Alexie as a professional Indian.

And though I felt I could do much of what he could, I was the one struggling to make a living.

Sherman Alexie wasn't the only well-known writer or musician I shadowed. From John Haines in Alaska to poets like Robert Bly, Billy Collins, David Lee, and also Li-Young Lee. From writers like David Sedaris and the late Spalding Gray to musicians and storytellers like Utah Phillips and the late John Hartford, to David Holt, Patrick Ball, John McCutcheon, and a host of other writers and musicians doing good work, appearing at a festival here, a university or arts center there.

No, despite my occasional and deep doubts, it wasn't that I wasn't good enough. It was something else. Maybe Amanda, an Anchorage writer I knew, was onto something when she said what was happening to me up in Alaska was karmic: it was a variation of something I'd heard hundreds of times—that prophets had to leave before getting respect in their homeland. The only trouble was I'd never thought of myself as a prophet, at least not enough to include it as part of the job description for my struggling small business. But it did seem pretty clear I ought to be heading elsewhere.

So we were back to finding a home.

Everywhere I drive, I think, Sure, I could live here, if only I had a reason, if only I had a girlfriend. And if I could find peace in the Atlanta suburbs for a few weeks, I really thought I could land anywhere.

I'd left Philadelphia to go to college, went as far as I could imagine, less than four hundred miles to Durham, North Carolina, a distance that had become more or less an everyday drive for a fiddling poet. But when I was turning eighteen, it was enormous. Since graduating college, I've lived all over—a year traveling, the year in Boston, several more back in North Carolina, the year in Seattle, then up to Alaska, which took me to Fairbanks, Juneau, Sitka, Nome, back to Juneau, and eventually to Anchorage. Then there's the touring I've been doing. When I visit schools now, sometimes I'll mention this, and the elementary-schoolers will be amazed at the number of places I've been. They get even more amazed when I mention that, No, I haven't had a television in almost thirty years, and for a few years in Fairbanks, I didn't even have a phone. But it's the lack of a TV that always gets the oohs and ahhhs. Some youngster might exclaim, How do you live? And then I'll say, By not watching television, that's when I found time to read all the books I read, write so many poems and stories, learn to play the fiddle.

As I toured those fourteen weeks in winter and spring 2005, wondering what next, sometimes I'd feel weary when I'd find myself in a motel room outside Paterson, New Jersey, or in Ashland, Ohio, or else in Pierre, South Dakota, or Missoula, Montana. Often the first thing I'd do would be to find the remote control, hit the power button. For awhile it felt useful, like I was learning things about the culture. Going to Comedy Central, watching The Daily Show juxtapose words and images to provide a context to the stories, and then later watching a straight news program utterly miss the point, I'd thank Russell and Alane for introducing me to the show. Watch enough television, understand a little more about what is not being said, and it is the network news that begins to seem like parody, though a little too dead-pan maybe. But it has its moments, working so hard to say so little.

It felt useful at first, watching. But as I continued viewing whatever was on—TBS, TNT, ESPN, HBO, CNN, C-SPAN—I'd fall asleep, wake up at 3 a.m. to a low hum and a blur, the box on the dresser the only light in the room. I'd find my glasses, fumble for the remote, properly turn off the television, fall back asleep. It was like going back to my unhappy childhood. Then I watched lots of television when I wasn't reading or outside playing sports. And if not television, there was radio. Nights, when there was a game on the West Coast, I'd fall asleep to the transistor, an announcer's play-by-play beneath the pillow. I'd wake up later to the faint buzz of another program, the game over—so I'd click off the radio, go back to sleep.

Where next?

Beginning in 2003, after a successful residency in and around Lafayette, Louisiana where I visited schools in two communities, when I had the time I returned there. I wasn't choosing it so much as it seemed to be choosing me. Jerry, the head of the Creative Writing Program at the local university, liked what I did, and there was talk he was going to book me at a major festival there in spring 2006. World-class musicians whom I admired lived in the area and some of them, like Mitch Reed and Al Berard, recognized my work, and seemed to like me. I wasn't totally committed, not yet, but I was spending more and more time there.

Fall 2004, I sublet an apartment in Lafayette for a month. December and January, I spent two more months, mostly in a small modern house in the country outside Opelousas, twenty-five minutes away. During that stint, I recorded half of a CD in a studio in Cecilia. The following spring and summer, I wrote most of this book there, the same house outside Opelousas. I was back in Opelousas again the end of the year and in April played a couple of performing arts series shows: one in Thibodaux, another in Eunice. July 2006, I was offered an opportunity to rent a spacious apartment in an old house a few blocks from downtown Breaux Bridge, a small town ten minutes from Lafayette. Though I'm still mostly on tour, the invitation was too good to pass up. When I'm there, I thoroughly enjoy the high ceilings, my several small rooms, the luxury of having a comfortable workspace where I can be productive, anonymous, and can quickly pedal on my bike across Bayou Teche to the post office.

I hadn't technically grown up in Philadelphia, but a suburb just a couple of miles from the northwest city limits. Lafayette Hill was the name of the suburb. It's funny, thinking of this place in Louisiana that's so flat. Lafayette-no-hill is what it is. It's nothing like where I grew up, yet it's also, somehow, like coming full circle.

Home? Though I'm renting an apartment in Louisiana, I still have my Alaska driver's license, which is good through 2011. My minivan, now within sight of 300,000 miles on the odometer, still has North Carolina plates, and it recently passed an inspection, making it legal through December 2008. When introduced to people who ask where I'm from, I never have a short answer. Alaska? Louisiana? The road?

At least when I'm in Louisiana there's always going to be great dancing. I can hole up, work, and still feel like I have a semblance of a social life. There's always that.

And if I find a girlfriend there, or elsewhere, that would be even better.

10
Opelousas, June 2005

George W. Bush: On Health Care

It's painful to find Americans sick.
No one's to blame, but people want to be
well. And I want to help. We can agree
that someone has got to pay. We can't kick
the dying from hospitals. The poor can't pick
doctors maybe, but they're promised to see
somebody. That's the system. Charity
is working well enough. Don't get sick—
that's my first piece of advice. Ride your bike
to work, which also saves big on gas.
Take aspirin. Eat what you really like,
which makes you happy. Most illnesses pass.
Specialists and tests aren't cheap. Insurance
has risen. I know it's tough on parents.

Late June 2005, the past eight weeks I've been in Louisiana, first in a sweet little house near downtown Breaux Bridge that I sublet from Jan, a French professor in Iowa who plays guitar. Other musicians have rented that house: a guitarist and singer, Marce; an accordion player, Steve. It was a good house for someone like me. Staying there four weeks, able to play late at night, I made up more than two dozen new fiddle tunes, tunes I somehow started playing and thought to record on a portable cassette player. Some felt like real keepers, but I won't know until I listen back, which won't be until July, August, or later. Aside from the tunes, I took care of paperwork, ran errands.

What kind of paper work? What kind of errands? I addressed more than two thousand envelopes by hand, just because I had the time and energy. A few hundred of these I stuffed with sheets, then handwrote personal notes, and mailed off. I also did my taxes, which for the first time I mailed late, more than a month after the April 15 deadline. And with a new book and new CD out, I had to make last-minute edits and find folks to write blurbs for the poetry collection, then had to work with a local graphic artist on both book and CD design. I made a few phone calls too, landed a job in California for early March, another in Ohio for October. I spent an hour or two daily doing e-mail. One day I applied for another credit card. Occasionally, I'd drive into Lafayette to make copies or buy groceries.

Today I'm in the country several miles outside Opelousas, where I've been almost four weeks now. I have one more to go in this modern three-bedroom house owned by a woman from Rhode Island, who bought in Louisiana because she loves zydeco dancing so much she'd like to retire here. I love the Cajun and zydeco dance scene too, but this month I've been holed up, working as if on an artist's residency, albeit a retreat I had to arrange myself. Four years continually on the road now, I'll be 50 years old in October. Sometimes I think, Yeah, I really am getting older. When I began, I joked I was going to continue until I was established or had gone bankrupt. Three or four years it would take, I thought, and assumed I'd become established. Of course I'd become established, despite the odds. Why else bother in the first place?

But I haven't become established. Nor have I gone bankrupt. Instead, I'm simultaneously approaching both. In a few months, my third poetry collection will be coming out. Later this year, my fourth CD, a two-CD set. This one was the most expensive to make. Already I've spent $8,500, which has paid for the recording, mixing, and mastering of both CDs. I've also already paid the designer, though we're still working on that end. And I've even paid a manufacturer to make 500 demo copies of each, so I can have some finished CDs even earlier for marketing. I do it all as efficiently and economically as I can, and it's still relatively expensive. It seemed easier that first time when I didn't know what I was doing. It was certainly less costly. I'd like to make 3,000 of the new ones, but with a 24-page booklet and professional-looking packaging, I may only be able to afford 2,000, which will cost $8,000 more. When I put that on my credit cards, I'll be over $50,000 in debt.

In August, it looks like I'll be recording a CD of material I do for children's shows. As for the novel and my story collection, I haven't given up. But very little has come easy. Everything costs money. Everything.

Mid January through the end of April I toured from Alabama to Alaska, driving cross-country and back. I grossed almost $26,000. Yet none of the music festival dates I'd applied for this summer came through, which set me back financially. I'm worried, but not all that worried, because though deeper in debt than I've ever been, I have a fair bit of work in October, one especially nice job in November, a few dates lined up in February, March, April, and the possibility of many more for next spring, summer, fall, and beyond. Business as usual. And the time off this summer has given me time to write, and, God knows, I've been needing to write. It's seemed especially appropriate to write about the touring I'd been doing the past four years. People are curious. People who I thought might know better ask: How do you get mail? How do you get jobs? What do you listen to on the radio? Do you miss not having your own place? How do you do it, all of it?

Sometimes people look at me enviously. Sometimes, like I'm dangerous. Sometimes, pathetic. Four years earlier, I left my apartment in Anchorage. Four years. And I'm happy these weeks parked in front of the keyboard, remembering. And, remembering, I'm more than ever aware of my mortality.

Last month, Memorial Day morning, I woke in the house at Breaux Bridge, and immediately felt something was wrong. This was no simple lightheadedness. Just past 6 a.m., I got up out of bed, and wished I could crawl back in, but I couldn't undo my rising, not this time. It wouldn't have helped. The first step, and I thought to myself, *I shouldn't be feeling like this.* Dizzy, but this was no mere dizziness, and I hurried to the bathroom, urinated, then knelt to vomit. When I was through, I tried to rise, but the feeling of being unwell didn't pass. If I stood, I felt like I might puke again. If I tried lying down, again I felt like puking. The best I could do was sit by the toilet, my head down, eyes on the tile floor.

In Breaux Bridge, there's a church with a clock that rings the quarter hour, and I sat that morning through a dozen of those rings. Time passed neither quickly nor slowly. My mind was clear; there was nothing to do now but wait. This would pass, I knew. But when? Each time I tried to stand, or lay down, I felt violently ill, so resumed my sitting position, which wasn't painful, and came to remind me of an enforced meditation.

After 9 a.m., sitting for three hours, it occurred to me that as a precaution I better call someone. It wasn't easy scrambling to find the cell phone on the desk in the front room, and the numbers I was looking for. It took me two tries, but I found them, and returned to my spot in the bathroom. One friend was out, but the second was in, and when she answered, I mentioned what was happening. I thought I'd be okay, I said, but there was also a chance I wasn't, and I wanted someone to know, just in case. This friend lived nearby, and stopped by a half hour later with crackers, ginger ale, a few pieces of fruit, some medicines. I tried eating a few crackers, drinking some of the soda, but couldn't keep it down.

I was reminded of what had happened to me nineteen months earlier in Las Vegas, staying at Jarret and Jennifer's. I'd gone out to dinner with friends, but while they'd continued the evening elsewhere over drinks, I felt tired and returned to my lodgings. I went to sleep, then woke an hour later, past midnight, nauseated. Until nearly 4 a.m., I had to camp by the toilet, as I was camped by one now, unable to stand or lie down. During the worst of it, I contemplated a trip to the hospital. Damndest case of food poisoning, I thought at the time, blaming it on the Caesar salad I'd ordered for dinner. When it was finally over, I wobbled back to bed, slept a few hours, and woke the next morning, feeling surprisingly well. I hadn't given the episode a second thought.

But now I was remembering. 10 a.m., 11 a.m., I wasn't feeling worse, but I wasn't feeling much better either. Near noon, my friend called back and asked how I was doing. She said she'd checked about walk-in clinics in Lafayette, and there was one open on the holiday. For $130, I could show up, wait my turn, and be seen.

Let me see how I feel, I said, and I'll call you back. I pushed myself up off the floor. I was feeling better, I could tell. Walking didn't feel as foreign. I didn't feel as bent over and old. But a minute later, I could feel a whirling from someplace inside my head, so scampered back to the bathroom just in time to vomit once more into the toilet. A minute later, I called my friend back, and said I was feeling a little better, but was not totally well, and if she didn't mind driving, I'd take a ride with her to that walk-in clinic. Just be sure, I added, to bring a pail or wastebasket along in case I have need on the way.

Fortunately, I didn't have need on the way, just kept my head down as we drove the two-lane to Lafayette. The weather had been sunny, sticky, hot for days now, and we kept the air conditioner on. It wasn't unpleasant in the waiting room, which wasn't too crowded. I sat, breathing easily, able to read a magazine. It was the best I'd felt all day by far. An hour earlier, I couldn't have even imagined reading. Two months earlier, near the end of my tour, I'd seen my naturopath, Darla, in Seattle, who pronounced me fine. It had been the first time I'd seen her in nearly a year, though we consulted once on the phone the past fall. With no health insurance, I depended on her implicitly and had been seeing her almost twelve years now.

Aside from Darla, though, I avoided doctors. I was the poster child for health care reform in this country, my pal Bob wrote in a recent letter. I could take my car in for preventive maintenance; that was one thing. But for my own self, I couldn't afford it. The last time I'd even been in a walk-in clinic had been fourteen months before, early March. The preceding week I'd been staying with my friend, Harry, north of New York City, and biked downhill into town, then uphill back. The return trip, I felt my heart really pound as I pedaled hard up a steep incline. Interesting, I thought, then turned to other things, including my performance at a nearby college that evening. The next morning, a Thursday, rummaging through the debris in the front seat of my car, parked in Harry's driveway, I found the next month's credit card bills stashed in the pile. I had a few minutes, so rooted around for my check-book, decided to sit, pay the bills, get them out of the way for the month. It was then I felt a fluttering, then a brief pressure in my chest, a quick attention-getter, nothing more, nothing less, and that was it, almost nothing, but something. Odd, I thought, finishing the task, fishing around for stamps. Finding them, I stuck them on the envelopes. I'd mail the bills later in the day. Noon, I walked the mile into town, mailed the letters, then walked back. That afternoon, I took the train into the city, found a subway to the East Village, played music that night, spent the weekend in Manhattan, did a couple of gigs, and even went dancing one night. I had the sensation, though, of wanting to stretch my chest, loosen everything up in there, like the time I'd once bruised a rib.

Tuesday, I was performing at a college in Rockland County, and my host there asked if I was completely comfortable. No, I admitted, I just felt a little tight, like last week I might have pulled something somewhere in my chest. He looked at me, asked how old I was. When I told him, he said it was probably nothing, but I should get it looked at. The next two days, driving from North Jersey across Pennsylvania and Ohio into Michigan, I was extra-gentle with myself. I ate fruits and salads, called friends, one night wrote a letter to Darla describing my symptoms. I wondered if I was okay; maybe I wasn't. Staying with a friend in Ann Arbor, thumbing the yellow pages, I found a walk-in clinic several miles away and drove there. After I described my symptoms, the practitioner studied my blood pressure, my heart rate, then suggested an EKG. Though I was in normal range, he said, everything did look a little low. There was nothing more he could do, but prescribe an appointment with a cardiologist. He gave me his card and one with a cardiologist, who he said would be able to see me next week.

The following week was to be one of my busy ones. I had two jobs six hours north in Sault Ste. Marie on the Michigan and Canada border, another two jobs later in the week not far from Ann Arbor. I expected to earn $2,500, more if I sold a reasonable number of books and CDs. Weeks like this kept me in business. And the week after next, I had a conference in Chicago, as well as a concert there. I'll talk with my friends in Ann Arbor, I decided, maybe call other friends, wait to hear back from Darla, hold off at least until Monday from making an appointment.

My friends in Ann Arbor had been happy to ask around. Saturday morning, they told me they thought it would be smart to get looked at more closely here, while I was by a first-rate medical facility. I couldn't disagree. I'd been jumpy the past week and been getting jumpier. Though I hadn't been concerned at the time I felt any of the symptoms, now I was. Why not stop by the hospital, I thought, and get a second opinion? Sunday, I was supposed to drive north. But Saturday was completely free, the rare day with nothing pressing.

The morning was cool and crisp, and I decided to walk to the hospital, located on the far side of a big medical complex adjoining the university. Construction caused me to backtrack, then loop back even further. Finally on the correct road, I saw a Honda roll through a four-way stop sign and hit a Volvo that had just begun accelerating through. The lone witness, I waited a half hour to tell the arriving patrolman what I saw.

In retrospect, as someone who from time to time looks to the universe for signs, I couldn't have been given a much clearer one that morning: go get a massage, treat yourself to lunch, go to a movie, anything but the hospital. It had been eight years since my plane wreck, the last time I'd had any contact with doctors and the traditional health care system. And four years prior to that, there had been my illness time. I'd forgotten, maybe, what I was walking into, having enjoyed good health for so long. I didn't realize the hospital had no walk-in clinic. So when I strolled in early Saturday afternoon, answered a few questions, I was treated with the utmost gravity, and admitted into emergency.

I didn't mind the tests that next hour, my gown, the team of technicians administering tests, the intern who was a world music fan. He seemed to be on my side. The supervisory doctor on call that afternoon, he confided, was more concerned though. Given my lifestyle, he said, she was lobbying that I should remain hospitalized until Monday, when I could be given further tests.

Monday, I said. I have to be in Sault Ste. Marie on Monday. Wait a second, I just came here to get looked at . . .

. . . and that's what we're doing, he said, putting a hand on my shoulder to comfort me. You're going to be fine. I don't think you'll be needing to stay, but she's the senior doctor and she has concerns. That's all I'm saying.

Fine, I said, then lay there awhile, listening to someone sob nearby. Sometime later, the intern reappeared, but looking tenser this time. One test surprises us, he said. We definitely want you to stay through the weekend. We think you had a cardiac event, and unless we do further tests, there's no telling what happened.

What? I said. What?

One test shows an abnormality. We're preparing a room to admit you through the weekend, and on Monday you'll go through tests, and from there we'll likely schedule a procedure . . .

What? I said.

We think you had a cardiac event, he said. A heart attack. We want you to get this taken care of.

Wait, I said, and then heard myself shudder. Heart attack. I couldn't believe it. This couldn't have happened. No. No way. And yet, what did I know? I didn't know what to think. Look, I sputtered, I have no health insurance. I'm supposed to work this week. I'm meeting friends for dinner tonight. I can't stay here. How much is this going to cost?

You're already through the worst of it, just coming in. Getting admitted, that's what's expensive. Now we need to take care of you. I'll send in a social worker. There are things you need to address now.

Wait, I said. I can't afford this.

You can't afford not to take care of this, the intern said, soothingly, and put his hand on my shoulder.

When he left, I started crying, thinking about what would happen, then tried not to think about it. When the social worker arrived, she couldn't answer my questions when I told her I had financial issues, and couldn't come close to paying, whatever the cost. When she left, I started crying once more.

A second intern peeked in to say hello. He'd been in briefly earlier. Now he asked if I minded if he had a few words.

I shook my head. I didn't mind.

Listen, he said. I just want you to know that, yes, one of your tests showed an elevated enzyme, but it was also within the normal range. Personally, while I think it would be in your best interest to stay overnight, I think it's highly unlikely, *highly unlikely*, there's anything wrong with your heart. I just don't think you had a heart attack. It doesn't add up.

So what is it? I asked.

I don't know, he said. Which is why you should stay and get this checked.

When he left, I thanked him, and then I lay there alone for awhile, listening to the occasional sobs still coming from the same nearby cubicle. Soon after, I had a thought, or, rather, a voice from within saying I should leave the hospital that afternoon and not stay overnight. I didn't know where it had come from, but it felt like a clearer place.

The first intern returned then to say my room upstairs was ready.

I don't think I can take it, I said.

What's this about? he said.

I mentioned what the other intern had said.

The supervising doctor and I were in strong disagreement with him about

202

this. We didn't know what he was talking about.

He said the one enzyme was within normal range.

It should be zero, he shot back. And your event was, what, nine days ago. It likely was much higher then. You likely had a heart attack.

I don't think I can be admitted, I said. I'm going to have to leave.

He shook his head, and sighed. If you leave, you'll be signing out against doctor's orders. We can't guarantee you won't run into trouble, or that we'll have a cardiologist to see you. Ordinarily they're booked weeks in advance.

I nodded.

He shook his head one more time, sighing.

That night, I had dinner with friends, and had a story to tell, though I didn't relish telling it. Sunday, I drove north, worked two successful jobs in town, one at a Native school, one at the university. My naturopath, Darla, called to leave a message. She'd received my letter, which had detailed my concerns and symptoms. She said that while she saw need for concern, there was nothing major. She prescribed a pair of remedies. For my heart, she prescribed antioxidant pills I could find at most natural foods stores and pharmacies. For fatigue, she had a homeopathic solution that she would mail me.

The following weeks on tour that spring had been difficult, but each day I put the episode further behind. I concentrated on eating as best I could, and treating myself tenderly, as I'd always tried, but sometimes forgot. When I could, I'd go out walking. Two months passed, and when I received the hospital bill for that Saturday afternoon in emergency, I groaned, and paid the balance immediately. I couldn't afford the expense, but I was well under the limit on one of my credit cards. There it went; I just wanted closure. Since then I've been extra-conscious of my health, especially my heart. More than a year later, I've had no symptoms other than occasional tightness in my chest if I drove too long and too hard for too many days in a row, or otherwise obviously overdid an activity. Darla thought the same as before. I was fine, given everything I was doing—though it was proper to be concerned, there was nothing major wrong with me.

Maybe it was just that I was in my late forties. Or maybe it was as a friend of mine in Seattle said, that I could choose to undergo all the tests in the world, but even if they did find something wrong, it's already happened. And if something had happened, it was something very minor that hadn't actually damaged me or I'd have known it. And if I hadn't been permanently damaged, the best program would be to eat well and exercise regularly, which surpassed any medical procedure.

That morning in Breaux Bridge, though, was something different. I didn't think it was food poisoning this time. It had been hot, sure, and I hadn't had the air conditioner on much. Maybe it was that, or a bug, or God only knew. The past week, I'd gone out near sunset a few times, jogged slowly up and down a nearby football field. Sweating had felt good, and besides, the last time I'd gone out running had been three days earlier.

Pulse is a little low, the doctor said, after examining me.

I was not feeling 100%, but I wasn't feeling badly. I didn't feel nauseated.

Maybe it's inner ear vertigo, he offered. Or maybe something else. It might have to do with your arteries. If you want, you could get a monitor from a hospital clinic, check your pulse rate for a day. That's a start.

How much would that cost?

Probably about $600.

And then what? Either I'm fine, or I'm not. And if I'm not, and need more tests, what would that mean?

Maybe an angiogram, he said.

I knew what that was, but didn't know the cost. How much? I asked.

That'll run several thousand.

And the way I understand it, I said, I'll either be fine, or still won't know, and then there'll be another procedure. Is that right?

He nodded.

I shook his hand, said I knew enough for now, and would call my doctor in Seattle the next day.

Tuesday, I called Darla and left a message. We talked on Wednesday. According to Darla, it was not my heart, but more likely a bug, and I was fine. But if the symptoms returned, I should let her know immediately. Friday morning, my last full day in that house before I was to move for Opelousas, I awoke at 4:30, spent two hours typing my concerns. After all, I'm a writer, I said, so I could at least use my talents to give a few more details here to help my naturopath with a diagnosis. Besides, I added as I ended the letter, in the next months I expected to be writing a memoir: writing this was practice, and, who knew, might even give me a possible ending to my story.

The past month, I've been up in Opelousas, living in a clean, comfortable house that put me in the mind of being up in Fairbanks. But instead of staying in and writing through the subzero winter dark, here I have the sticky summer heat inviting me in. The TV was broken and I had a cell phone which I'd disciplined myself not to use except in the evening. It hardly mattered anyway since it never rang since virtually no one knew the number. I had no internet, few distractions but the fiddle and mandolin, a refrigerator and stovetop. When I picked up either of my music instruments the past month, which was often, I don't know how or why it happened, but invariably I'd find myself making up some new melody, something with a groove. It was as if the preceding month, where I'd made up a couple of dozen, was only the warm-up. I wasn't seeking these new tunes; they were somehow seeking me. I dutifully recorded them on my little $30 tape recorder. Every other day, I might drive five miles to town to mail a few letters or check e-mail, but this summer the air-conditioner in the library was broken and was taking awhile to get fixed so the building was often open from 8 a.m. to 9 a.m. only. Though I'd have preferred to use that time to write, I adapted, and was back by 9:30, so had the rest of the day at the desk.

Once a week, I'd drive to Lafayette to buy groceries at the store I preferred (thereby avoiding Wal-Mart), run a few more errands, maybe catch a band.

Under house arrest, I joked to a friend when asked what I'd been doing. But in truth, I didn't mind so much. It took four weeks to compose a reasonable draft. So often the past few years, it seemed, I'd sifted through boxes, weighing my possessions, had to decide what to keep, what to throw out. Already light, without much of a physical space besides a minivan, I'd had to become even lighter.

The past four weeks of writing had been the inner equivalent of the same process. I've lived almost fifty years: eighteen outside Philadelphia; ten more off-and-on in the North Carolina Piedmont with time off for five summers and one winter in Boston plus travel; a year in Seattle; and then twenty as a resident of Alaska, the last several of those years barely there at all.

What to keep? What to toss? What was to show for it all?

Stubbornness. Self-righteousness. Integrity, even if misguided. Luck, both good and bad. Not much money. Occasional recognition.

I sometimes joke that if an actor came along who could do a one-person show about a guy in Alaska who went around telling interesting stories and reciting equally interesting poems he himself had written about living up north—even a few poems about surviving a plane crash—and if he could play the fiddle, well, he'd likely have one of those Will Rogers, or Mark Twain, or Ernest Hemingway shows you sometimes saw. He could stay pretty busy. In fact, he'd be a whole lot busier and more successful at it than me, even though I was the original guy, doing it now in real life.

But then, I wondered. Someone in Seattle tried producing that once, and no one was interested in backing it.

So what next? Try again? June 2005, I had two published books, one more about to be published, another ten written. With this manuscript, I'd have an eleventh. I had three CDs, and a double-CD about to come out. I'd be recording a children's CD that August. I performed all over the country. It could be better, could certainly be worse.

What more could I do? Work harder? Work smarter? Become more perfect in my writing, my fiddling, my stagecraft? Leave the country?

I remembered Ed, a poet from Vancouver I met down in Seattle at one of those festival book fairs. Ed grew up in New York, fled to Canada to avoid the draft, and last time I saw him, he mentioned how he'd spent his 40's running around, trying to get ahead, wondering if he was doing the right thing. Then once he'd turned 50, it felt like there he was, this was his life, he'd better make peace with it, and he had, and things had gotten easier. He didn't feel as if he'd had as much to prove, didn't feel the need to rush or push. Ever since, he's been enjoying his life immensely.

Less than four months, I'd be turning 50 myself.

206

11
Postscript:
Breaux Bridge, December 2007

At the Survival General Store

We begin each day with two dollars
and a choice: a loaf of bread,
or a map. And always we've chosen
a round wedge of warm sourdough
with thick crust, and enjoyed it
hunk by hunk, wandering the earth
under lit gray skies through which
we could almost see tomorrow.

Yesterday, hemmed by rock and ice,
we chose map for the first time,
and learned we were in Survival,
a semi-depressed mineral town
halfway between Payne and Salvation.
Accordingly, we swiped a loaf,
ran for the cutoff, and entered
the trailhead that led to the pass.

The past three days, I've been sitting at a desk in a narrow little hallway, one of the eight rooms in my Breaux Bridge apartment. At least, I call this hallway a room. I've been working on this book, taking the manuscript I wrote in Opelousas two and a half years previously and putting it in publishable form. In the ideal world, this would have been done long ago, the book already published. July 2005, after finishing the major draft of this manuscript, I drove to San Antonio for a reading and workshop, returned to Louisiana, a friend's trailer near Breaux Bridge. I still had three weeks before leaving for Clifftop. I spent one of those weeks revising this manuscript. The next, researching literary agencies online, where I went to websites, made a list of specific agents who, according to their profiles, should have been absolutely interested in a project like this. While fiction is a notoriously difficult sell even for established writers, it is common knowledge that there is a continuously growing market for non-fiction. Travel books sell. Quintessential American journeys sell. Writers who already have some kind of marketing plan in place sell. Some agents specifically sought books like this one by writers like me. I confidently typed my single-page query letter, pointing out the strengths of the manuscript, my unique background. After individually addressing them, I printed them out, and mailed with the requisite self-addressed stamped envelopes. Every agent I researched still preferred doing business by mail like this, and I was happy to comply. The final week, I caught up on some of the work I'd put aside the past two months in order to write.

Before leaving Louisiana, I sent queries to just over thirty agents, and then I tried to forget about it. There was nothing more to immediately do. Clifftop, of course, occupied me fully for a week. Afterwards, I drove to Chicago, where I'd been invited by my friend Jordan to record a children's CD and then stay through September. Jordan was a high school ESL teacher, having made a career change in his late thirties. Previously, he'd been a full-time musician, a freelance writer, had managed the big folk music school in the city. He understood the challenges of an artist's life.

We recorded the CD in his living room, his first recording project as engineer—though he was no mere engineer since he also played banjo, guitar, fiddle on the project, and, as co-producer, helped persuade friends to play on several tracks. I spent the rest of the month dealing with the final mixing, the mastering, the graphic design, the manufacturing. This was my fifth CD. They may all be different, but they're similar too. I knew how to get this particular one done quickly and economically.

Fortunately, I was too busy to dwell on the manuscript because I was reminded of that business with each batch of forwarded mail that found me in Chicago. Surely, several of the agents should have jumped on the prospect. Instead, the rejections trickled in. Four one week, five the next, then three more. All were form letters, though a few had a scrawled SORRY on the bottom, which gave the impression of at least a brief consideration. But had they really considered it? The majority of agents never did respond. One, though, did e-mail that he'd like to see the complete manuscript, so I rushed a packet to New York City. Ironically, this was the agent I'd hesitated most to put on my list, since even though his agency represented a few literary writers, the vast majority of clients were celebrity authors, known for movies, sports, media work, politics. It wasn't much of a surprise that I was turned down by this one a month later, the explanation that though he liked the book, he'd have nothing to say when he approached editors and they asked, Who's he?

Had you actually read the book? I wanted to respond, but at least knew to fold because responding to this one would be an obvious waste of time. If the agent had read the manuscript and couldn't get excited enough to say who I was, this was no one to represent me.

Earlier that year, driving from Vermont to Ohio on an overcast late February Sunday, I'd ruminated most of the day on my upcoming fiftieth birthday. At the time, it wasn't yet clear where I'd be or what I'd be doing, only that I had a job two weeks earlier in Wisconsin and another a week later in Ohio. I knew I wanted to perform somewhere, and have something more than just the birthday itself to celebrate. It was in the midst of that long drive that it became obvious I should shoot for having both the new poetry book and the new double-CD come out for the occasion.

Late August in Chicago, my birthday was just a couple of months away. The next weeks, I'd be flying to Albuquerque for a conference, then driving to Indianapolis and Memphis for two more. Jordan and I were getting along well enough that we agreed I could extend my stay through October and I wouldn't be in the way. My birthday fell on a Friday and I managed to book a date at The Hideout, a music club not far from downtown. Though most shows were in the back room, where there was a stage, they also featured happy-hour music on Fridays in the front bar. Best, the club was string-band friendly, so what I played was viewed as good regular fun, even with a few poems stuck in. Jordan would join me. And though we didn't have commitments right away from Clayton, Elizabeth, and Angela—friends of his who all contributed on the children's CD—we let them know they were welcome. I only had two problems with the birthday date:

the double-CD was going to be delayed a month by complicated design issues; the book looked to be delayed indefinitely by publisher problems.

Early September, I called Bryce Milligan, who I'd met in July in San Antonio when I'd read there the past summer. A writer and musician himself, he was also the director of Wings Press, a highly-respected small Texas publishing house. He'd bought one of my CDs after my reading, so I tossed in another, and may have thrown in one of my books. I don't recall. But since I didn't know where I stood with my Ohio publisher—my fiftieth birthday was much less important than the major grants I was applying for, as well as the dates I was booking that depended, in part, on having that third collection—I asked him what he would do in my position.

I'll do that book myself, he replied instantly.

But you haven't even seen it, I said

Doesn't matter. I've seen your other stuff.

Let me get back to you, I said, and went to work. Now that there was another offer, my original publisher who I couldn't reach for two months was suddenly responsive, and said he would get back on the project immediately, though I wouldn't have the book in my hands until November or December.

No problem, I said, then called back Bryce, who surprised me yet again by offering to do a different book of mine as long as I could get it to him within the week. He had a small hole in his schedule, he said, and could fit mine in as long as I could promise to buy 500 copies up front.

500 copies was no problem, I assured him. For my first two books, I'd needed to buy that many almost immediately from John Crawford so I could supply personal orders and do my own marketing.

It only took two days to revise the unpublished collection I thought would be the best fit for Wings Press. *The Secret Visitor's Guide*, I titled it. They were mostly Alaska-set poems, a few plane wreck poems, a mix of others. I was happy to get both hard-copy manuscript and computer disk in the mail. Since I knew Bryce was politically inclined, I also included copies of a sonnet, a sestina, and a villanelle I'd recently written about George W. Bush. They'd make him smile, I thought.

Within a week, I received a proof in the mail. Here, Bryce surprised me again, this time by deciding to include two of the George W. Bush poems, placing them at the end of the sequence of dated poems that began with September 11, 2001. He was shooting for a run of 2,000 copies and let me know that if 500 books weren't in my hands for my birthday, at least they'd be close. And if I needed a few review copies for grants or gigs, he promised to rush them my way.

After the long wait that accompanied my first collection and the difficulties I'd been having making arrangements for the third book, this seemed like no small miracle. Similarly, though I wasn't going to be able to do anything about the double-CD, the one that had been almost two years now in the making, the children's CD was on its own fast track. Though it had just been recorded in August, it appeared likely I'd have my couple of thousand copies by mid October, a week prior to my birthday.

Also that month, Tom Hunley, a poet in Bowling Green, Kentucky, who had recently founded Steel Toe Books, accepted a collection of my poems about health, healing and relationships. The publication date was mid-2006. One new section consisted of heart-related poems, written after my experience at the Ann Arbor hospital. Another section, the one that really sold him, was a sequence of seventeen comedy sonnets, the subjects ranging from Laurel and Hardy to Buster Keaton to Woody Allen to Cheech and Chong.

In several weeks, I'd gone from having one upcoming new book to three new books, and a new children's CD to go along with the bigger double-CD project. I'd also gotten totally absorbed with my urban Chicago routine. Except to leave town for my tours, I barely had reason to move the minivan, so kept it parked in front of Jordan's house. I rode my bike daily, pedaling several miles most afternoons to buy groceries, make copies, mail packets. I'd also found an internet cafe a few blocks away—a decidedly Polish internet cafe, since so much in the neighborhood was Polish. There were Polish newspapers in the convenience stores, Polish foods on the cafe menus. I'd overhear people speaking Polish, especially at the internet cafe. The business charged only $29 per month for unlimited internet time and I spent mornings and early afternoons in front of one of the computers. I'd advanced far beyond the hour per day limit the Chicago libraries allowed. My massive computer needs, I saw, were becoming a real problem and I wasn't sure yet what to do about it. If I allowed myself, I could stay busy online all day, everyday.

My birthday? The children's CD arrived in time. The Wings Press book arrived a few days late, a small box of them catching up with me at one of my Ohio jobs. I'd wanted to feature the new book from the Ohio press for those Ohio jobs, but that wasn't to be. Instead, those books eventually reached me in December near Opelousas. They were worth the wait and aggravation; well-edited, they looked beautiful, and I was grateful to have them. My double-CD arrived in time for a November CD-release show at a performing arts center in rural Kentucky where two of my band mates accompanied me.

So much for the books and CDs I'd wanted to get myself for my fiftieth birthday. Keeping all this fiddling poet work going was getting more and more complicated. Maybe that's why it was a relief, finally, to have a fiftieth birthday that turned out so simply. With no stage in that front room, Jordan and I set up in the corner and ran through a number of tunes, just fiddle and banjo, some traditional standards, mostly my originals. Though some of the happy-hour bands, I learned, decided against mics, I wanted at least one, if I decided to recite a few poems. I was glad I had it since a few poems were in order that early evening; people arrived who expected more than an anonymous fiddler and banjo player knocking out tunes in the shadows. I'd invited some of the people I'd met the preceding months working, and several showed up, who brought friends. Jordan also had friends who came, as did Clayton, Elizabeth, and Angela, who all eventually arrived and played a few tunes. I got to display the new children's CD along with my other CDs and books. Elizabeth and Angela bought dozens for Christmas gifts. Though there was no cover charge or guarantee—we were treated to beers, however—we passed the hat and earned enough to have several pizzas delivered. I offered to divide the remaining forty dollars. Everybody waved me off so I wadded the fives and ones and stuck them in my pocket. Triumphant or not, the Fiddling Poet had turned fifty.

Of course, the books, the CDs, the conferences, the touring of August, September, and October had cost money. Plus, I'd had virtually no income May, June, or July except for a few CD sales at Clifftop, a few gift shop orders from Alaska. For a few years, I'd wavered between $30,000 and $50,000 in credit card debt, which still felt manageable. But it kept getting harder. The laws had changed, so my monthly bills rose. That was one thing. I'd been paying for that big double-CD projects in stages, and only had one more $8,000 stage to go. But that alone was going to put me over that $50,000 threshold. And while Jordan didn't charge me for recording the children's CD and his friends played for free, the final mixing wasn't free, the mastering wasn't free, the graphic design wasn't free, and certainly the manufacturing of 2,000 CDs wasn't free. Though I once again produced a good-looking, good-sounding product on a budget, I'd spent another $4,500 I didn't have. And pre-buying 500 copies of the Wings Press book cost me $3,500. Steel Toe Books wanted a deposit with my promise to buy two hundred books, which, again, was no problem. But that was more money. And though I wasn't contracted to buy any books from the Ohio press, I needed two hundred books to get me started, which cost more than $1,000. It was at that time that West End Press, my original publisher, went through some changes and decided to let my books go out of print. While there were only a few copies left of the *Nome Poems* collection, there were still several hundred remaining of the second one, which had gone into a second printing. While I could have let the books disappear, that was nonsense. I could always use books, so I purchased all I could at 15% of the cover price: $1.80 each. That equaled another $1,200. In addition, the conferences in Albuquerque, Indianapolis, and Memphis were expensive: booth space, hotel rooms, transportation, showcasing all cost money. Somehow, in several months I'd gone from $30,000 in credit card debt to a figure more than double that. My interest payments were now approaching $2,500 monthly. If I could only sell this new inventory, I rationalized, I wouldn't be doing all that poorly—in fact, I'd be out of debt. And if I sold the non-fiction book, that would help—surely somebody would recognize the market for it and offer me a contract. And if I got a major fellowship like a Guggenheim, which paid more than $35,000, that would be a huge help—writers with my credentials got these every year and sometime it would have to be my turn. At worst, if I just landed a few of those $5,000 to $10,000 gigs to supplement the work I could continue to get, that too might be enough. I was going to fight my way through this. I just had to.

Having just typed that last paragraph, I sit here two years later in my Breaux Bridge apartment and shake my head. The church bells are ringing. It's 5 p.m. on Friday afternoon December 14. For more than two years, I've been hanging in there, some seasons more confident of my ability to continue, some seasons less. April 2006, I managed to earn almost $13,000, my best month ever. It didn't even seem that hard at the time. I began by working two performing arts series shows at colleges in Louisiana, then did a series of nine library shows in Oklahoma City, then a coffeehouse show in Newton, Kansas, then a day-long residency in Salina, Kansas, then a week-long residency in Socorro, New Mexico, even a little coffee-house show in Alpine, Texas on the last day of the month. I might have cut the debt to $40,000 after that flurry. But May was quieter. Overall, none of the grants have come in, at least not yet: not even the one for Alaska artists, which I still legally qualify for. That's the one that still puzzles me because I see the names of people who do earn the money. Fine people, all. But that's an old story, and I only allow myself to be puzzled momentarily before I go on to the next chore of that particular day. Though I'm still unwilling to give up my Alaska residency—it's just not the time for it and even though I'm paying rent now in Louisiana, I'm not here much and my situation could change quickly—I've long stopped depending on Alaska for support even if it's still the backdrop of so many of the stories and poems I share onstage. Yes, I still have deep ties. I'm still Alaskan.

December 2004, one night at the Blue Moon Saloon in Lafayette, someone came up to say hello and I was momentarily taken aback at this stranger's misplaced familiarity. And then I saw it was Scott, who I'd known peripherally for years up north. We'd originally met at the airport in Seattle; he was playing a concertina as we both awaited the city bus to take us downtown. We talked, found that though we'd never previously met, we'd had near-parallel experiences. The next years, I saw him once in Fairbanks, another time at a blues club in Anchorage, then once in Juneau at the festival. Where I grew up playing tennis and had even taught in Fairbanks and Juneau, he originally arrived at University of Alaska Fairbanks to play basketball. Where I later traveled rural Alaska as a visiting artist and played my fiddle, he also traveled rural Alaska, but as a basketball ref who in his free hours might accompany local musicians on his concertina. Now I performed nationally and shared Alaska with all kinds of people, and he'd moved to Skagway in Southeast Alaska where he performed summers for tourists from all over the world. But where I was single, he had a girlfriend in Whitehorse. The Yukon was one of my favorite spots anywhere. If I wasn't living my life, I might wish to live his. Having heard of the music scene in this part of Louisiana, he was visiting—and was as surprised to see me as I was him.

We spent a few nights that month going to clubs together, and in early 2006, he returned for 10 weeks with his girlfriend. Our time then barely overlapped since I was touring. But on one of his last nights south, we had dinner, and he mentioned I should think hard about coming up to Skagway for the summer. Though he said the tourism industry was different, he thought I might like the work, at least for one season. If I e-mailed him, he'd send along contacts.

I was grateful for the suggestion. Even though I recently had the three new books and the two new CDs and had applied yet again to summer festivals, it looked like I was going to be once more shut out from those kinds of jobs. We talked in early March. Summer was fast approaching. The prior months I'd had nice write-ups in *The New Yorker*, the *Boston Globe*, the *Chicago Reader*. Early readers had liked the new books; early listeners had liked the CDs. That double-CD was an epic, I thought. Over two hours and fifteen minutes of music, it was beautifully designed, and only cost $20. But this was just like the non-fiction manuscript, which had received virtually zero interest. There was already so much material competing for attention that it took great amounts of money—or superior connections—to distinguish yourself. I certainly didn't have the money or those kinds of connections. And I'd long realized I was spread too thin trying to work in so many directions, even if every one of them fully engaged me. As for the music and my so-called epic project: who realistically was going to pay any attention to fiddle tunes and poetry? That was my dilemma. I was reminded one more time of the woman who'd tried handling bookings for me in 2001 and 2002—people will like what you do, she'd said, though your problem will be getting presenters to take a chance on you. And while the children's CD got raves from both parents and children, and a strong review in *School Library Journal*, I was hampered because I could only market it so much with my limited resources.

I told Scott he'd likely hear from me. I'd just been in Alaska in early February, had sold enough books and CDs to make the trip worthwhile, but needed to follow up. Besides, I said, all the time I've spent in Alaska and I've hardly been in Skagway and had never once worked a tourist job. Maybe this would be the summer for it.

Early May 2006, I flew to Anchorage where I spent a night at David McCormick's, then flew to Juneau where I stayed with Fiddling Jim Stey. In both cities, I filled a few orders for the new books and CDs and thoroughly enjoyed seeing friends, reconnecting with that part of Alaska. Sunday afternoon, I boarded the ferry from Juneau and arrived in Skagway that evening, where Scott met the ship, drove me to the Gold Dredge, two miles out of town, where we'd both be working. He showed me my lodgings, a tiny cabin-like structure on the tourist park grounds. There were two other similar cabins nearby as well as a bigger cabin with kitchen, shower, and toilet. The next day, I walked through the gift shop, the gold panning area, and the gold dredge itself, a huge monster hulk of a machine that had originally been shipped in parts to Skagway, then transported by rail to near Dawson. Several years earlier, it had been transported back by road to Skagway and been reassembled for the tourist trade.

I'd arranged to work through the middle of July only. Though I'd been originally contracted to work as an entertainer, there had been changes in the business, and now Scott was going to take those duties. I ended up as a tour guide, my first time not working wholly for myself in almost fifteen years. Something wasn't right with the job; every shift, trouble dogged me. If I didn't check the schedule an hour before I was to show up to meet the next tour bus, I'd miss a late update, so arrived at the wrong spot or wrong time. If I grabbed a portable microphone and didn't check it, the battery would be run down. The one tour all season that seemed to go perfectly ended with a passenger suffering a heart attack. It was as if I were back in Nome, where things inevitably ended badly, no matter what. Though I did learn Skagway history and was happy to share what I could, I was virtually indistinguishable from college students up for the summer who'd been in Alaska for weeks, and didn't know Nome from Barrow from Homer.

Postscript: Breaux Bridge, December 2007

Because the job was unfulfilling, I busied myself in other ways. After all, the fiddling poet had better stay productive. I rented a cheap one-speed bike so had an efficient way to get around town, at least the flat parts. I sold books and CDs to a few shops. At the last minute, I applied to play two festivals in Canada and was accepted at both, so twice caught rides across the border and played—and, yes, had checked so we were legal. I also played mandolin with the band Scott put together, my first time playing back up like that, and each Tuesday night rode in to do a short solo fiddle set during the Red Onion Saloon's weekly open mic. What engaged me most, though, and what felt most important was the new writing project I'd begun earlier that spring.

March 2006, AWP was in Austin, and prior to the conference I read in San Antonio in support of the Wings Press book. Afterwards, Bryce Milligan casually mentioned if he could find a book of good political poems, he'd publish it in a second. I reflected on the statement and was sorry I didn't have a backlog of good political poems to submit. Two weeks later, house-sitting in Breaux Bridge, a house with cable TV, I watched the Daily Show one night and was inspired to write a Jon Stewart sonnet, something like those I'd written as part of my comedy sequence, the Steel Toe Press book that was due out later that spring. The Jon Stewart poem referred to George W. Bush and Dick Cheney, which made it political, I supposed, so I had one new one. A few days later, watching the news, I wrote an Abu Ghraib sonnet. That made two. A few days after that, I wrote a sonnet about Laura Bush, so I had a third. The poems trickled out through March and April. When I flew to Alaska in May, I wrote three political sonnets on the plane, and my night at David McCormick's, I wrote two more. In Juneau at Jim Stey's, I wrote two more, and the poems had already started shifting. While many of the first ones could be considered commentaries, now I was writing sonnets in George W. Bush's voice, as if I were one of his speechwriters, albeit one with an aptitude for formal verse. Or it was as if the president himself had had discovered a knack for ten-syllable lines that rhymed and I'd been called in as stenographer.

In the 5 a.m. light then, I'd wake early in Skagway, lay in my sleeping bag in my faux little cabin, and write one or two of these poems daily before working my shift for the dredge. Some days I wrote even more, three or four of the fourteen-

217

liners, taking the concept as far as I could, exploring not just policy, but the dreams I imagined George W. Bush might have. By early June, I had 64 poems, enough for a collection. The challenge my next month was cobbling the book together, which meant long sessions at one of the two internet cafes—at either $3 or $5/hour—accessing my web mail account. Or else I'd slip in the occasional strategic visit to the library, which was open in the afternoons and early evenings. The computer policy there was a strict half-hour daily limit on the machines, the slots reserved by appointments that could be made no earlier than a day in advance.

Mid June, several new employees arrived at the dredge, so I was barely working there at all, only a few shifts a week on the busiest two tour days. Others were grumbling because they'd been promised more money. I didn't mind, as long as I could keep my accommodations there, which was not guaranteed. I hadn't been a stellar employee to begin with and now almost all my energy was going into the new book. By the time I left Skagway mid July, my friend Jerry had designed the full text, another friend M. L. Liebler had offered to publish it (Bryce at Wings Press had found a new distributor, which meant he could only publish on schedule now, so this would have to wait a year, and besides, he had some doubts about this particular project), and I'd found a commercial printer in Austin that specialized in short-run projects like this. It made sense to contract with their in-house designer for the cover art. Mid August, I planned to be in Austin anyway, so could pick up the books at the warehouse. Thanks to a friend in Haines, I had a title: *As the World Burns*. Its subtitle: *The Sonnets of George W. Bush and Other Poems of the 43rd Presidency.*

Also mid July, Jordan flew to Skagway from Chicago and we toured Alaska for two weeks, performing twice in Skagway, then Haines, then Juneau. Then we flew to Anchorage and performed in Fairbanks, Talkeetna, Palmer, Girdwood, and Seward. In Fairbanks, we visited Pat and Robin—I got to show Jordan the studio I'd used three times previously, and then we used it ourselves. In a single afternoon, we recorded a CD to go along with the book. At every stop in state, I tried peddling books and CDs. I didn't fill massive orders, but I filled some, and over the next months, I'd be receiving checks in the mail for a few thousand dollars.

But renting a car in Alaska for ten days in the summer was expensive, almost as expensive as my round-trip flight to Anchorage had been. And though I'd just paid Pat and Robin for the studio time, the CD had to be mixed, mastered, designed, and manufactured. Even though M. L. Liebler was publishing the book with Ridgeway Press, we agreed that I was going to be paying for it. The other month, the books from Steel Toe Press found me in Skagway. I'd sent a check there too. So I left Alaska having broken even, but with a new book in hand, another to be published that was going to cost $4,000 or more, another CD that was going to cost $1,200 or more. Though I continued to pay the credit card bills on time, I hadn't paid attention to the terms. These banks kept merging and interest rates were climbing: one or two had numbers like 27.99%.

I tried not thinking about the money as I flew back to Louisiana, moved immediately into the house in Breaux Bridge, and then drove to Clifftop, leaving late Saturday afternoon. The same evening, after dinner in Hattiesburg, I thought I might as well look under the hood since I hadn't had time the past few days with all the busyness of moving. It wouldn't budge; the latch had broken. I couldn't even add a quart of oil if I wanted to, unless I wanted to wait until Monday. So I drove through the night, sleeping a few hours in a rest area outside Chattanooga and again near Bristol. Arriving at Clifftop, the minivan starting overheating. I'd barely made it. The next morning I left my campsite, prayed the car would get to a mechanic without needing a tow. I found one twenty miles away just as the gauge was starting to show the engine was running hot. By mid afternoon, the shop had figured out how to refashion a latch and had fixed the radiator.

I continue to do it all though I still don't know how. Occasionally, I'll try one more time to find an agent for performances, or an agent for my writing, or for some other kind of help. But nothing has happened and it's time away from everything else I'm doing. The past two and a half years, I've driven another 50,000 miles, and most of those miles I've been listening to the six tapes I made of those tunes I invented May and June, 2005. Summer 2006 in Chicago, the week after Clifftop, Jordan and I recorded twenty of them at his house, just fiddle and banjo. It helped that we'd just spent two weeks playing in Alaska. My recording process was evolving yet again. I didn't know the tunes myself, but I'd played them once, and having listened to them for years now, I played them in Jordan's living room, picking them up almost instantaneously. Jordan, a stronger musician, only had to hear them just a few times to play them on banjo. This past summer, July 2007, we had two half-days, so only recorded another dozen. This summer, I'm looking to do thirty more and finish the project. We're talking about spending a weekend in Alaska to record at Pat and Robin's. I need to be up in Alaska anyway and have a frequent flyer ticket I can offer Jordan. I also have another children's CD to record, something different, a recitation of the two children's books I'd written, but for which I haven't had time to seek publishers. Of course, we'll put music on it. Then there's still more work to do on this non-fiction book plus I still have that novel, the collection of stories, and the additional poetry collections that are already written.

How do I do it all?

I don't.

After I picked up the George W. Bush book in Austin, I sent a few out in a flurry. Jarret in Las Vegas thought I'd sell ten thousand easy, which I was happy to imagine. If the books cost approximately $2 each and netted $6 to $8 wholesale, depending on terms, and $12 for the ones I sold outright, and if I sold those ten thousand, plus a few CDs here and there, then I'd have done it, climbed out of debt yet again.

December 2007, however, I haven't sold ten thousand, not even close, am still on my first run of two thousand. But the book continues to find readers here and there. The day after I picked it up in Austin, I drove to San Antonio, dropped twenty off with Bryce since he thought he could sell a few. Naomi Shihab Nye lives several blocks away from Bryce. For years, I'd had an open invitation to visit but never had. That day I knocked on her door. She was busy, though graciously allowed me to interrupt her writing for ten minutes, and ended up taking a half dozen of the books, promising to get them in people's hands. In one case, this has already directly led to a residency in Pittsburgh, which included a major reading series, a full day in a school, good publicity, and a healthy honorarium. It's a good thing, I suppose, they don't sell much quicker because that would mean reprinting or remanufacturing, and right now I can't afford it. But if I had to reprint or remanufacture, of course I would.

Though I've continued to apply for major grants and fellowships, the past year I was shut out one more time. And though none of my books or CDs sell quickly, they continue to sell slowly, steadily. In a side note, after the *As the World Burns* CD was released, I sent it to djs at several dozen public and community radio stations. The music director at KMUD, in Humboldt County, Northern California, called to say she really liked it, and was giving it lots of airplay so it was on the charts—and when I went to look at their website, there I was at #8, directly behind Dylan and Beck, and above Eric Clapton, Willie Nelson, Sting, Los Lobos, and Elton John.

Am I famous?

Famous enough right now for me, though one musician friend, Keith, just shakes his head at the Fiddling Poet's finances. Another one, Jeff, has long counseled me to declare bankruptcy.

I recently told Jeff I'll be grossing $50,000 this year.

If you weren't paying all that interest, you'd be doing well, he said. You're making more than practically anyone I know in this business. But you need to erase that debt.

But if I declare bankruptcy, I can't use credit cards to get on a plane, rent a car, make more CDs or buy more books if I need them.

You're not going to pay them off, even if you live to a hundred. Even if you live to a hundred and forty, he added, which reminded me of what a friend in Athens, Georgia said just the other week, Hey, if you die, you beat them, don't you.

That's not the plan, I answered grimly.

Instead, in lieu of the big grant which could halve my debt, and in lieu of the big book and CD sales that could melt my debt, I slog through it, day-by-day, week-by-week, month-by-month. I continue to invest in my business how I can, where I can. This past March in Chicago, Jordan marched me one Saturday afternoon to an Office Depot. There was a sale on laptops and with WiFi now so widely available, owning a computer with internet access finally made sense. I didn't need much convincing, so hauled the box to the register and threw down the credit card that still had a few thousand under the limit. This past week as I was finishing this manuscript, I really should have been shooting off e-mails across the continent for jobs next month in New York, jobs next summer in Alaska, jobs everywhere in between. I should have been making phone calls. But I just can't do it all. Writing takes time, and I'd like to see this book out in the world. I never did find the time to contact a second round of agents. I never did find the time to contact publishers directly. It's not that any of it would have made a difference. But it might have, and this is all part of the work.

In the end, if I don't have the writing, I'm a fraud. And at least I have the writing, have had it for years—and it does help to have the books, which I use to convince some of those skeptics out there, if only the skeptics take the time to read.

My car has over 285,000 miles and I just spent $600 in Georgia for work on the suspension and alignment after it started shaking and rattling. But what was I going to do? I was performing that night in Savannah. So I got my car fixed and was off, though got stopped on the way, pulled over by a cop in rural Eatonton, ostensibly for the broken side view mirror on the passenger side. But there was something else going on. He called a backup, so soon a second patrol car pulled in behind his, now two rows of blue lights flashing.

Then the first cop asked me to get out of the vehicle with my hands up— *keep the hands out of those pockets!*—my hands raised now against the back of the van so he could frisk me, first up and down my legs, then my chest, then my arms. Then, after he was through, he had me stand by his partner as he went through the debris of my car, looking, he said, for guns.

Afterwards he let me off with a warning and put out his hand. I thought about not shaking it, but what good would that do? I'd already explained I was playing that night at a church in Savannah, had shown him the North Carolina inspection dated earlier in the week, the car having passed two days earlier. No, I just shook his hand and was glad to be off, happy that he hadn't found his way into the box of the George W. Bush-inspired poetry books, which would have been awkward to explain. There were terrorists out there, the cop said to me, and they were bad people and the rest of us can't be too careful.

The rest of the way to Savannah I mulled over what that cop might have done if I were black or Hispanic. Or if I were an Arab.

Postscript: Breaux Bridge, December 2007

On that same Georgia trip, in an Athens parking lot, I had a phone consult with Darla in Seattle, my naturopath who I still consulted approximately twice a year. God knows I could be healthier. December 2005, I'd had a physical in Louisiana and been declared "healthy." But though that felt like an oversimplification, I wasn't going to press it. And even that had been two years earlier. Last I spoke to Darla was this past May. September and October I hadn't always felt quite right—one week a little more tired than usual, one week a chest cold, one week something with my skin. But what was right? I called mid October for an appointment and it wasn't until early December that we could talk.

As I sat in a parking lot in Athens talking on my cell phone, Darla sat listening in her Seattle office. What did it mean that at first she saw toxicity, some internal inflammation, something of concern? What did it mean that she did what she always does, seeing me in ways I still barely know anything about? I finished the hour feeling clearer though; Darla claimed I'd done well. She was going to send two new remedies, which indeed have just arrived here in Louisiana the other day. One is for my heart. The other is for my confidence.

Though I know I should see a dentist, I haven't seen one in over a decade. Though I know I need to see an ophthalmologist, I'm putting that off too. Though I used to get bodywork sessions regularly, I haven't been in more than two years. And while I walk and bike as I can, I'm far too sedentary for my own good. September 2008, it's all going to get easier, I keep telling myself. Happiness. Health. And, sure, why not, money too. How or why, I don't know, but I do know it'll come to be. I don't doubt it. That's my own remedy.

Mostly it's the money that's most difficult for now. Though there's also the matter of time—there's just never enough. Last night, at least, I went out dancing, saw a band that's as good as any in the world if you like fiddles and an accordion. In just a few minutes, I'm going to take a shower, then get in my minivan, and go out again. Where I'm going there will be another world-class band, plus I'll be running into more friends, meeting a new one or two, probably ordering a bowl of gumbo, maybe some jambalaya.

A long time ago, in the midst of a difficult illness time, a card reader predicted for me an unlucky love life, a premature death. At least now I can say with certainty that was a different me. And that one did have an unlucky love life. That one did die prematurely.

These days, I do believe I'll be holding on for another twenty-five to thirty years. It should be a lot of fun seeing what all happens. The past eighteen months, I've been meeting all kinds of women I like, who like me.

The one I'm waiting for is waiting for me.

Afterword

As someone who has actually ridden shotgun for a few days with Alaska's Fiddling Poet in his road-ravaged and stuffed-to-bursting van—stopping for Thai soup in Richmond, Virginia, fully expecting a young Bruce Springsteen and his pals to walk in to that perfect New Jersey bar and grill with that perfect loud talking sweetheart of a New Jersey waitress, hobnobbing with the famous poets at the Dodge Festival who dubbed us "the country boys" because of our peculiar folk music and poetry thing—I can truthfully say I always figured that the Tao of the Fiddling Poet that can be named is not the true Tao of the Fiddling Poet. But as he has done so many times to so many people, Ken Waldman has proved me wrong. In *Are You Famous?*, Ken not only elaborates his own inimitable saga, replete with fascinating and richly detailed characters and places and scenes, he also offers, with characteristic generosity, a kind of self-help roadmap for aspiring performers, a comprehensive and insightful how-to manual for doing the crazy thing he's done with his life.

Beginning with a downer chronicle of his mysterious, protracted illness, Ken quickly draws from it the Nietzschean lesson, "What does not kill me, makes me stronger." Plane crash? No big deal. Insurmountable debt? I'll get by. Heartbreak, insult, neglect? Piece of cake. Alaska of course looms large in this tale, always there, whether in the foreground or background. Maybe Jesus was right about a prophet not finding honor in his home country, but ultimately Ken's story is bigger than Alaska. It's all our stories, collected and distilled by a roving poet/musician possessed of a clear eye and a big heart. Waldman is clearly in the tradition of Walt Whitman, Woody Guthrie, John Steinbeck, Jack Kerouac, Allen Ginsberg, Ken Kesey . . . out there soaking it all up and crafting his unique take on the big story of a big country.

Maybe you won't immediately go buy a van and give up your day job to travel around the country after reading *Are You Famous?*, but you'll be glad somebody's out there doing that work. And I guarantee you, nobody's better at it than Ken Waldman.

Jim Clark
Jordan Professor of Southern Literature and Writer in Residence
Barton College
Wilson, North Carolina

Thank you

First, to Denise and Pauline Bourdon, Jan Boney, Kathy McInnis, and Miss Gussie de la Houssaye, for places to live in Louisiana which allowed this book to get written. Then to John Crawford of West End Press, Bryce Milligan of Wings Press, David Baratier of Pavement Saw Press (now of Montpelier OH!), Tom Hunley of Steel Toe Books, M. L. Liebler of Ridgeway Press, J. L. Powers of Catalyst Book Press for publishing my books so far. Then to Yvonne Olivier, Jim Stey, and Carol Cook Hagood for being the first to read the manuscript. Then there are others who need mention for all sorts of reasons (apologies to those I'm forgetting—and there are many!): Pat Fitzgerald and Robin Dale Ford, Mike Welsh and Cindy Hardy, Pam Miller, Kate Wool, David McCormick, Jan Myers, Duke and Marie, Jim Kloss and Esther Golton, David Cheezem and Melissa Behnke of Fireside Books, Paul Morley and Deb McKinney, Jerah Chadwick, Nancy Lord, Jim and Martha Stey, Tom Paul and Jan Caulfield, Dan Henry, Gershon and Kerry Cohen, Len Feldman, Scott Pearce, Andrea Cooper and Mark Roberts, Cat Fox, Suzanne Todd and Sean Beesley, Betsy Donahue, Jamie Hascall, Anita Anderson, Greg Spatz and Caridwen Irvine Spatz, Ned Leager and Tia Regan, Dan Berkman and Nancy Hiss, Keith Knight, Tim Wilson, Barb Hansen, Michelle Mills, Jack Webb, Celia Sigmon, Aaron Parrett, Mike Shay, Brad Benz, Burt Baldwin, Jarret and Jennifer Keene, Woody and Chris, Bob and Beth Cooperman, Lisa Chavez, Rus Bradburd and Connie Voisine, Eddie Holland and Susie Byrd, Jerry and Megan Hagins, Michael and Naomi Nye, Miss Mars, Jordan Wankoff and Susan Marx, Robin Metz, Norbert and Katie Sarsfield, Juan Romano and Karen Holden, John Fabke and Shauna Wells, Deb Shebish, Patrice Melnick, Al Berard, Mitch Reed, Lisa Trahan Reed, Hogie Siebert, Judy Card, Jim Richardson, Jeff Talmadge and Susan Davidson, Lisa Marcusson, Bobb Head, Bryan and Barbara Blake, Jim Clark, Russell Braene and Alane Hartley, Doug Van Gundy, Mark and Hilarie Burhans, Mark Tamsula, Don Shean, Howard Nelson, Charlie Shaw, Harry Bolick and Pat Schories, Eli Smith, Gladys Miller-Rosenstein of the Puffin Foundation, Tim Blunk of the Puffin Cultural Forum, Sallie Mack, Lloyd Graves, Scott Schnapp and Heidi Almy, Lisa and Hal Tovin, Kent Aldrich, Rachel and Charlie, and Mike and Janet Levin.

While this whole story is how I've remembered, I've changed some names to protect those people's privacy.

Other books from Catalyst Book Press

Labor Pains and Birth Stories
essays edited by Jessica Powers, intro by Tina Cassidy
ISBN 978-0-9802081-1-5, $18.00

Giving birth is a time when one's best dreams and ideas—and worst fears and nightmares—coalesce into a single moment of anticipation. Out of such moments are birthed stories that reach into the deepest place of what it means to be human, what it means to be a spiritual being, what it means to love and be loved. Includes essays by Frederica Mathewes-Green, Ariel Gore, William Pierce, Elisabeth Aron, Jennifer Mattern, Diana M. Raab, and many more.

Creating a Life
by Corbin Lewars
forthcoming in December 2009
ISBN 978-0-9802081-1-5

In this memoir, founder of *Reality Mom* zine Corbin Lewars tells the story of her decision to reclaim control of her body by giving birth at home and recovering from her memories of getting raped as a teenager. Though the topic is heavy, Lewars excavates her memories with self-deprecating Annie Lamont-style humor.

Forthcoming in 2010
Watch for an anthology on miscarriages and an anthology on the adoption triad.